Routledge Revivals

I0113004

Palestine

First published in 1978, *Palestine: A Modern History* traces the history of Palestine from the late nineteenth century to the outbreak of World War II. It examines the Palestinian Arab response to Jewish immigration and Zionist expansion in Palestine. From the outset the Palestinian Arabs viewed all Zionist activity in the country as foreign invasion and strongly resisted it. However, in 1917 the British occupation of Palestine entirely altered the political environment and the Palestinian response had to change accordingly.

Based on both British and Arab primary sources this book develops a number of interesting arguments about the history of Mandate Palestine. It demonstrates the high level of political consciousness amongst the Palestinian Arabs and it shows the importance of social stratification in the nationalist movement. It also makes clear the incompatibility of the declared aims of British Policy with its implementation in Palestine. In this regard the book explores the important conflicts between the local mandatory authorities and the imperial policies adopted by the British government in London. This is an important historical reference work for scholars and researchers of Palestine studies, Middle East politics, peace and conflict resolution, and international relations.

Palestine

A Modern History

Abdul-Wahhab Kayyali

Routledge
Taylor & Francis Group

First published in 1978
by Croom Helm

This edition first published in 2024 by Routledge
4 Park Square, Milton Park, Abingdon, Oxon, OX14 4RN

and by Routledge
605 Third Avenue, New York, NY 10017

Routledge is an imprint of the Taylor & Francis Group, an informa business

Publisher's Note
The publisher has gone to great lengths to ensure the quality of this reprint but points out that some imperfections in the original copies may be apparent.

Disclaimer
The publisher has made every effort to trace copyright holders and welcomes correspondence from those they have been unable to contact.

A Library of Congress record exists under ISBN [if unavailable then LCCN]:

ISBN: 978-1-032-90482-5 (hbk)
ISBN: 978-1-003-55824-8 (ebk)
ISBN: 978-1-032-90484-9 (pbk)

Book DOI 10.4324/9781003558248

PALESTINE
A Modern History

A.W. KAYYALI

CROOM HELM LONDON

© Abdul-Wahhab Said Kayyali

Croom Helm Ltd, 2-10 St John's Road, London SW11

British Library Cataloguing in Publication Data
Kayyali, Abdul-Wahhab
    Palestine: A Modern History
    1. Zionism — History 2. Arabs in Palestine
    3. Jewish-Arab relations
    I. Title
    956.94′001   DS149
    ISBN 0-85664-635-0

Printed and bound in Great Britain by
Billing & Sons Limited, Guildford, London and Worcester

Endorsements For "Palestine: A Modern History" By Abdul-Wahhab Kayyali

"Palestine: A Modern History" is a groundbreaking, in-depth study of the early decades (1881-1939) of the still unresolved conflict between Palestinian and Israeli national aspirations. It is a must-read for anyone seeking to understand the fraught political relationships between the imperial policies of Great Britain and the national aspirations of the Palestinians and Zionists during the crucial early decades of the ongoing conflict.

- *Janice Terry, Professor Emeritus, Eastern Michigan University*

This classic, pioneering work was the first account of the modern history of Palestine from the late 19th century until 1939 to utilize newly opened British archives, while incorporating a novel study of the cleavages in Palestinian society, and emphasizing the significance of the great Palestine revolt of 1936-1939. Written half a century ago, it retains the freshness and potency of its analysis, and contributes to our understanding of both the history and the current situation of Palestine.

- *Rashid Khalidi, Edward Said Professor of Modern Arab Studies Emeritus, Columbia University*

Almost five decades after it was first released, *Palestine: A Modern History*'s insightful narrative has only grown in relevance and poignancy with time. As the world grapples with the injustice and ongoing colonization faced by Palestinians, Abdul-Wahhab Kayyali's work continues to offer the rigorous historical analysis required to understand the contemporary political moment. It continues to present an assessment rooted in the highest standards of scholarship, with its depth and expansive outlook. This masterful work stands as an embodiment of wisdom in scholarship and as a testament to the enduring power of history, bridging past and present with profound insight.

- *Karam Dana, Alyson McGregor Distinguished Professor of Excellence and Transformative Research, University of Washington Bothell*

Preface for Reissue of "Palestine: A Modern History" by Abdul-Wahhab Kayyali

Written by Randa Abdul-Wahhab Kayyali

When Routledge approached me to authorize a reissue of "Palestine: A Modern History," I eagerly agreed. My motivation extended beyond preserving my father's legacy or keeping his seminal work in print. This historical account, covering the critical period from 1881 to 1939, remains a vital resource due to its unique synthesis of English and Arabic sources, offering fresh insights into Palestinian history from the perspective of a Palestinian historian.

This book challenged dominant colonial narratives of twentieth-century history. At its first publication in 1970, histories on the Palestinian mandate were from a British colonial mindset about the Middle East (a British colonial office term) or from a European Zionist point of view. Rashid Khalidi, author of "The Hundred Years' War on Palestine: A History of Settler Colonialism and Resistance, 1917-2017," which is Amazon's number one bestselling book on the history of Palestine and Israel in 2024, sought out the English and Arabic editions in the early part of his career as a historian. A dog-eared copy of the book lives on the library shelves of the School of Oriental and African Studies (SOAS), University of London -- a testament to its use by generations of students of modern Middle Eastern history.

The backbone of this book was the recently declassified Cabinet Papers and correspondence between the British Consul in Jerusalem and the Colonial Office in London, housed at the Public Record Office in the 1960s and 1970s. Some of these documents were later redacted or relocated to the National Archives in Kew and the University of Exeter. My father skillfully compared these official documents with private collections and coverage in 23 Arabic-language newspapers to capture the impact of British colonial policies and the immigration of European Jews, as well as their purchase and settlement of land, on employment and local attitudes over time. My father interviewed Hajj Amin al-Husseini to capture the nuanced reactions of various segments of Palestinian society. He also accessed documents, manuscripts, and private papers from Professor Walid Khalidi's and Neville Mandel's collections.

Abdul-Wahhab Kayyali, known as Abed to his friends and family, was born on November 4, 1939, in Jaffa, Palestine. His father, my grandfather, Said Abdul-Wahhab Kayyali, was a merchant, and his mother, Massarah Ghusain, was a high school graduate literate in Arabic—an unusual achievement for a Muslim woman of her standing at the time. Abed was the eldest of six children, including his brothers Zafer and Maher and his sisters Maha, Nuha, and Suha.

From origins neither privileged elite nor fellahin (countryfolk), the family was forced to leave Jaffa in March 1948 for Lebanon, believing they would return. In 1950, they moved as a family to Amman, Jordan. At age eleven, young Abed traveled alone by taxi from Amman to Damascus and then to Beirut to begin studying at Brummana High School, a Quaker boarding and day school with an English-language curriculum.

Like many of his Brummana classmates, Abed enrolled in the American University of Beirut (AUB) for undergraduate studies. After graduating, he briefly worked as a translator in Kuwait to support his sibling's education. Upon returning to AUB for graduate studies, he met Susanne Denkmann Sweeney, an American undergraduate student. In 1966, they married at the Islamic Center in Washington, DC, and moved to London, where Abed pursued a Ph.D. in Modern Middle Eastern History under the supervision of esteemed Professor Vatikiotis. While a doctoral student in the late 1960s in London, he wrote editorials and was the editor-in-chief of a monthly journal called "Free Palestine."

In 1969, he completed his doctoral degree and founded the Arab Institute for Research and Publishing (AIRP). AIRP's first publication was his doctoral dissertation, written in English and translated into Arabic as "Tarikh Filastin Al-Hadeeth." Several years later, a more concise Arabic version was published. Later editions appeared in English, French, Spanish, and Persian. Croom Helm—now a division of Routledge—published the book in 1978. This fortunate circumstance is how Routledge came to reissue the book in its Revivals series.

Abed became a father with my birth, and in 1975, my sister Kinda was born, making him a father to two daughters. By the mid-1970s, the Lebanese Civil War forced my family to relocate to London, using it as a base for the family and the publishing company. My father continued to travel to Beirut for business. Tragically, on December 7, 1981, he was assassinated at his office desk in Beirut.

His sudden death at age 42 was a devastating blow that shattered my world as an 11-year-old girl. Though I was too young to grasp the concept of targeted killing, I keenly felt his absence, and living in the UK, apart from my Arab family, felt like its own form of exile from my Arab heritage.

At Oberlin College in January 1990, I read this book for the first time and heard the late Edward Said lecture on campus a few months later. With a deeper understanding of how academia intersects with activism, I joined a group called Oberlin Students for Middle East Peace. Collectively, we renamed the student organization, and I chaired Students for a Free Palestine in my first and second years of college.

During my junior year abroad at the American University in Cairo, I sought out my father's past friends and colleagues in London, Beirut, Amman, and Cairo. Through these connections, I learned more about his life from an adult's perspective and embarked on a mission to uncover the identity of his assassins. To Palestinians, he is a martyr, someone who died for the cause of Palestine. While I cannot be sure of all the circumstances surrounding his death, I know that he was a brilliant Palestinian intellectual whose vibrant personality endeared him to many.

After his untimely death, his brother and my uncle, Maher Kayyali, took over the publishing company, which continues to thrive in the Arabic-language publishing industry. My first book, "The Arab Americans," was published in English and then translated and printed in Arabic by AIRP, which now has offices in Beirut and Amman. That my late father's publishing company translated and published my book on Arab Americans in Arabic is validation that the legacy of his vision continues under my uncle's leadership and how my first book, like my father's, can be written in English, yet claim a space in the Arabic book market.

My father's rigor in writing and exhaustive research remain examples of excellent, heartfelt scholarship. While he focused on Palestine, I honor my mixed American and Arab heritage by writing about Arab Americans. Like him, I am a public historian who educates others about diverse, seldom-heard historical experiences.

The reissue of "Palestine: A Modern History" is not just the reprinting of an old text but a revival of a voice that powerfully speaks of the impact of the past. Through this book, readers can engage with the complexities of modern Palestinian history and perhaps be inspired to contribute to the ongoing conversation about justice, peace, and freedom for Palestine in the contemporary moment.

Reissuing this book is not just an academic exercise but a personal journey. Writing this preface, collecting endorsements from outstanding academics, and working with Routledge Revivals have been a profound privilege. It is a way to honor my father's memory and contributions to Palestinian historiography. His untimely death deprived the world of a passionate and insightful historian, but his voice continues to be heard through this book. Its revival ensures that my father's scholarship will continue to educate and inspire future generations because it provides a foundation for more informed dialogue and, hopefully, a path toward a free Palestine.

Randa A. Kayyali, Ph.D.
Independent Scholar

CONTENTS

ACKNOWLEDGEMENTS

I am indebted to a number of persons whose help and guidance have been of immense value in completing this study. In particular I wish to express my gratitude to Professor P.J. Vatikiotis and to my wife Susanne for their assistance and encouragement. Thanks are also due to the Public Record Office for access to proven copyright material, which is published by permission of HM Stationery Office, to Dar al-Kutub, Cairo, and Miss Elizabeth Monroe of the Centre of Middle Eastern Studies, St Antony's College, Oxford; to Mr N. Mandel and Professor W. Khalidi for access to documents, manuscripts and private papers relevant to the present study.

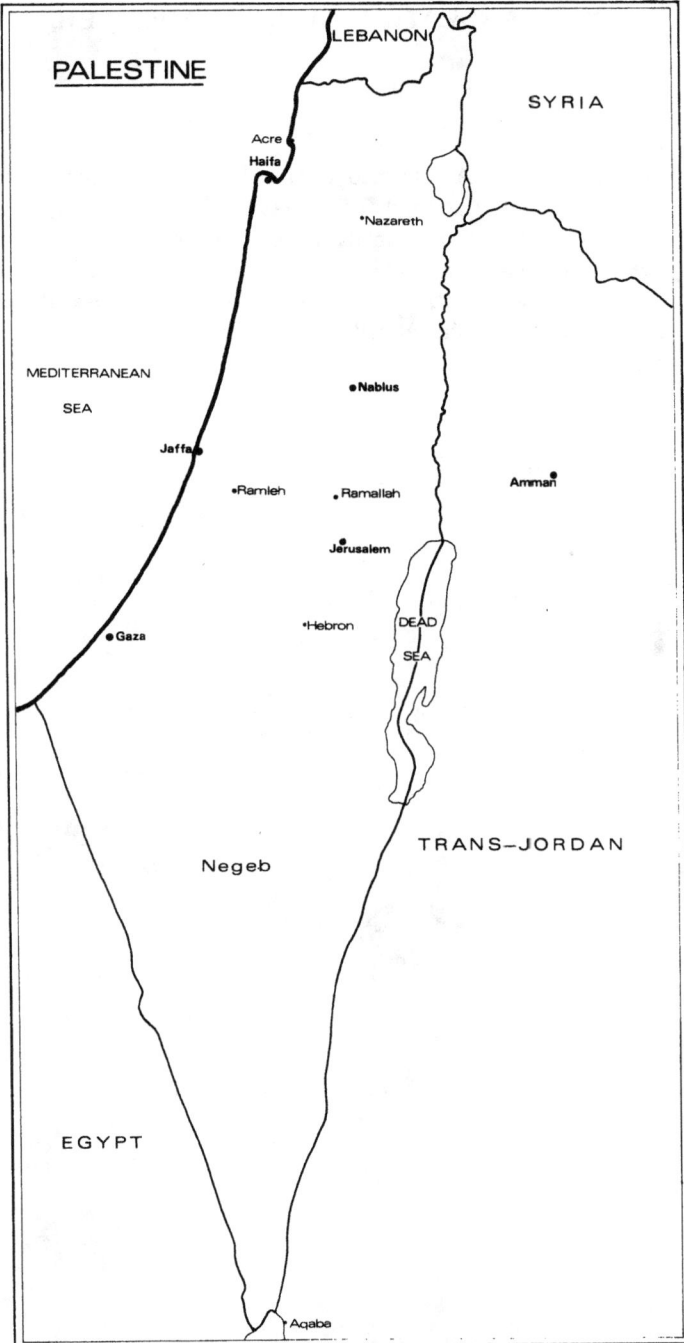

PALESTINE

LEBANON

SYRIA

Acre
Haifa

•Nazareth

MEDITERRANEAN

SEA

•Nablus

Jaffa

•Ramleh   •Ramallah   Amman

                •Jerusalem

•Hebron   DEAD

                SEA

                        TRANS—JORDAN

        Negeb

EGYPT

                Aqaba

NOTE ON TRANSLATION AND TRANSLITERATION

When translating from Arabic into English I have attempted to strike a balance between the strength of expression in the original and its exact meaning. In transliterating names of organisations and titles of newspapers I have used the same system adopted in the second edition of the *Encyclopedia of Islam* with slight variations. Names of personalities were rendered phonetically by the simplest possible English rendering.

1 SETTING FOR A CONFLICT: 1881-1908

At the same time of the Russian pogroms of the early 1880s and the ensuing first Jewish *aliya* (immigration), Palestine lay wholly within the Ottoman Empire. On the West of the Jordan, it comprised the independent *Mutasarrifiyya (Sanjak)* of Jerusalem (Quds-i-Cherif) to the south and part of the *Vilayet* of Sham (Syria) to the north. In 1883, the *Vilayet* of Sham was reorganised and the northern part of Palestine; namely, the *Sanjaks* of Acre and Nablus (Balqaʻ) were made part of the *Vilayet* of Beirut.

The *Sanjak* of Jerusalem was independent and directly linked to the Minister of the Interior in view of its importance to the three major monotheistic religions. It comprised the greater part of the territory of Palestine and more than three quarters of its population.[1]

The total number of villages was 672 with an estimated population of 457,592[2] (not including the Beduins). The number of educational establishments in Palestine amounted to 956 most of which were primary and elementary schools.

The overwhelming majority of the population was Sunni Muslim. Small numbers of Shiʻa and Druzes existed, while around sixteen per cent of the population was Christian, mainly Greek Orthodox, Latin and Greek Catholics. Arthur Ruppin put the number of Jews living in Palestine in 1880 at 25,000.[3] Both Jews and Christians were free to practise their religions and enjoyed a degree of autonomy through the Millet system.[4]

The majority of the Muslim population was engaged in agriculture and lived in villages. Apart from the peasants there was a considerable number of unsettled beduins, particularly in the vicinity of Beersheba. The urban population, both Muslim and Christian, was engaged in commerce, the crafts and modest agricultural industries, and some people held government posts.

Prior to 1880 almost the entire Jewish population of Palestine lived in its 'Four Holy Cities': Jerusalem, Tiberias, Safed and Hebron. A sizeable proportion of Palestine's Jewry was supported to a very large extent by the *challukah* system; the organised collection of funds in the Diaspora for the support of the pious scholars in Palestine. Nevertheless, piety was not the sole characteristic occupation of Jews in Palestine. As early as 1851, the British Consul in Jerusalem reported that Jews are the majority of artisans — which included the glaziers, blacksmiths, watchmakers, tailors, shoemakers, book-binders.[5] In addition they almost monopolised money-lending and the limited banking business in the country.

Under Turkish rule Palestine was dominated by the leading Arab families who, principally on the strength of their long established local position, were recruited into the governing class of the Ottoman Empire. It was a kind of feudal system consisting of a small number of land-owning families and a backward peasantry, whereby the *'Ulama'* (interpreters of Muslim laws and traditions) occupied a strong position, for they alone could confer legitimacy on the Ottoman government acts.

In his excellent study, *Ottoman Reform and the Politics of Notables*, Mr Albert Hourani analysed the relations of mutual dependence between the monarch and the notables; a concept which had far-reaching implications not merely under the Ottomans but throughout the period under study:

> The political influence of the notables rests on two factors; on the one hand, they must have access to authority, and so be able to advise, to warn and in general to speak for society or some part of it at the ruler's court; on the other, they must have some social power of their own, whatever its form and origin, which is not dependent on the ruler and gives them a position of accepted and 'natural' leadership.[6]

The Ottoman attempt to reform administration — the *Tanzimat* (1856) — tended to strengthen the position of the notables rather than limit their role:

> ... Notables became 'Patrons' of villages, and this was one of the ways in which they came to establish their claims to ownership over them.[7]

Palestine and the Great Powers

The effects of the decline of the Ottoman Empire were not confined to the growth of the power of the notables. As the Ottoman state became increasingly dependent on foreign protection *vis-à-vis* other foreign powers as well as ambitious vassals, the European powers sought to establish direct links with the various populations of the Empire. Thus, France became the 'protector' of the Catholic communities in Syria,

Lebanon and Palestine, while the Orthodox Christians came under Russian protection. The British Government's interest in Palestine was aroused by Napoleon's Palestinian Campaign (1799) which posed a threat to the British overland route to India. When Mohammad 'Ali of Egypt occupied Palestine and Syria and defeated the Ottoman armies, even threatening Constantinople itself, the British Government adopted a course of military intervention and was instrumental in driving the armies of Ibrahim Pasha (son of Mohammad 'Ali) back to Egypt. It was during that period (1838) that the British Government decided to station a British consular agent in Jerusalem and to open the first European Consulate in March 1839.

Mohammad 'Ali's advance into Syria opened the 'Syrian Question'. New British policies were formulated as a result. To begin with, Britain sought to emulate the French and the Russian approach in the area. It was during the 1840s and 1850s that the British Government, which had no obvious protégés of its own, established a connection with the Jews in Palestine, the Druzes in Lebanon and the new Protestant churches. 'Behind the protection of trade and religious minorities there lay the major political and strategic interest of the powers.'[8]

From its start, British presence in Palestine was associated with the promotion of Jewish interests. Albert Hyamson stated, '. . .this question of British protection of Jews became, however, and remained for many years the principal concern of the British consulate in Jerusalem'.[9] In a dispatch to the British Ambassador at Constantinople, Viscount Palmerston explained why the Sultan should encourage Jewish immigration to Palestine over and above the material benefits:

> . . . the Jewish People if returning under the Sanction and Protection and at the Invitation of the Sultan, would be a check upon any future evil Designs of Mehemet Ali or his successor.[10] -

The Rise of Political Zionism

Modern political Zionism could be said to have been the outcome of the failure of the era of liberalism and equality which had been heralded by the French Revolution, on the one hand, and the growth of nationalist and colonialist ideas and aspirations in nineteenth-century Europe on the other. For in spite of Rothschild's ascendancy in European finance, that of Disraeli (a converted Jew who gloried in his origins) in British politics and that of Lassalle in the leadership of German socialism, the *Haskalah*, the 'Enlightenment' or Jewish assimilationist movement, was not a complete success. This partial

failure could be explained by 'the obvious inadequacy of the assimilationist view of anti-Semitism, the fact that bitter Jew-hatred persisted
even where its objects were most completely de-Judaized'.[11] The
reaction to this failure took the form of a call for a national Jewish
entity, preferably a national return to Zion.

Thus, Zionism, with its inherent implication of loss of hope in the
future total acceptance of the Jew as an individual by the majority of
society, did not begin to find its way to popular appeal and acceptance
until after the Russian pogroms of 1881, which set a mass exodus of
millions, in eastern and western Europe, into motion.

There were a number of attempts to create Jewish agricultural
communities in Palestine prior to 1881. But philanthropy, not
nationalism, was the basis of the *London Hebrew Society for the
Colonization of the Holy Land,* founded by Jews in 1861.[12] The same
year witnessed the establishment of the *Alliance Israélite Universelle,*
an institution for the protection and improvement of the Jews in
general and of those in Europe and in the Muslim lands in particular. In
1870, the *Alliance* established the Agricultural School *Mikveh Israel*
near Jaffa, obviously aiming at the settlement of Jews in Palestine on a
considerable scale.

Following the assassination of Tsar Alexander II in 1881, and the
ensuing pogroms in Russia, the enthusiasm for *Haskalah* collapsed and
its place was taken by a new movement *Hibbath* (also, *Hovevei*) *Zion*
(The Love of Zion). Societies were formed in Jewish centres where the
question of settling in Palestine as an immediate practical prospect and
the study of Hebrew as a living language were discussed.

The first Jewish colonists belonged to an organisation of Russo-
Jewish students formed at Kharkov for the colonisation of Palestine,
known as Bilu. The growth of Jewish nationalism coincided with the
rise of Arab nationalism in the Arab provinces of the Ottoman Empire.

The Arab Awakening

In his well-known book, *The Arab Awakening,* George Antonius traced
the pioneering manifestations of political consciousness in the *Vilayet*
of Syria:

> It was at a secret gathering of certain members of the Syrian
> Scientific Society (1868) that the Arab national movement may be
> said to have uttered its first cry.[13]

There is no need to go into the question here in great detail. Suffice it to say that after centuries of political inertness the Arab East began to experience a certain political awakening and the beginning of a consciousness of a common Arab identity. On 13 December 1875, the British Consul in Beyrout (Beirut) reported:

> For some years past there has existed amongst certain classes, especially the Mohametans, of the population of Syria a secret tendency to desire annexation to Egypt which has gradually grown in intensity.[14]

On 28 June 1880, the British Consul-General in Beirut reported the appearance of 'revolutionary placards in Beirut'.[15] In subsequent telegrams the British Consul reported the main points of the first recorded statement of an Arab political programme (1880):

> (1) the grant of independence to Syria in union with the Lebanon,
> (2) the recognition of Arabic as an official language in the country,
> (3) the removal of censorship and other restrictions on the freedom of expression and the diffusion of knowledge.[16]

From the scanty evidence available we learn that Palestine was not insulated from the new political trends in the Levant. Following 'Arabi's stand against the British in Egypt, the British Consul reported riots and excitement in Jerusalem and Jaffa:

> It is quite certain that the native Moslems profoundly sympathised with Arabi, both as a Mohammadan fighting against unbelievers and more especially, as the champion of the Arab Mussulman race, upon whose success posed possibilities affecting the future of their race other than merely repelling the invasion of Egypt.[17]

Two years later, the British Consul reported the Palestinians' reactions to the revolt of the Mahdi in the Sudan in the following manner:

> Whilst the general feeling of the Moslems as regards the religious aspect of the (Mahdi) Movement is such as I have stated there is an undercurrent of sympathy carefully suppressed on their part in favour of the Mahdi as an Arab struggling for his race against Ottoman domination and misrule.[18]

This nascent nationalist feeling did not express itself in any particular form of anti-Jewishness. While civil strife and tension between the various religious sects were not infrequent, in his first report on the state of the Jews in Palestine (1839) Vice-Consul Young informed Viscount Palmerston that the Jews were being permitted to live 'in the Mussulman Quarter' and

> . . .were a Jew here to fly for safety, he would ask it sooner in a Mussulman's house than in that of a Christian.[19]

In 1853 the British Ambassador in Constantinople reported that 'a Jew was admitted to the meetings of the Mejlis (Council) of Jerusalem' four years earlier.[20]

The Shape of Things to Come

However, with the advent of Jewish agricultural settlements inspired by Zionist ideas of a national return to Zion, a definite change in the character of the Jew in Palestine occurred. The new immigrants were no longer old pious Jews coming to Palestine to pray and die, but rather determined young Jews coming to live and establish a Jewish nation of their own. The new Jewish settlers found reliable backing and support in Baron Edmond de Rothschild; and from 1896, Baron de Hirsch's *Jewish Colonisation Association* began to interest itself in Jewish settlement in Palestine.

The net increase in the Jewish population of Palestine between 1880 and 1910 amounted to 55,000. Almost from the beginning the new settlers caused friction and offended the local population, 'because they were ignorant of Arabic and of Arab ways. For example, the Jews, unfamiliar with the custom of Masha regarded the incursions of Arab shepherds with their flocks as trespass and expelled them forcibly etc.'[21]

Some of the wealthy landowners were willing to sell land to the new immigrants at profitable prices. However, 'the eviction of the peasants from the land caused serious clashes.'[22] It is interesting to note that in some instances lands were sold by the government to the Jews because the peasants were unable to pay their taxes, and on other occasions the peasants fell victims to usurers who in turn sold the lands to the Jewish immigrants.[23] It was not surprising, under those circumstances, that the evicted Arab peasants should, as early as 1886, attack the newly established Jewish colonies in protest against having their villages taken away from them.[24] The apprehensions of the peasants were shared by the small predominantly Christian, class of tradesmen and professionals who feared the threat of economic competition which was to follow.

The friction between the peasants and the Jewish colonists, among other things, might have prodded the authorities towards imposing restrictions on Jewish immigration. In March 1887, the British Consul in Jerusalem reported that, 'for some time past the local Turkish authorities. . .have been inhibiting foreign Jews from coming to reside in Jerusalem, or in Palestine generally.'[25] In 1890, the Arab notables of Jerusalem protested to Constantinople against Rashad Pasha, the *Mutasarrif* of Jerusalem, for his leanings towards the Jews. The protest was followed, on 24 June 1891, by a petition 'organised by the Muslim notables in Jerusalem to the Grand Vezir that Russian Jews should be prohibited from entering Palestine and from acquiring land there'.[26] We shall see later that this first protest spelled out the two cardinal demands which all ensuing protests against Jewish immigration and colonisation reiterated; namely, the prohibition of Jewish immigration and land purchase in Palestine.

The conflict over evicting Arab peasants from newly bought Arab lands continued during the last decade of the nineteenth century. Mandel described the pattern of reactions among the rural population of Palestine towards the new colonies as being one of 'initial resentment, suppressed or open hostility, giving way in time to resignation and outward reconciliation'.[27] In 1895, after talks with Palestinian Arab merchants, Najib al-Hajj, the editor of *Abu-al-Hol* of Cairo accused the Jewish colonists of expropriating the Arabs' means of livelihood.

Both Rashad Pasha, the Ottoman *Mutasarrif*, and the educated Palestinians were quick to perceive that the Zionists sought to establish a Jewish State in Palestine. Yusuf al-Khalidi 'viewed the Zionist movement with grave concern: he recognised the existence of a Jewish problem in Europe. . .but he also foresaw that a Jewish state could not be established in Palestine without hostilities and bloodshed because of Arab opposition'.[28]

The Mufti of Jerusalem, Muhammad Taher al-Husseini, fought Jewish immigration and agricultural settlement, and in 1897, he presided over a commission which scrutinised applications for transfer of land in the *Mutasarrifiyya* and so effectively stopped all purchases by Jews for the next few years.[29] In 1900 there was a campaign of protest by means of signed petitions against Jewish purchases of land.[30]

Fears and Apprehensions

In the same year, A. Antebi, of the Jewish Colonial Association (a non-Zionist institution) reported:

> The Zionists had made the Muslim population ill-disposed to all progress accomplished by the Jews. A year and a half later, illiterate Muslim peasants asked him, 'Is it time that the Jews wish to retake this country?' and in early 1902 the ill-will had spread to the Administrative Council, the law courts and government officials many of whom especially at lower levels were drawn from the local population.[31]

Religious sentiments were an additional ground of resentment:

> Muslim sentiments in Jerusalem were reflected in the following statement made in 1903 by a young (and, it is reported not very fanatical) Arab: 'We shall pour everything to the last drop of our blood rather than see our Haram Sharif fall into the hands of non-Muslims.'[32]

It is also worth noting that local government officials, Christians and educated Muslims, were interested in reading Zionist literature, and some of them even read *Ha-Po'el Ha-Za'ir*. This explains the presence of a state of alarm among the Arab population of Palestine following the Seventh Zionist Congress in 1905, which resolved that Zionist efforts must be directed entirely towards Palestine.

The Palestinians were not entirely alone in conceiving the implications of Jewish immigration and agricultural settlement in Palestine. Rashid Rida, one of the most prominent Islamic reformists and editor of the influential *Al-Manar,* recognised that the Jews were seeking national sovereignty in Palestine.[33] In his book, *Le Reveil de la Nation Arabe* (Paris, 1905), Najib Azoury warned that Zionists and Arab nationalist aspirations would come into conflict. Because Azoury called for Arab independence, copies of his manifesto had to be smuggled into Palestine as a result of which several Arab notables in Jaffa, Gaza and Ramla were imprisoned by the Ottoman authorities.[34]

Towards the end of the nineteenth century, an important event took place that was destined to have a most dramatic impact on the fate of Palestine. Organised Zionism was born at the First Zionist Congress, 1897, where the formulation of the Zionist Programme and the establishment of the Zionist Organisation were achieved. The Zionist

Programme, alias the Basle Programme,[35] declared that 'the aim of
Zionism is to create for the Jewish people a home in Palestine secured
by law', to be achieved by systematically promoting the settlement in
Palestine of Jewish agriculturalists, artisans and craftsmen, in addition
to strengthening the Jewish national consciousness through Zionist
Federations all over the world. After creating the Zionist Organisation,
its founder, Theodor Herzl,[36] proceeded to create the instruments of
systematic colonisation. Herzl had his misgivings about the haphazard
colonisation of Palestine supported by wealthy Jews as a mixed philan-
thropic nationalistic venture. For him, it did not prove to be the right
way for the fulfilment of Zionist aims. The chosen instruments for this
colonisation scheme were *The Jewish Colonial Trust* (1898), *The
Colonisation Commission* (1898), *The Jewish National Fund* (1901)
and *The Palestine Land Development Company* (1908).[37] With the
arrival in Palestine of the second *aliya* (1904-1907), a more determined,
better organised and ideologically committed attitude prevailed. The
attitudes between the first and second *aliya* colonists differed in a
number of aspects, of which the most important constituted their
attitude towards the Arab population of Palestine. An outstanding
leader of the second *aliya*, David Green (Ben-Gurion),[38] spoke about
the state of Jewish affairs at the time of his arrival in 1906:

> Among the early disappointments was the spectacle of Jews of the
> first *aliya*, now living as *effendis*, drawing their income from groves
> and fields worked by hired workmen or from occupation of the kind
> imposed on our people by their exile. It was clear to me that we
> could never achieve national rehabilitation that way.[39]

According to Ben-Gurion the aims and achievements of the second
aliya were radically different from those of the first *aliya*: 'Pioneer *aliya*
gave birth to a Jewish community radically unlike all others,
independent in economy, culture and speech, able to defend itself.'[40]
Here we find the prototype, as it were, of the embryo of the
contemplated Zionist state: exclusively Jewish, motivated by Zionist
ideals and almost completely insulated. The key Zionist concept in this
context was *Kibush Avodah* (Conquest of Labour). In *Ben-Gurion
Looks Back*, the Zionist veteran explained this concept, and the fight it
entailed against Jewish landowners who preferred Arab labourers to
inexperienced Jewish hands, and the dismissal of Circassian guards with
the resulting emergence of the organisation of watchmen called the
Hashomer, the forerunner of the *Haganah*.[41]

This rigid and doctrinaire attitude *vis-à-vis* the 'natives' left no room for conciliation. The Arab tenant farmers were not merely dispossessed, they were prevented from being employed as hired hands. The reaction was one of widespread resentment, and by 1907, 'anti-Jewish feeling had intensified among the most influential segments of the Arab population and was latent among fellaheen who had contact with the *Jewish settlers*'.[42]

Notes

1. Vital Cuinet, *Syrie, Liban et Palestine, Géographie Administrative, Statistique, Descriptive et Raisonnée*, Paris, 1896, p.520.
2. Ibid., pp.93, 180 and 520.
3. Arthur Ruppin, *The Jewish Fate and Future*, London, 1940, p.54.
4. A practice which granted non-Muslim subjects a limited autonomy under the chief ecclesiastical leaders of the various religious sects.
5. James Finn to Viscount Palmerston, 7 November 1851, FO 78/874, no.20.
6. Albert Hourani, *Ottoman Reform and the Politics of Notables*, unpublished manuscript, pp.6-7. (Subsequently published in *Beginnings of Modernisation in the Middle East: The Nineteenth Century*, edited by William R. Polk and Richard L. Chambers, Chicago, 1968, pp.41-68.)
7. Ibid., pp.30-31.
8. Ibid., p.35.
9. Albert Hyamson, *The British Consulate in Jerusalem in Relation to the Jews of Palestine, 1838-1914*, London, 1939-1941, part I, p.xxxiv.
10. Viscount Palmerston to Viscount Ponsonby, 11 August 1840, FO 78/390, no.134.
11. Arthur Hertzberg (ed.), *The Zionist Idea: A Historical Analysis and Reader*, New York, 1959, p.29.
12. Nahum Sokolow, *History of Zionism: 1600-1918*, 2 vols., London, 1919, II, p.256.
13. George Antonius, *The Arab Awakening*, Beirut, n.d., first published 1938, p.54. Also see Albert Hourani, *Arabic Thought in the Liberal Age 1798-1939*, London, 1962; Zeine N. Zeine, *Arab-Turkish Relations and the Emergence of Arab Nationalism*, Beirut, 1958; and William Yale, *The Near East*, Ann Arbor, 1958.
14. 13 December 1875, FO 226/183.
15. 28 June 1880, FO 195/1306.
16. Antonius, op.cit., pp.83-4.
17. 1882, FO 226/204, No.37.
18. 14 March 1884, FO 195/1477.
19. 25 May 1839, FO 78/368, No.13.
20. 11 August 1853, FO 78/962, No.26.
21. Mandel Neville, *Turks, Arabs and Jewish Immigration into Palestine, 1882-1914*, unpublished D.Phil. dissertation, St Antony's College, Oxford, 1965, p.32.
22. Ibid., p.37.
23. Ibid., p.36.
24. Ibid., p.40.
25. 5 March 1887. FO 195/1581, No.9.
26. Mandel, op.cit., p.44.
27. Ibid., p.56.

28. Ibid., p.57.
29. Ibid., p.155.
30. Ibid., pp.102-3.
31. Quoted, ibid., p.132.
32. Ibid., p.133.
33. *Al-Manar*, Vol.IV, 1902, pp.801-9.
34. Mandel, op.cit., pp.145-6.
35. It is commonly referred to as The Basle Programme because the First Zionist Congress met at Basle, Switzerland.
36. For Herzl's ideas and activities see Theodor Herzl, *The Complete Diaries of Theodor Herzl*, 5 vols., edited by Raphael Patai, translated by Harry Zohn, New York, 1960.
37. For further details of the Zionist organisational structure see Sokolow, op.cit., I, pp.263-131 *passim*.
38. Ben Gurion soon became the pillar of the Jewish Community in Palestine and was the most outstanding Zionist leader from the thirties onwards. In 1948 he was declared the first Prime Minister of Israel.
39. David Ben-Gurion, *Israel: Years of Challenge*, London, 1964, p.7.
40. Ibid., p.42.
41. Moshe Pearlman (ed. and trans.), *Ben Gurion Looks Back*, London, 1965, pp.25-7.
42. Mandel, op.cit., p.148.

2 CRYSTALLISATION 1908-1914

By 1908 resentment against the incoming Jews backed by foreign protection, endowed with the privileges and advantages of the Capitulations, began to assume new dimensions. Following the Ottoman Revolution of 1908, a Palestinian newspaper, *Al-Asma'i,* seized the occasion of parliamentary election, and drew a comparison between the conditions of the Palestinian Arab peasant and his Jewish counterpart, then went on to point out the harm done by Jewish immigration:

> They harm and do evil to the indigenous population, by relying on the special rights enjoyed by foreign powers in Turkey and on the corruption and treachery of the local administration. In addition they are free from most of the taxes and heavy impositions on Ottoman subjects; they compete with the native population with their labour, and create their own means of sustenance and the (native) population cannot stand up to their competition.[1]

As a remedy the paper proposed that its readers buy local rather than foreign products and called upon wealthy Arabs to support the development of native commerce and industry.

The Palestinian peasants resented the Jewish colonists and were hostile from the moment of the settler's arrival in some cases.[2] 'In December, 1908, villagers from Kafr Kama tried to seize some land belonging to J.C.A. in the *Caza* of Tiberias.'[3]

The Land-sellers

Hand in hand with this resentment went the indignation at feudal landowners profiting from land sales to Jews at high prices:

> In November, 1908, it was reported that the peasants in the region of Haifa and Tiberias were adopting an aggressive attitude towards Arab landowners with large estates (Mustafa Pasha, Fu'ad Sa'd and the Sursuq family) and also towards Jewish colonies.[4]

This raises the issue as to the exact identity of the landowners who profited at the expense of obvious harm done to Arab tenants with utter disregard for the pressure of public opinion against the sale of land to the colonists.

A hitherto unpublished manuscript written by a prominent member of the Khalidi family[5] and completed in 1911, sheds light on the general state of political information in Palestine at that time, as well as providing valuable information on Jewish colonies. This manuscript, entitled *al-Mas'ala al-Sahyuniyya* (The Zionist Question), left its imprint on a number of individuals who later played key roles in the national movement in Palestine, like *Haj Amin al-Husseini.*[6] The author started by defining Zionism, its origins, history and aims; the establishment of a Jewish State in Palestine being the most important of all aims. With some detail and considerable knowledge, the author described Herzl's efforts, the Zionist Congresses and the institutions designed to serve and achieve Zionist aims. Furthermore, he drew a subtle and definite distinction between Zionist and non-Zionist Jews. After a short account of Jewish history, the author dealt in a careful and informative fashion with the activities of Jewish immigrants and their colonies. The author provided his readers with a list of all the Jewish colonies, the area of each colony, its original name in Arabic, and from whom the land was bought.

In the overwhelming majority of cases the lands were sold by one or the other of the following three categories:

(1) Absentee landlords, mostly Lebanese families — Sursuq, Tayyan, Twainy, Mudawar and others.

(2) The Ottoman Government, apparently through auctions owing to the inability of the Arab peasants to pay their taxes.

(3) The Palestinian landlords, mostly Christian families, — Kassar, Rock, Khoury, Hanna and others.[7] Some lands were sold by Muslim notables, but the author did not always disclose their names. In two cases, he wrote, 'one of the effendis of Safad or Ramleh'. Only three villages were reported to have been sold by the peasants and represented less than 7% of the total land bought by the Jews.

In all, the Jews at that time owned 28 villages and a total area of 279,491 *dunum;* a fraction of Palestine's cultivable area. In a letter published in *al-Ahram* on 4 August 1909, a Palestinian studying at *al-Azhar* accused the Jews of employing devious means; namely, bribing the Ottoman governors of the *ancien régime* as a means of obtaining land in Palestine. There were other attempts by Palestinians to make capital out of associating the previous regime with concessions made to the Zionists, including laxity in the application of laws regarding Jewish immigration and land acquisition by them. Furthermore, members of the (Ottoman) ruling *Committee for Union and Progress,* with branches in Palestine, endeavoured to exercise inter-party pressure to draw the attention of the ruling junta to 'the danger which menaces the country and the peasants from Jewish immigration'.[8]

The Forms and Forums of Arab Opposition to Zionism

By the end of 1909 sustained vocal opposition to Zionist immigration had become the order of the day. The mounting Palestinian opposition was promoted and adequately expressed by the only Arabic newspapers in Palestine *al-Asma'ī* and *al-Karmal.* The editor of the latter paper played a leading role in publicising the Zionist threat to Palestine and the Palestinians. Najib al-Khuri Nassar, a native of Tiberias, had worked with the Jewish Colonisation Association as an agent and thus was able to speak with authority on the aims and the means of Jewish colonisation in Palestine. He founded al-Karmal (1909) with the express purpose of writing against the Yishuv in Palestine as that the Arabs would not continue to sell land to the Jews.[9] Complaints from Jews about articles which had appeared in *al-Karmal* resulted in its temporary suspension in the early summer and again in the winter of 1909.

The notables found in the new Ottoman Parliament an opportunity to articulate Palestinian Arab opposition to Zionism and Jewish immigration. At the beginning of June 1909, Hafez Bey al-Sa'id, the deputy from Jaffa, submitted a question to the Chamber, asking what Zionism implied and if the national movement of the Jews was compatible with the interests of the Empire. He also demanded that the port of Jaffa be closed to Jewish immigrants.[10] Though the forum was modern, the old role of the notable as an intermediary between the ruler and the ruled persisted.

Towards the end of the year there was a note of exasperation in the air. In October, *al-Ahram* sent a correspondent to Palestine to report on the local situation. 'The Palestinians are concerned about the Zionist Movement; constant immigration creates fear and anxiety for the country is now almost in the hands of foreigners.'[11] Furthermore, the reporter recorded that the Palestinians accused the Zionist Movement in Palestine of seeking to establish an independent kingdom, and asserted that some rich Jews had undertaken to pay sums of money to the Ottoman Government so that the Ottoman Jews in Palestine would be spared military service and could devote all their efforts towards colonisation, at a time when Muslims and Christians had no alternative but to undergo the hated military service.

Amidst resentment and suspicion of Governmental collusion, a significant development took place in the same year; opposition to Zionism and Jewish settlement began to assume an organisational form. In October 1909, Albert Antebi observed that a group was being formed among the local population to prevent sales of land to Jews.[12]

In addition to the familiar platforms of protest — newspaper articles, telegrams and delegations — to the various levels of authority, the year 1910 witnessed the emergence of a call for an Arab boycott of Jewish goods and businesses in retaliation for Zionist boycott of Arab labour and shops.

In May 1910, the Arab press attacked the Sursuq family for their intention to sell the villages of Fulah and 'Afulah to the Jews. The inhabitants of Nazareth and Haifa despatched two telegrams to the Central Government protesting against Jewish land purchases and accusing the Zionists of seeking to deprive the local population of its land.[13] Al-Karmal warned against mortgaging any land with the Anglo-Palestine Company because of its Zionist identity. In the middle of May, a group of Arab deputies demanded an assurance from Tala't Bey that Jews would not be permitted to take possession of the local population's lands and that mass Jewish immigration would not be tolerated.[14]

Protestations to the Ottoman authorities were not in vain. When an official of the British Embassy in Constantinope spoke to Tala't Bey about the renewed land restrictions, he was told that they were 'the outcome of complaints of the local inhabitants who feared a foreign Jewish invasion'.[15]

By the summer of 1910, several influential Arabic newspapers in Damascus (*al-Muqtabas*) and in Beirut (*al-Mufid, al-Haqiqa*, and *al-Ra'i al-'Am*) were won over to the campaign against the sale of Arab lands to Jewish settlers and became part of the anti-Zionist press campaign. In some cases Najib Nassar's efforts were instrumental in drawing the attention of the editors to the Zionist danger.[16]

During debates in Parliament the Palestinian deputies urged the Government to take action against Jewish immigration and land purchases and were energetically promoting and propagating the notion of the incompatibility between Ottoman interests and Zionist aims in Palestine. 'During March and April Dr. Jacobson reported from Constantinople that the Arab deputies, especially Ruhi Bey al-Khalidi, were conducting a campaign for new legislation against Jewish immigration into Palestine.'[17]

Sa'id al-Husseini, deputy of Jerusalem, well-versed in Zionist ideas and activities owing to his proficiency in Hebrew, was another active anti-Zionist. Albert Antebi reported that, since accounts of speeches by Ruhi Khalidi and Shukri al-Assali had spread among the peasants, anti-Jewish feeling had widened.[18] A telegram signed by one hundred and fifty Arabs was dispatched from Jaffa to the President of the Chamber, to the Grand Vazir and to various newspapers in protest against the continual purchase of land by Jews and urged Parliament to take steps against Jewish immigration and land purchase.[19]

On 24 May 1911, *ha-Herut* carried the text of a leaflet which proclaimed the emergence of organised Palestinian Arab opposition to Zionism. The leaflet was signed *al-Hizb al-Watani al-'Uthmani* (The Ottoman National Party). The Party addressed itself to the Arabs of Palestine in the following terms:

Zionism is the danger which encompasses our homeland; [Zionism] is the awful wave which beats [our] shores; it is the source of the deceitful acts which we experience like a downpour and which are to be feared more than going alone at the dead of night. Not only this; it is also an omen of our future exile from our homeland and of (our) departure from our homes and property.

Suleiman al-Taji al-Farouqi, a founder of the Ottoman National Party, sought to mobilise public opinion in the neighbouring Arab districts of the Ottoman Empire against what he and his associates regarded as Zionist invasion. On 19 August 1911, this able writer and poet wrote an important long editorial in *al-Mufid*, a leading Beirut newspaper run by 'Abdul Ghani al-'Arisi, a prominent political figure. Al-Farouqi stated that Palestine had virtually fallen within the sphere of Zionist influence, and that Zionism in Palestine constituted a government within a government with its own laws and courts, its own flag, its own school system etc. Jewish immigrants, he contended, were equipped with education and money, and the Palestinians were threatened with poverty and eviction. These conditions prodded a group of young men to establish;

A National (Patriotic) party to promote everything beneficient to the nation, and to direct all efforts towards lawful opposition to the Zionist Movement and fighting it with the weapon of justice, in addition calling the attention of the *Ummah* (Nation) to the grave consequences and reminding the government of its duties: First, stoppage of immigration by applying the Red Passport.[20] Second, prohibition of sales of land. Third, carrying out a census among the Jews and giving the Ottomans among them clear identity cards. Fourth, imposition of governmental control and official curriculum over their schools. Fifth, prohibition of their special meetings unless they obtain special permission from the authorities in accordance with the laws governing such meetings. Sixth, carrying out land surveys in the colonies, and imposing the various taxes, tithes and Wercos, and reasserting the lost rights of the Treasury.

The growth of Arab opposition to Zionism was reported by the Palestine correspondent of *Ha'olam*, the central Zionist organ, in the following terms:

The greater force in Palestine is the Arabs. . .we forgot altogether that there are Arabs in Palestine, and discovered them only in recent years. . .we paid no attention to them; we never even tried to find friends among them. The greatest enemies of Jewish efforts are the Christian intellectuals among the Arabs.[21]

The last sentence was an acknowledgement of the efforts of Najib Nassar, editor of *al-Karmal*, whose unyielding perseverance in combating Zionism was effective in stirring public opinion inside and outside Palestine against Zionist immigration and settlement. On 7 June 1911, Nassar published in *al-Karmal* an open letter addressed to all newspaper editors who shared his views, suggesting that they unite in a common front against the Zionists. Within a few days his suggestion found support from Taha al-Mudawwar of Beirut's *al-Ra'i al-'Am* who proposed a common stand among the newspapers against Zionist settlement, in an endeavour to bring about appropriate government action to prevent it. On reviewing the Arabic newspapers of the second half of 1911, the reader would readily notice the expanded circle of anti-Zionist articles.

During the same year Najib Nassar also published a book entitled, *al-Sahyuniyya: Tarikhuha, Gharaduha, Ahammiyyatuha* (Zionism: Its History, Aims, and Importance), where he told his readers that the Zionist Movement rested on a racial base, and its aims were both national and political. He laid stress on its independent institutions, its para-military gymnastic societies, its flag and its emblem. After stating that Zionism aimed at gaining 'mastery over our country and the sources of our livelihood', he pointed out that 'unwavering leadership and bold, ambitious plans were required. . . We the Arabs need to rely upon ourselves and to stop expecting everything from the Government'.

The Palestinians were discovering that the Government was not very keen on protecting them from the Zionist danger. Calls for organisation found receptive ears. After the second debate on Zionism in Parliament, Nassar drew the attention of the readers of *al-Karmal* to the lax manner in which entry restrictions and regulations were enforced by the Ottoman authorities in Haifa. He succeeded in setting up a citizen's watch committee, which was successful in gaining permission from the *Mutasarrif* of Acre to supervise the disembarkation of Jews from all ships docking at Haifa in order to see that the entry restrictions were fully implemented. Nassar's efforts left an imprint on a number of Arab journalists, like *'Isa al-'Isa* of *Falastin* and 'Izzat Darwaza, the writer-politician who played a role in the Arab national movement in Palestine as we shall see later on.

Opposition to Zionism found some expression in literary works like *al-Sahir wa al-Yahudi* (The Wizard and the Jew) by Is'af Nashashibi, March 1909, and *Fatat Sahyun* (The Young Girl of Zion) by Ma'ruf al-Arna'ut, November 1911.

By the beginning of 1912 the Zionists were already speaking of 'the spirit of enmity which has begun to gain a foothold among the masses in the Mutasarriflik of Jerusalem'.[22]

The anti-Zionist campaign in the Arabic press continued unabated. *Al-Munadi,* a newspaper which began to appear in Jerusalem in the spring of 1912, was candidly anti-Zionist from its first issue. An article by Muhammad Salah al-Samadi al-Husseini of Jerusalem in *al-Ra'i al-'Am* declared that the dangers of Zionism and Jewish immigration were ten-fold. Zionist-inspired Jewish immigration would lead to: Jewish settlement in places of the greatest commercial and strategic importance; the sale of the local population's houses and land; the loss of the most valuable land; the return of the Jew's money to their own pockets through places of entertainment and the like which they would open for the Arabs; the subjugation of the local population to the Jews; the usurpation of all educational affairs by Zionist schools; the theft of industry and trade by Zionist banks and institutions; the defeat of the most powerful Arab leaders; and finally, the economic domination of Palestine through which political power would be generated.[23] Echoing the tone of this article *al-Muqtabas* alleged in its issue of 25 December 1912, that 'Zionism sought to destroy the totality of our economics and politics'.

Falastin, which was on its way to becoming the foremost anti-

Zionist paper, informed its readers, in its issue of 28 August 1912, that active immigrants own thirty colonies or villages, that immigration is proceeding at a terrific pace and that Hebrew will become the official language of the country someday. The Zionists have advanced schools and numerous important newspapers and have powerful societies backing them. The article concluded by exhorting the Arabs of Palestine to wake up to prevent a catastrophe before it is too late. Three days later the same paper called for the unity of all Palestinians to combat the Zionist danger.

Among the Ottoman provinces Palestine alone was free of the prevailing strife and tension between Muslim and Christian Arab communities due to the Balkan War. The relations between the two communities in Palestine were remarkably good owing to solidarity against the common Zionist danger.[24]

On 17 November 1912, *Falastin* published an article accusing the *Mutassarrif* of complicity in selling lands to the Jews in the face of Arab opposition and widespread protest. By the end of 1912 *Falastin* was so outspoken against Zionism that *ha-Herut's* correspondent in Jaffa called for its boycott.

The pace was set for 1913 by *al-Karmal* in an editorial of 3 January. That editorial dealt with the general political situation as well as giving an evaluation of the outcome of the paper's four-year campaign against Zionism. It referred to the efforts of some Arab deputies like Shukri al-'Assaly and Ruhi Khalidi in particular to combat Zionism in debates in the Ottoman Parliament. Then it proceeded to attack other leaders who, while pretending to safeguard the national interests, were in fact indulging in brokerage and sales of land to the Zionists. The article concluded by stating that 'a good number of enlightened people, journalists and (local) government officials, recognised the menacing Zionist danger and were fighting this danger with us'.

Throughout the summer of 1913 Syria witnessed a general campaign of protests against the sale of state lands in Beisan to the Jews. In June *Falastin* published two telegrams from the leaders of the villages and tribes of Beisan addressed to the Sultan and the *Vali* of Beirut. In these telegrams the inhabitants explained that the lands in question were usurped from them and registered in the name of the previous Sultan and that the state was now contemplating selling it to foreigners. The telegram reminded the Sultan that it was the duty of the ruling authorities to safeguard the interests of their subjects whom they taxed and conscripted. 'We prefer to die defending our nation and our possessions rather than emigrate to unknown destinations and perish from starvation.'[25] On 29 June, *Falastin* hinted that what Palestine, 'the beloved nation', needed was the bliss of independence but that 'we dare not spell it out'. The same issue carried an article contributed by a reader in which he emphasised that words cannot stand in the face of finance, science, zeal and national solidarity of the Zionists. Only action can stand in the face of action. The writer suggested the establishment of a national Palestinian land company financed by a group of wealthy Palestinians to buy lands that were not under cultivation and to exert pressure on the government to confine cultivated land sales to peasants. He concluded by calling for unity and co-operation to defend the country.

In these articles, published in the early part of the second decade, two things merit remark. The first is the implicit and permeating feeling of admiration for the advanced technological and organisational methods employed by the Zionists. The second is the underlying and sometimes explicit realisation that only through acquiring knowledge, skill and organisation could Arab opposition to Zionism be effective.

The First Arab Congress

The political stirrings and cross-currents of political ideas and aspirations culminated in the convening of the First Arab Congress in Paris during June 1913, which included an impressive number of prominent political personalities from the Levant.

It was an attempt at articulating a political programme demanding partnership and equality between the Arabs and the Turks within the Ottoman Empire. Delegates demanded recognition of the Arabs as a nation entitled to autonomy within a decentralised Ottoman state and to representation on all legislative and executive levels. They also demanded cultural independence and promotion of the Arabic language to the status of an official language.

Among the participants listed in the book published on the proceedings of the Congress, there were a number of Palestinian notables and students. The more striking aspect of the Palestinian presence in the Congress were the telegrams sent from Palestine to the Congress. These telegrams revealed the existence of two literary groups in Jaffa. *al-Multa' am al-'Adabi*[26] (The Literary Meeting Place) and *al-Jam'iyya al-Khairiyya al-Islamiyya* (The Islamic Benevolent Society). Telegrams were also sent by the inhabitants of Nablus and Haifa who pledged their support and called for reform and decentralisation. Other telegrams from the headmen and local notables of Beisan and Jenin urged the Congress to declare its opposition to the sale of lands in their district which they claimed were usurped from them by the Ottoman *ancien régime*. The signatories considered the delegates as 'representative of the Arab Nation', and the loss of the Beisan lands as a threat to the whole Arab Nation.[27]

It was extraordinary that the First Arab Congress did not discuss fully the Zionist danger in Palestine and that no resolutions were passed in relation to this important and preoccupying issue. The fact was that the incipient Arab national movement was contemplating ways and means to attain political independence for the Arab provinces of the Ottoman Empire. In a paper published in *Middle Eastern Studies,* Neville Mandel reported contacts between certain members of the Arab Decentralisation Party and the Zionist Executive. These contacts must be viewed, 'within the context of the nationalists' search for allies against the Turks'.[28] However, the Palestinians were unwilling to endorse the policy of taking the Zionists as temporary allies in the struggle against the Turks. In its issue of 9 July 1913, *Falastin* rebuked a leading figure of the Arab Congress, Sheikh Ahmad Tabbara, 'For he did not mention what dangers were connected with the immigration of the Zionists into the country and what problems for the future are being brought by the Government's attitude on this issue'. What is of interest to us in this context is the degree of Palestinian participation in th attempts at the 'Arab-Zionist entente'. According to Mandel, 'Some Arab notables were disturbed by the (anti-Zionist) popular mood. One such notable was Nassif Bey al-Khalidi, a native of Jerusalem, who in 1914 was Chief Engineer in Beirut.'[29] Nassif Bey's efforts to convene an Arab-Zionist conference were unsuccessful.

Zionist contacts with Palestinian Arabs in Constantinople were also abortive. Their demands were unacceptable to the Zionists. The Arabs desired the Zionists:

(i) to assist Arab education, by supplying expertise and funds; (ii) to give assurances that the fellaheen would not be deprived of all their land or proletarianised by the Jewish settlers; and (iii) to find large capital sums to finance extensive public-work projects for the development of the Arab provinces.[30]

In Palestine itself there were unmistakable signs of a hardening of Arab anti-Zionist feeling, in the months immediately following the Congress. In August, *Falastin* informed its readers that it had to increase the number of its pages in order to publish the increasing number of petitions and protests against Zionist encroachment. On 12 August, *al-Karmal* reported in its front page a huge demonstration in Nablus against the intended sale of the Beisan lands to the Jews, where spirited and vehement speeches were delivered, and telegrams of protest despatched to the authorities. Three days later, *al-Karmal* proposed that an anti-Zionist congress be held in Nablus to discuss ways and means of combating the Zionist peril. The proposed congress would discuss the establishment of societies to mobilise the people, improve the conditions of the peasant, create wealth and preserve it and encourage the quest for applied (practical) sciences. *Al-Karmal* argued that promoting the peasant's well-being and dignity would sharpen his sense of duty towards his nation. Knowledge, patriotism and solidarity were not enough to combat the encroaching danger. What was at stake, *al-Karmal* concluded, was survival and in this context organised and enlightened action alone could save the day.

Many Arab newspapers and a few political groups endorsed *al-Karmal's* proposed congress. As no enthusiasm was shown by the leading notables, the proposal was not carried out. However, *al-Karmal's* agitation for organisation was instrumental in preparing the ground for the emergence of an Anti-Zionist Society with headquarters in Nablus and branches in other Palestinian towns. This Society called for demonstrations against the Government's intended land sales by public auction, despatched telegrams of protests and proposed that the preservation of the peasant's rights in their lands which were usurped by the Government could be achieved through annual instalments. The Anti-Zionist Society led the agitation and struggle against Zionism in Palestine by setting the pace and pattern of articulation from Nablus where no Jewish element or influence existed to counteract the Society's activities. As early as 3 August, Antebi reported that, 'The Anti-Zionist Society was gaining adherents and was moving into its active phase.'[31]

Throughout September 1913, *Falastin* and *al-Karmal* devoted a great deal of space to Zionist activities in a deliberate attempt designed to inspire a desire for emulation. On 20 September, *Falastin* reported that a group called The Society of Jewish Youth had been formed to ensure that the Jews boycotted the local population. Less than a month later, the same paper attacked the communal Jewish law courts in Tel-Aviv and some of the Jewish settlements, suggesting that such institutions were laying the basis of 'a state within a state in Palestine'. On 4 November *al-Karmal* published a telegram that declared all those cooperating with the Zionists to be traitors, and on 8 November Suleiman al-Taji Farouqi of the National Ottoman Party, published a poem entitled, *The Zionist Danger.* In this poem Farouqi did not merely denounce Jewish designs to usurp Palestine from its inhabitants, but also warned the Turkish rulers and reminded them of their duty to protect Palestine where many holy Muslim sites existed.

The Ottoman authorities were not altogether happy with the vehemence that characterised Arab opposition to Zionism in the Arabic newspapers and took disciplinary action from time to time against these newspapers. The suspension of Arab papers began to arouse Arab suspicions that the Young Turks and the Zionists were allies in their battle against the incipient Arab national movement and Arab independence.

Organised Anti-Zionism

During the months that preceded the First World War, anti-Zionism in Palestine was at its peak. There was more evidence of organised opposition to Zionism; people who co-operated with the Zionists were unequivocally denounced; the press was extremely vocal against Zionism; and anti-Zionism played a prominent part in the campaign of most candidates to the Ottoman Parliament in Palestine.

On 24 February 1914, *al-Karmal* reported that Arab youth in Constantinople had founded an anti-Zionist Society. Towards the end of April, 'Ibry wrote to Dr Ruppin that he was sure that there existed both in Jerusalem and Jaffa special organisation of youth, both Christians and Muslims to fight us throughout Palestine by all means.'[32]

On 14 June *Falastin* published a letter from R. Abu al-Sal'ud which disclosed the names and programmes of four nationalist and welfare societies which had recently been founded in Jerusalem to 'stand in the face of the impending dangers threatening their homeland and save their existence from destruction'. These societies were the following: *al-Jam'iyya al-Khayriyya al-Islamiyya, jamiyyat al-Ikha' wal-'Afaf, Shirkat al-Iqtisad al-Falastini al-'Arabi* and *Shirkat al-Tijara al-Wataniyya al-Iqtisadiyya.* The correspondent added that a reading club was under way where magazines, newspapers and books would be available for purposes of public education. All the above-mentioned societies preached patriotism, promoted education[23] and supported national industries.

In its issue of 21 June, *al-Iqdam* published a letter from Jawdat Qandus which stated that the Palestinian students in Constantinople, together with the youth from Tyre and Marji'yun:

established a society whose aim is to unite the word and bring together the hearts of the Arabs in general and the Palestinians in particular to promote what is good for the country, and in particular, resist Zionism by all our means, if not through finance then through science, literature, and sincerity.

The founders of the Society planned to have headquarters in Jerusalem and branches in all other Palestinian towns. In the same message Qandus stated that the members of the Society were already lobbying the members of Parliament. On 5 May another newspaper, *Fata al-'Arab* reported the existence of a society at al-Azhar called *Jam'iat Muqawamat al Sahiyuniyyeen* (The Society for Resisting the Zionists), which had been founded by Palestinian students. On 19 July, *al-Iqdam* published a Manifesto of considerable length issued by the *al-Azhar* Society at the end of which the aims of the Society were stated:

(1) To oppose the Zionists by all possible means; by awakening public opinion and uniting views on this point; and by propagating the Society's programme among all classes of the Arab nation in general and in Syria and Palestine in particular.

(2) To found branches and societies in all the towns of Syria and Palestine for this purpose.

(3) To endeavour to spread the spirit of unity among all the elements of the inhabitants.

(4) To activate and support economic, commercial and agricultural projects and enlighten the ideas of the farmers and peasants, so that they may be able to protect themselves from the dangers of Zionism.

(5) To make representations before all those interested in this question to halt the stream of Zionist immigration.

Also in July, reports were published in *ha-Herut* of two societies formed under the influence of Najib Nassar. The first, in Beirut, was made up of a hundred young men from Nablus studying there and was called *al-Shabiba al-Nabulsiyya* (The Youth of Nablus).[34] Its aims were to protect the rights of the Arabs and to agitate for the good of the Arab people and for the good of Syria. The Second Association was a mixed Muslim and Christian society in Haifa called *al-Muntada al-Adabi* (The Literary Association), whose objectives were openly nationalist and secretly anti-Zionist.

In July 1914 Palestinian Arab women emerged on the political scene when they founded *Jam'iat al-Ihsan al-'Am* (Society for General

Charity) and *Jam'iat Yaqzat al-Fatat al-'Arabiyya* [Society for the Awakening of the Arab Girl). Both societies were nationalist and advocated support for local industries.[35]

On 7 July *al-Karmal* published a *General Summons to Palestinians* which was received from Jerusalem and presumably distributed by one of the newly founded organisations in that city. The summons reflected the tense political atmosphere that prevailed in the country and attempted to mobilise Palestinian public opinion as a preparation for more drastic action:

> ... Do you wish to be slaves to the Zionists who have come to kick you out of your country, claiming that it is theirs... Are you, Muslims, Palestinians, Syrians, Arabs, happy at this?

We shall die rather than let it happen.

The summons then urged the people to undertake the following action:

> (1) Apply pressure on the Government to act in accordance with its law stipulating that it is completely forbidden to sell *miri* (state) lands to foreigners.
>
> (2) Try to develop local (*wataniyah*) trade and industry. Do not trade except with your own people, as they (the Zionists) do because they do not trade with the Muslim and the Christian.
>
> (3) Do not sell them your lands and use your power to prevent the peasant from selling. Henceforth, scatter the land agents and revile them.
>
> (4) Be concerned to stop, by all means you can, the stream of migration from and to Palestine.
>
> (5) Demand of your *awqaf* to found Arab religious schools and also other schools for crafts, agriculture and science.
>
> (6) Trust in God and in yourselves; do not trust in the Government because it is occupied with other things. Strive that Arabic will be the language of instruction in schools.
>
> (7) You must implant in the hearts of the local population, especially the youth, love of agricultural work, of trade and industry ... The dangers threatening your country are many the greatest of all is 'the Zionist danger' so beware of it, strive, act and God will favour your deeds.

At the end of the summons *al-Karmal* inserted its own advice to the organisers:

> Mobilize public opinion so that you can achieve these objectives. You should not blame the Zionists as much as you should blame the leaders of your country and government officials who sell them lands and act as their brokers. Prevent those selling and you will halt the Zionist Movement.

The Summons revealed that as the Palestinians lost hope of any Government action against Zionist encroachment they moved towards self-organisation and self-reliance.

During the first seven months of 1914, the Palestinian Arab press played a key role in mobilising public opinion and preparing the ground for organisational and concerted action against the Zionists. The press assiduously denounced, 'Those rich and influential people who were blinded by self interest; they do not see the encircling Zionist danger, and preferred to have a golden present at the expense of a dark future for their sons'.[36] The same article warned that, "he who controls the land and the economy is the real master, and the political sovereign is merely his vassal".

On 2 April 1914, *Falastin* published an article on 'The Zionist Danger and the Arab Press' where it expressed gratification on witnessing a general anti-Zionist campaign in Cairo, Beirut and Damascus. *Falastin* paid tribute to the pioneering role of *al-Karmal* 'in the patriotic struggle' against Zionism, which was taken up soon afterwards by *Falastin* itself as well as *al-Muqtabas, al-Ra'i al-'Am, Fatat al-'Arab* and *al-Islah* successively. The article alleged that the few papers that failed to participate in the anti-Zionist campaign were receiving material benefits from the Zionist Movement. The writer of the article was apparently impressed by the participation of the prestigious *al-Hilal* magazine of Cairo in the fight against Zionism and referred to the long article published by it on the autonomous and totally insulated life led by the Jewish colonists in their settlements. The writer also acknowledged the role of *al-Iqdam* which was the keenest of all in exposing the Zionist danger and stirring public opinion on the issue.

The Electoral Platform of 1914

Al-Iqdam was a weekly paper published in Egypt in 1914; the editor was Muhammad al-Shanti, a Palestinian. For all intents and purposes *al-Iqdam* was a paper devoted to Palestinian affairs and was endowed with a certain immunity on Palestinian issues, since Egypt was not under Ottoman control. From the outset *al-Iqdam* sought to make the Zionist danger the heart of the matter in Palestinian public and political life. It invited debate and attention through a series of interviews with the notables and political personalities. It was instrumental in bringing to the fore the Zionist danger as the main issue in the Parliamentary elections of 1914. On the 22 March 1914, *al-Iqdam* published three interviews with Sa'id Husseini, Ragheb Nashashibi and Salim Husseini.

Sa'id Husseini pledged, if elected, to continue the fight against Zionism in Parliament as he had done in the past. He advocated the improvement of the *fellah*'s condition and providing him with owner-ship titles to the land he looks after in order that he may cling to it and never give it up. He criticised the government for not fighting Zionism, which was a political as well as an economic peril, and warned that negligence would lead to grave consequences.

Ragheb Nashashibi, another incumbent Parliamentary candidate, called for special legislation aimed at the prevention of Zionist acquisi-tion of land in Palestine. He resented the fact that many Zionists were non-Ottoman subjects who exploited the Capitulations, did not speak Arabic, and 'looked at our sons and brethren with contempt'. He pledged to fight Zionism and Zionists without injuring the feeling of Ottoman Jews.

Salim Husseini expressed admiration for the Zionists and called for their emulation. He also advocated special legislation to prohibit all land sales.

A week later, *al-Iqdam* published an interview with Khalil Sakakini, 'one of the founders of the Constitutional School in Jerusalem where the spirit of antagonism to Zionist colonialism was being propagated'. In the course of the brief interview Sakakini submitted a profound statement on the nature of the Zionist challenge:

> The Zionists want to own Palestine, that is, the heart of the Arab countries and the middle link between the Arab peninsula and Africa. Thus, it appears as if they want to break the chain and divide the Arab Nation (al-Ummah al-Arabiyyah) into two sections to prevent its unification and solidarity. The people should be conscious that it possesses a territory and a tongue, and if you want to kill a nation cut her tongue and occupy her territory and this is what the Zionists intend to do with the Arab Nation.

Another political personality, Faydi 'Alami warned that if matters continued to take the same course, 'The Zionists would own the country and we would be aliens'.

Jamil Husseini put the whole problem, including the dilemma of the notables, in a nutshell:

> Resisting Zionism is a priority because it is harmful to the inhabitants of the country and aims at dispossessing them of their lands. But how can we resist it and fight it when the Government lends it backing and support, and when the inhabitants are simple ignorant people. The Government employees are working in the direction of facilitating a Zionist takeover.

At about the same time a number of notables from Jerusalem, Jaffa and Gaza appealed to the members of *al-Muntada al-Adabi* in Constantinople and to the Turkish newspaper *Pyam*. The appeal spoke of the plight of the Palestinian peasant, as well as the merchant and the Government employee, because of Zionist designs and influence. 'If sincere people did not come to the rescue of the Palestinians', the appeal asserted, 'their fate, will be similar to that of the American Indians. Zionism, a state within the Ottoman state, threatens the very existence of the Arabs in Palestine'.[37]

In mid-April Ahmad al-'Aref, a former member of Parliament, told the editor of *al-Iqdam* that 'The sole topic of conversation among Palestinians at present...is the Zionist issue; all are frightened and scared of it'.

On 11 April, *Falastin* had to publish a supplement, 'owing to the great deal of material on the Zionist Movement'. That issue carried an important article on the economic boycotts and pressures applied by th Anglo-Palestine Bank against merchants and businessmen who had signed a telegram of protest against Zionism. The article named the merchants in question, and how they had to withdraw their signatures, and even to deny that they had signed the telegram in the first place, before the boycott of the Bank was lifted. Only one merchant refused to withdraw his signature and continued to suffer from the Bank's boycott. *Falastin*, then, added that economic boycotts were not new but had become strict of late: 'Jews do not buy from Muslims and Christians, there is hardly any trace of native labour in Jewish enterprise'.

On 20 April 1914, the local authorities suspended *Falastin* on orders received from the Ministry of Interior, on the grounds that an article which had appeared on 4 April was deemed guilty of exacerbating relations between the races. Subsequent to its suspension, *Falastin* issued a circular to its readers and subscribers which attacked the Government for regarding the Zionists as a race, whereas the paper contended that they were merely a political group. The paper distinguished between a Jew and a Zionist and blamed Zionism for the prevailing tensions:

> Ten years ago the Jews were living as Ottoman brothers loved by all the Ottoman races. . .living in the same quarters, their children going to the same schools. The Zionists put an end to all that and prevented any intermingling with the indigenous population. They boycotted the Arabic language and the Arab merchants, and declared their intention of taking over the country from its inhabitants.[38]

The circular quoted Dr Urbach of the Zionist Movement as saying in Haifa that Zionism should rise against the Arabs, divide them and evict them, thus serving Ottoman interests.

Furthermore, *Falastin* warned the authorities that Zionism was no longer a ghost but a tangible menace. The central government could suppress *Falastin,* but there were other patriotic papers to 'carry the torch', and there was the youth of Palestine, 'boiling with anxiety over the threatened future'.

The British Vice-Consul in Jaffa as well as the Consul in Jerusalem testified that the circular 'faithfully mirrors the growing resentment among the Arabs against the Jewish invasion'.[39]

The anti-Zionist campaign in the press continued unabated until the eve of the First World War in August 1914. However, the outbreak of the War did not stop the Arabs from contemplating action against the Zionists. According to Pearlman, 'Papers seized by the Turks in 1915 outline a plan for getting rid of Zionism; the colonies were to be razed by fire, and the Jews driven out. The Zionists it was argued were the worst enemies of the Arabs, that was why the Turks were so ready to assist them'.[40]

The Palestinians came to view the Zionists and the ruling Turkish nationalists as allies against Arab regeneration. It was not surprising that the Palestinians started contemplating violent means to overthrow Turkish hegemony on the eve of World War I as the only effective method of ridding themselves of both hostile forces. The two secret revolutionary organisations *al'Ahd* and *al-Fatat* which were active in promoting the Arab Revolt against the Turks during the war comprised many Palestinian Army Officers. Although the Arabs fought on the side of the Allies, the Allied victory brought forth a new occupation by a power that had promised the Zionist movement a Jewish national home in Palestine through the Balfour Declaration of 2 November 1917. The British occupation and rule in Palestine marked a new fateful era in the country's history which forms the subject of the subsequent chapters of this study.

On reviewing the reactions of the various socio-economic groups to Zionism, i.e. Jewish immigration and Jewish settlement between 1881 and 1914, certain patterns emerge. These patterns of reactions were related, by and large, to socio-economic factors.

The big landowners who were willing to sell their lands to the Zionists were mostly absentee landlords from outside Palestine proper, e.g. the Sursuqs or city merchants who had minimal contact with the peasants and no sympathy for their plight. Besides, these two categories of landowners did not derive their social power from land ownership. The traditional landowning families whose social standing depended on their land holdings and who constituted the 'notables' were reluctant to sell their lands to the Zionists for fear of undermining the base of their status. Some, like Nassif Khalidi, were disturbed by popular agitation and sought accommodation with the Zionists. However, in as much as Zionism aimed at taking over the country, the notables recognised the threat to their existence and position and sought to combat the Zionist peril by performing their role as intermediaries between ruler and ruled. The notables sought to fight Zionism by appealing to the authorities, the *Mutasarrif*, the central Government and Parliament, to restrict Jewish immigration and prohibit land sales to the Zionists. This role could only be effective, or indeed feasible, as long as the authorities were willing to respect the notables' appeals and maintain their position in society. Following the Young Turks Revolution, the notables' position and importance in articulating political demands was undermined.

The middle classes, professionals, artisans and literary groups were apprehensive of the professional competition and the political challenge introduced by Zionism in Palestine. Newspaper editors and students belonged to these classes and were instrumental in mobilising the public against the 'Zionist peril' as well as forming the backbone of political and semi-political organisations established to combat Zionism. It was the vocal and active groups of newspapermen and students that were outbidding the notables in the fight against Zionism.

The reaction of the peasants was less sophisticated and more violent as they were the direct victims of Zionist land acquisitions, especially after the second *aliya* and the introduction of *Kibush Avodah*. Almost all attacks on Jewish settlements were undertaken by destitute peasants who were evicted as a result of land sales to the Zionists.

Thus, within the ranks of the nationalist movement in Palestine, the notables performed the role of the diplomats, the educated middle classes that of the articulators of public opinion and the peasants that of the actual fighters in the battle against the Zionist presence.

Notes

1. Neville Mandel, *Turks, Arabs and Jewish Immigration into Palestine 1882-1914*, pp.164-65.
2. H. Frank to Antebi, 8 November 1908, AIU VIII E.25, quoted in Mandel, *op. cit.*, p.168.
3. For clashes between the peasants and the colonists, see Mandel, op. cit., pp.171-9. J.C.A. stands for Jewish Colonisation Association.
4. Ibid.
5. The Manuscript is presented under the custody of Professor Walid Khalidi. The authorship is not definitely known though it is almost certainly that of Ruhi al-Khalidi, a leading politician and intellectual in Palestine in the first two decades of the twentieth century.
6. Interview with Haj Amin el-Husseini, Beirut, Summer 1966.
7. The prefix (al) before family names is henceforth eliminated wherever convenient. It is possible that withholding of these Muslim notables' names was an act of political prudence on the part of the author.
8. *The Jewish Chronicle*, London, 18 June 1909.
9. Mandel, op.cit., p.204. *Al-Karmal* was founded in Haifa.
10. *The Jewish Chronicle*, 18 June 1909.
11. *Al-Ahmed*, 7 October 1909.
12. Albert Antebi to Frank, 18 October 1909, AIU IX E.27 quoted in Mandel, op.cit. p.214.
13. *Le Jeune Turc*, Constantinople, 7 May 1910.
14. Mandel, op.cit., pp.209-10.
15. 13 June 1910, FO 195/235, Minute on folder to No.25.
16. For Nassar's influence see *Falastin* (Palestine), 2 April 1914.
17. Arthur Ruppin (Jaffa) to ZCO, 31 March 1911, CZA Z2/635, quoted in Mandel, op.cit., p.251.
18. 21 June 1911, JCA 268/ enclosure No.195. Ibid pp.268-9.
19. Arthur Ruppin to ZCO, 31 March 1911, op.cit.,
20. The Red Passport was a measure initiated to stem the flow of immigrants posing as tourists. The original passport of the tourist was retained at the point of entry and a red slip was issued as a receipt which would entitle the owner to redeem his passport on leaving Palestine.
21. *Ha'olam*, vol.V (1911), quoted in Moshe Pearlman, 'Chapters of Arab-Jewish Diplomacy', in *Jewish Social Studies*, 1944.
22. See Mandel, op.cit., p.300.
23. Arthur Ruppin to ZAC, 2 May 1912, CZA Z3/144 8, quoted in Mandel, op.cit. p.296.
24. *Falastin*, 24 November 1912, accused the Zionists of sowing the seeds of Muslim-Christian strife through publishing letters, under Muslim names, designed to cause ill-will between the two communities.

25. *Falastin*, 5 June 1913.
26. Very little is known about this society beyond the fact that it included Christians as well as Muslim.
27. For names of participants and texts of telegrams see *al-Mu'tamara al-Arabi al-Awwal* (The First Arab Congress) published by the Supreme Committee of the Decentralisation Party in Egypt (Cairo, 1913).
28. Neville Mandel, 'Attempts at an Arab-Zionist Entente, 1913-1914', *Middle Eastern Studies*, vol.I, no.3, April 1965 p.241.
29. Ibid., p.251.
30. Ibid., p.258.
31. Antebi to President of JCA, 31 August 1913, JCA 268/no.218, quoted in Mandel, op.cit., p.390.
32. Quoted in Mandel, op.cit. p.476.
33. An educated Arab, Husni Khayyal, advocated the establishment of a college with Arabic as the language of instruction (*al-Iqdam*, Cairo, 14 June 1914). An unsigned manifesto distributed in Jerusalem in July 1914 called for the establishment of industrial and agricultural schools (*al-Karmal*, 7 July 1914).
34. In June 1914 Nablus's Administrative Council prohibited all sales of land to the Zionists irrespective of their nationality (*Falastin*, 27 June 1914).
35. *Al-Karmal*, 7 July 1914.
36. *Falastin*, 26 March 1914.
37. *Falastin*, 29 March, 1914.
38. Ibid., 29 April 1914.
39. McGregor to Mallet, 30 April 1914, FO 371/2134/2236, no.31.
40. *Jewish Social Studies*, p.125.

3 POLARISATION: THE MILITARY ADMINISTRATION 1917-1920

Between the summer of 1914 and the autumn of 1917, Palestine's internal political scene was overtaken by the First World War. Politically active elements in Palestine — Southern Syria as it was known then — were plotting against the Ottoman Empire in the interests of the Arab Revolt and Arab independence. The Palestinians, nevertheless, were not unmindful of the dangers posed by the Zionists.

In a report prepared by the Arab Bureau (a British military institution based in Cairo) during the early months of 1917, British officials were informed that 'There has already been formed in Jerusalem a society of the better class and better educated young Moslems for resisting Jewish colonisation'.[1]

A more revealing report on the political situation in Palestine was filed during the first weeks of January 1917 by Captain William Ormsby-Gore of the Arab Bureau.[2] The report described certain aspects of the political power structure in Jerusalem, and the attitude of the Palestinian Arabs towards the Turks, the British and the Zionists. 'In Palestine nobody — except the German Colonists — likes the Turks, least of all do the oppressed peasantry'.[3] The notable Muslim families — the Hussainis, the Khalidis, the Nashashibis and the Dawudis — were pro-British and sent their sons to English schools to be educated;

> The Moslems of Jerusalem and neighbourhood are well disposed toward the Christians, but very anti-Jewish, or to be more precise — Anti-Zionist. They strongly object to the growth in number and influence of the Jewish colonies in town and country and particularly to the purchase of land by the Zionists and consequently dispossession of the Moslem population.

The writer further added that the opposition of the old Turks and Arab representatives in the Ottoman Parliament to Zionist acquisition of land was quite ineffectual.

The ineffectiveness of the anti-Zionist Arab effort in the Ottoman Parliament encouraged the Palestinian Arabs to join secret Arab societies which were dedicated to Arab autonomy and later worked for Arab independence. The Palestinians conspicuous role in these secret societies was made public when Jamal Pasha, the Ottoman supreme military commander in charge of the Arab front, sent a number of Arab political leaders to the gallows on charges of conspiracy against the state. Salim 'Abdul-Hadi, 'Ali Omar Nashashibi and Muhammad al-Shanti were among those who were hanged. Hafez al-Sa'id and Sheikh Sa'id al-Karmi had their sentences commuted to imprisonment for life on account of their advanced years and Hasan Hammad had a miraculous escape. When the Sharif of Mecca, later King Hussein, declared the Arab Revolt against the Turks, a number of Palestinian officers joined his ranks.[4]

Before the Sharif declared his revolt, he reached an understanding with the British High Commissioner (H.Cr.) in Egypt, Sir Henry McMahon. In the correspondence between McMahon and Hussein, Britain pledged to recognise and support Arab independence within certain specified frontiers in the Syrian provinces of the Ottoman Empire in return for Hussein's declaration of war on Turkey.[5] The question whether Palestine was to be included within those frontiers or not became a controversial question after the end of the War. Whatever the British real intentions at that time, the Arabs were under the impression that Palestine was included in the proposed independent Arab state which Britain promised to recognise. It is certain [6] that Palestine was included in the Arab State which Britain would, through McMahon, be pledged to recognise. The cause of the controversy over this can only be understood in the light of other commitments to the Zionists and to the French during the war.

Simultaneously with the Hussein-McMahon correspondence, the British were secretly negotiating with their French allies the respective territorial desiderata in the Ottoman Empire. These negotiations culminated in the Sykes-Picot Agreement of 16 May 1916, according to which Palestine was to have

an international administration, the form of which is to be decided upon after consultation with Russia, and subsequently in consultation with the other Allies, and the representatives of the Sharif of Mecca.[7]

But before the end of the War Britain undertook another major commitment regarding the future of Palestine in the form of a letter dated 2 November 1917, from Lord Balfour, Britain's Foreign Secretary, to Lord Rothschild, the leading Jewish personality in Britain:

His Majesty's Government view with favour the establishment in Palestine of a national home for the Jewish people, and will use their best endeavours to facilitate the achievement of this object, it being clearly understood that nothing shall be done which may prejudice the civil and religious rights of the existing non-Jewish communities in Palestine, or the rights and political status enjoyed by Jews in any other country.[8]

Aware of the nature of Arab feeling regarding the future of Palestine,[9] the British Government tried to prevent any discussion of the Zionist subject during the War. When the Sharif's newspaper *al-Qibla* published, in the latter part of 1916, an article about Zionism, General MacDonogh of British Intelligence directed General Clayton, Chief Political Officer, Egyptian Expeditionary Force and head of the Arab Bureau, to communicate a 'serious and personal warnings to the Sharif and to urge him 'to do his utmost to prevent discussions of this dangerous topic.[10]

These British efforts prevented the erosion of Arab goodwill and 'British troops were welcomed as liberators' and 'the attitude of the Arabs in Palestine, passive and active, contributed to their success,[11] General Allenby and his Egyptian Expeditionary Force (EEF) entered Jerusalem 11 December 1917, less than six weeks after Balfour's Declaration.

Days after Allenby's entry into Jerusalem, Colonel Deedes of the EEF reported the initial reactions to the Balfour Declaration as follows:

The news of Mr Balfour's declaration regarding Palestine is new to Jerusalem and had caused no little apprehension amongst other elements, the latter I am warned are trying to see me.[12]

During the same week Deedes reported exacerbation of relations between Arab and Jew in Palestine as a result of the Declaration. Jewish Colonists

profess to wish to be self-supporting without Arab labour. . . There is also occasionally noticeable an anti-Arab feeling which is reciprocated and recently rather accentuated, as you are aware, by the Balfour pronouncement. In a word friction is not absent.[13]

General Clayton of the Arab Bureau lost no time in drawing the attention of London to the ramifications and likely effects of the Declaration on future Anglo-Arab relations in Palestine:

> The policy which is enunciated in clause No.4 (regarding Jewish Colonization in Palestine) will meet with strong opposition from both Christian and Moslem Arabs who have already shown distrust of the lengths to which H.M. Government are prepared to go as consequence of Mr. Balfour's announcement to the Zionists.[14]

Two weeks earlier, Clayton had laid the alternatives before Sykes. 'We have therefore to consider whether the situation demands out and out support of Zionism at the risk of alienating the Arabs at a critical moment.[15] In a memorandum to the War Cabinet circulated to the Middle East Committee, Sykes indicated his choice as to the two alternatives set out by Clayton. 'Palestine and our Zionist declaration combined gives us and the Entente as a whole a hold over the vital, vocal and sentimental forces of Jewry'.[16]

A Crowd of Weeds

Sykes added that a 'crowd of weeds' were growing around British (political) assets in the area; the first of the weeds on his list was 'Arab unrest in regard to Zionism'.[17]

In view of Palestinian Arab reactions to the Balfour Declaration and the JNH policy, the Military Authorities, who were primarily bent on winning the War and preserving peace and order in the country, withheld publication of the Declaration in Palestine throughout the period of the military administration and attempted to stick to the Law and Usages of War.[18] However, according to Colonel Ronald Storrs, the Military Governor of Jerusalem during the period of the Military Occupation:

> The Military Administration notably contravened the Status Quo, in the matter of Zionism. . . General Allenby's very first proclamation and all that issued from me were in Hebrew, as well as in English and Arabic. Departmental and public notices were in Hebrew and, as soon as possible, official and municipal receipts also. We had Jewish officers on our staffs, Jewish Clerks and interpreters in our offices. For these deliberate and vital infractions of military practice OETA was criticized both within and without Palestine.[19]

This, however, did not satisfy many leading Zionists in Palestine who were anxious to turn Palestine into a Jewish State 'as Jewish as England is English'[20] as soon as possible. Dr Weizmann, the Zionist leader, proposed that 'the whole administration of Palestine shall be so formed as to make of Palestine a Jewish Commonwealth under British trusteeship'.[21] Zionist impatience led to a certain amount of friction between the home authorities, who were willing to give way to Zionist schemes and pressures, and the local British authorities in Palestine and Egypt who were responsible for carrying out the Zionist policies in the face of Arab resentment and counter-pressures.

Indicative of the pace contemplated by Balfour and Weizmann was the interview in December 1918, at the Foreign Office, where the Zionist leader revealed his plans to the British Foreign Secretary:

> a community of four to five million Jews in Palestine. . from which the Jews could radiate out into the Near East. . .But all this presupposes free and unfettered development of the Jewish National Home in Palestine not mere facilities for colonisation.[22]

The British were less concerned about these grandiose plans at that time than they were about preserving their war position in the area. To achieve this end an Arab-Zionist understanding was deemed necessary. Forcing the hand of King Hussein on the Zionist issue was the first step in this direction:

> In this matter it should be pointed out to the King that the friendship of world Jewry to the Arab cause is equivalent to support in all States where Jews have political influence.[23]

Furthermore, as a result of Clayton's efforts, the Arab Committee in Cairo, alias the Syrian Welfare Committee, undertook to send emissaries to Palestine to persuade the Palestinian Arabs to take a more conciliatory attitude towards Zionism.

These efforts did not allay Arab suspicions in Palestine. Clayton's weekly reports from Jerusalem consistently talked of Palestinian uneasiness at Zionist activity and distrust of Britain's 'Zionist policy'. Towards the end of February 1918, Clayton reported that 'Educated Moslems are still much disturbed at what they deem preferential treatment of the Jews and at the possibility of Jewish domination.'[24]

Owing to the general war considerations, the British Government was anxious that a Zionist Commission visit Palestine, headed by Weizmann with Captain W. Ormsby-Gore as its liaison officer. The Foreign Office informed Wingate that the

Object of Commission is to carry out subject to General Allenby's authority any steps required to give effect to Government declaration in favour of establishment in Palestine of a national home for Jewish people. . .and at the same time allay Arab suspicions regarding true aims of Zionism.[25]

Before the Zionist Commission reached Palestine the Palestinian Arabs were able to transform their feelings of shock and apprehension into organisational effort as a means of promoting the expression and the effectiveness of their opposition to Zionist aims in Palestine. Inevitably the temptation to imitate the enemy's techniques was present. From Jerusalem, Clayton reported to his superiors:

Moslems are still nervous regarding progress of Zionist movement. There are indications that Moslems think that British Authorities intend to set up a Jewish Government but that France will intervene and oppose a Zionist State, . . .Christians share Moslem's apprehensions. There is a movement in Jaffa amongst the Moslems and Christians to appoint an official committee to further Christian and Moslem interests on similar lines to Jewish Committees.[26]

This movement culminated in the emergence of the Muslim-Christian Committees which were similar to Zionist and Jewish organisations in an effort to act as a counter-force to the Jewish organisation. Muslim-Christian Committees were mainly dominated by the leading notables and merchants in the major cities and towns of Palestine.

The British officials in the area endeavoured to create a conciliatory atmosphere on the eve of the Zionist Commission's visit and made a concerted effort to bring forth an Arab-Zionist entente.[27] These efforts were directed at the traditional centres of political influence and power. Thus towards the end of March the Commander-in-Chief of the British forces paid a visit to the Mufti in Jerusalem which 'produced an excellent effect throughout Moslem community'.[28]

Clayton lost no time in convincing pro-British Syrian politicians in Cairo, working for an Arab state in Syria, that Weizmann was working for a 'British Palestine'. He succeeded in persuading 'Fawzi el-Bakri, an El Azm, a Nashashibi, an Abd el-Hadi, Dr Farouk. . to communicate with their friends in Palestine to quiet their fears and reassure them'.[29]

Yet when Weizmann and his Zionist Commission reached Palestine during the first week of April 1918, he discovered that 'Arab agitators lost no time in proclaiming that "the British had sent for the Jews to take over the country"'.[30]

In a more optimistic frame of mind Clayton expected 'that meetings between members of the Commission and leading local notables will do much to dissipate apprehension of Christians and Moslem committees in Palestine.[31]

Clayton's hopes notwithstanding, the Commission's visit did little to promote an Arab-Zionist entente. In a long report to the Foreign Secretary (Balfour), Ormsby-Gore gave a detailed account of the reception accorded to it by the various communities, as well as its activities and the problems thereof. The report, though restrained, did not fail to reflect Palestinian opposition to the Balfour Declaration and the JNH policy:

> . . .It would be idle to deny the existence of a good deal of mutual suspicion on the part of both Jews and Arabs. . .The Arabs are generally apprehensive of expropriation by the Jews and the loss of social and political prestige; on the other side the Jews are frightened of Arab fanaticism, intrigue and attempts at domination'.

A Symptomatic Incident

Ormsby-Gore then reported a symptomatic incident signifying the political deadlock in the triangular Arab-British-Zionist relations in Palestine. The incident was referred to as the 'language controversy', which was precipitated by a recommendation submitted by the Arab majority of the Municipal Council of Jaffa (nominated by the Military Governor) that Arabic should be regarded as the only official language. The Jewish minority (two out of nine members) protested and the British Military Governor refused to enforce the Council's recommendation. The 'language controversy' engendered political tension in Jaffa and barred the establishment of friendly contacts between the Zionist Commission and the town's notables. It also pointed out the course of action the Arabs were likely to adopt in representative councils, and the incompatibility of Palestinian Arab self-determination with the Balfour Declaration and Zionist aims in Palestine.

In Jerusalem, however, Storrs managed to arrange a meeting in his office between the members of the Commission and a representative gathering of the leading personalities of the City. This gathering included the three chief members of the Husseini family who,

> from the official positions which they hold and from the universal respect they command, not only in Jerusalem but in the whole of

Southern Palestine, may be regarded as being the most represent-ative arab leaders in the occupied part of Palestine.[33]

On the following day Weizmann paid a visit to Ismail Husseini, where his cousin the Mufti Kamel Husseini was also present. Weizmann tried to allay the fears of his hosts on various questions which have caused alarm among the Palestinians and

> touched upon the question which agitates most closely the minds of Arab leaders, viz, the Land Question. He assured his hosts that expropriation or the driving out from Palestine by economic means of the Arab proprietors or Arab fellaheen was the last thing he desired.[34]

Ormsby-Gore reported that the two Arab notables were guarded in their replies. His report, however, overlooked an important incident, which reflected the political mood in Palestine, that took place in Jerusalem during the Commission's visit to the Holy City.

The incident has three known versions. *The Palestine News* which was issued by the British in Cairo towards the end of the War, reported, in its issue of 25 April the following item:

> A group of Muslim literary figures in Jerusalem presented, on the 11th and 12th of April, a play 'The Maid of Adnan and Arab Chivalry' at the Rashidiah School Club. A big map of Palestine was conspicuously displayed in a prominent place in the club with the following lines of poetry inscribed under it:

> > The Blessed Land of Palestine
> > Is the Land of the sons of Ya'rub
> > O the best land of all do not despair
> > I have no other love but you,
> > We shall sacrifice our souls for your sake
> > And you shall soar to great heights
> > Until you become like the sun in its zenith
> > Giving light to East and West.[35]

An agitated Weizmann provided a more animated account of the same incident, which took place on the 11 April, in a report to Ormsby-Gore on the political situation in Palestine:

. . .Both speakers used the kind of language which would be appropriate if an attempt were on foot to enslave and ruin the Arabs of Palestine. They called on the Nation to awake from its torpor, and to rise up in defence of its land, of its liberty, of its sacred places against those who were coming to rob it of everything. One speaker adjured his hearers not to sell a single inch of land. Nor is that all. Both speakers took it for granted that Palestine was and must remain a purely Arab country. In fact, a map of Palestine, bearing the inscription 'La Palestine Arabe' was prominently displayed, and the speeches concluded with the expressions 'Vive La Nation Arabe'.[36]

In contradistinction to the Arab attitude, Weizmann described a Jewish meeting where a warm tribute of gratitude was paid to the British Government for Balfour's Declaration. In view of these considerations, Weizmann concluded that the British should authoritatively explain to the Arabs the exact meaning and scope of the Balfour Declaration and then proceed to tell them 'that it is their duty to conform to it'.

A week after Weizmann submitted his report to Ormsby-Gore, Storrs retorted with a strongly worded rejoinder in which he described Weizmann's account as misleading and blamed the Zionists for the prevailing tension in Palestine. He also criticised the Zionist Commission for refraining from making public announcements of a nature that would 'dispel the pardonable anxieties of the Arab population of Palestine'.[37]

An Intelligence Report filed during the third week of April provided 'a good idea of the angle from which the man in the street regards the whole business':

The political effect of the visit of the Commission is not a favourable one so far. . .Christians and Moslems do not feel any easier in their minds about their future, and are still fearful of their rights being interfered with in case of the realisation of what they imagine are the Zionists' aspiration; they are going ahead in forming Committees to look after their own interests.[38]

In a revealing letter to Judge Brandeis, a leading American Zionist, Weizmann confirmed the above report of the situation:

The non-Jewish Community, especially the Arabs, both Mohammedan and Christian, interpreted the Declaration as an intention of the British Government to set up a Jewish Government at the end of the War, to deprive the Arabs of their land and cast them from the country. They looked upon the Commission as the advanced guard of Jewish capitalists and expropriators, and naturally have received with the greatest amount of suspicion.[39]

As for the British authorities in the area Weizmann informed Brandeis that 'the British officials have tried their best before our arrival to allay the suspicions of the Arabs both in Egypt and Palestine'.

On 8 May, the Military Governor of Jaffa summoned the political and religious notables of the Arab port to meet Weizmann. After listening to Weizmann's speech, an Arab spokesman assured the Zionist leader that 'both Moslems and Christians shall treat their compatriots the Jews as they treat one another so long as the Jews regard and respect the rights of these two religions, thus confirming their words by their action'. The Palestinian spokesman availed himself of the opportunity to demand

that Great Britain will allow representation of the Moslems and Christians to attend the sittings of the Convention or the body of men that have to consider and settle the question of this country.[40]

Shortly after hearing the Palestinian demand Weizmann hastened to write to Balfour arguing against the application of the democratic system as it 'does not take into account the superiority of the Jew to the Arab, the fundamental qualitative difference between Arab and Jew'[41]. In the same letter Weizmann put forth proposals for the founding of a Hebrew University, the handing over of the Wailing Wall to the Jews and the acquisition of Crown, waste and unoccupied lands in Palestine by the Zionists.[42] The Zionist leader then proceeded to submit to the British Foreign Secretary a plan to circumvent Palestinian Arab opposition to Zionism:

The problem of our relations with the Palestinian Arabs is an economic problem, not a political one. From the political point of view the Arab centre of gravity is not Palestine, but the Hedjaz, really the triangle formed by Mecca, Damascus and Baghdad. I am just setting out on a visit to the son of the King of the Hedjaz. I propose to tell him that if he wants to build up a strong and prosperous Arab kingdom, it is we Jews who will be able to help him and we only. We can give him the necessary assistance in money and in organising power. We shall be his neighbours and we do not represent any danger to him, as we are not and never shall be a great power. We are natural intermediaries between Great Britain and the Hedjaz.

Weizmann's meeting with Faisal took place on June 1918 at Wahida. According to Colonel Joyce's report the meeting was cordial but Faisal was non-committal:

Sharif Faisal declared that as an Arab he could not discuss the future of Palestine either as a Jewish Colony or a country under British Protection. These questions were already the subject of such German and Turkish propaganda and would undoubtedly be misunderstood by the uneducated Bedouins if openly discussed. Later on when Arab affairs were more consolidated these questions could be brought up.[43]

At a meeting of the London Zionist Political Committee held on 16 August, Nahum Sokolow, who was in the chair, confirmed the purpose of the Zionist contacts with the Arabs outside Palestine (Cairo and Hedjaz), when he said that the Zionists 'hoped to entertain the best relations with the real representatives of Arabs outside Palestine so as to influence the Arabs inside Palestine'.[44]

The Zionist efforts in this direction were spurred by the tactics of the Palestinian Arab leadership. For as the convergence in British policies and Zionist aims in Palestine became clearer, the Palestinian Arabs sought to restore the balance of power by closer alliance with the main Arab movement. During the second half of May 1918, the Palestinians adopted the 'Arab Flag' and the 'Arab Anthem' (of the Arab Revolt) as Palestine's own.

The Palestinians quest for greater Arab concern and backing was not their sole reaction to the impending dangers. Spurred by the Zionist challenge, the Palestinians tried to set up political, social and educational institutions in an effort to achieve greater internal cohesion and revival, which was deemed all the more necessary in view of the possibility of being politically isolated and denied contact with the neighbouring Arabs.

On 6 June *The Palestine News* reported the founding of the following societies in Jaffa: *Dar al'Ulum al-Islamiyya* (The Islamic

School for Sciences), *Jam'iat al-Shabiba al-Yafiyya* (The Jaffa Youth Society), *Jam'iat al-Ta'awun al-Massihi* (The Social Christian Welfare Association), and *Al-Jam'ia al-Ahliyya* (The National Society) which was similar to the local Zionist Organisation, composed of Jaffa's leading Muslim and Christian families and was responsible for dealing with the Government.

Other efforts were directed at thwarting Zionist efforts by practical means. During June a member of the British political staff in Palestine reported that in Jerusalem

> ...a society was being formed by Christians and Moslems with a program to combat Jewish predominance; to counteract Jewish influence and to impede by all possible means, the purchase of land by the Jews.[46]

Another important literary-political association *al-Nadi al'Arabi* (The Arab Club) was reactivated in Jerusalem during June 1918 by Haj Amin al-Husseini (brother of the Mufti Kamel al-Husseini) and other young Jerusalemites ostensibly dedicated to the revival of the Arabic language and literature.[47]

During August 1918, it was reported that *al-Jam'ia al-Islamiyya* (The Islamic Society) founded some years earlier in Jerusalem 'with a view to preserving Muslim property from being acquired or exploited by Christians or Jews', was reactivated.[48] Another society *al-Ikha'wa al-'Afaf* (Brotherhood and Chastity) closely connected with guarding Muslim property was reported as being active on a later date.[49]

In one of his more perceptive reports on the political situation, Clayton provided an account of the economic factors at play within the ranks of Palestinian Arab opposition to Zionism:

Class Attitudes

> The great majority of the more or less educated Arabs regard any prospect of Zionist extension with fear and dislike. The small land-owner with his shiftless and antiquated methods of cultivation realises that he cannot hold his own against Jewish science and energy; the trader foresees the day when Jewish enterprise, backed by Jewish money and employing modern business methods will inevitably squeeze him off the market; the small Effendi, whose one ambition has always been to secure a Government appointment, sees an administration in which the better educated and more intelligent Jew, will predominate, thereby lessening the chances for him and for his class of obtaining the coveted official post. . .the

classes to which I have alluded above will spare no effort to induce in the peasantry a hostile attitude towards the Jews. They are in closer touch with the lower strata of society than any other class, and it is not difficult for them to persuade an ignorant and gullible population that Zionism is only another word for robbing them of their lands and even of their means of livelihood.[50]

Clayton apparently neglected to add the city and town workers (porters, dock-workers, labourers engaged in traditional industries, etc.). According to Ormsby-Gore, 'The main problem is the competition between Jewish and Arab labour'.[51]

It should be pointed out that some of the classes referred to in Clayton's report had, in spite of their opposition to Zionism, a vested interest in befriending the prevailing government on which their economic well-being and ambitions depended. Thus, in spite of a clear convergence of British policy and Zionism in Palestine, no public manifestations of Palestinian Arab antipathy to British military occupation on a mass scale were discernible and recruiting for Faisal's army was still going on.[52] Some Palestinian notables were trying through personal contacts and diplomacy to dissuade British officials on the spot from supporting Zionism.

In August 1918, Ormsby-Gore reported that 'The Moslem-Effendi class which has no real political cohesion and above all no power of organisation is either pro-Turk or pro-British' and in any case they 'will not dare to do anything to embarrass a British military administration backed with British bayonets'.[53]

This did not mean that the Palestinian Arabs were not constantly protesting and complaining against the British pro-Zionist policy:

The Christians complain of favouritism shown by the authorities to the Jew. The Moslems complain among other things that the Sharif has no representative and played no part in the entry into Jerusalem and that recruiting for Feisal's Army has only just been allowed as we have only conceded it because we had to send the majority of our troops to France... It is incontestable that the policy has greatly added to our difficulties.[54]

The considerations that Ormsby-Gore referred to were real and as long as the War was going on, the political notables and their Muslim-Christian Societies were unable to articulate Palestinian Arab opposition to Zionism in any effective manner. On 4 August Clayton reported that

> The Moslem-Christian Committee at Jaffa have resigned, having
> entirely failed to fulfil its purpose of watching over interests of
> Moslem and Christian Arabs. The Military Governor is taking steps
> to form a new Committee.[55]

Inability to change the situation by the application of internal
pressure led to an abortive attempt at a world-wide Christian-Muslim
appeal on behalf of the Arabs of Palestine, which was published by
al-Mustaqbal, the Parisian Arabic paper.[56] In a letter of protest to Picot,
Sykes described the article as 'incendiary and seditious' as it called for
an 'anti-Zionist War Fund'.[57]

Strategic Considerations

As the War drew nearer to its conclusion the local British authorities
found it increasingly difficult to apply pro-Zionist policy in Palestine
and requested greater leeway and more autonomy in the carrying out of
this policy.[58] Simultaneously, the British were inclined to adopt an
increasingly intransigent attitude regarding the necessity of retaining
control over Palestine in view of its strategic importance to the defence
of the Suez Canal. A memorandum on 'The Future of Palestine' by L.S.
Amery of the War Office, later Colonial Secretary, stressed that

> Strategically Palestine and Egypt go together. Not only is Palestine a
> necessary buffer to the Suez Canal, but conversely, any defence of
> Palestine would have its main base at Kantara... Palestine is
> geographically practically in the centre of the British Empire.[59]

The logical conclusions of this line of thinking were drawn in a
memorandum by the General Staff at the War Office:

> The creation of a buffer Jewish State in Palestine, though this State
> will be weak in itself, is strategically desirable for Great Britain so
> long as it can be created without disturbing Mohammadan sentiment
> and is not controlled by a power which is potentially hostile to this
> country.[60]

The first anniversary of the Balfour Declaration was a testing ground
for the emerging attitudes and relationships of the three sides of the
Palestinian triangle. When the Arabs heard that the Zionists intended to

celebrate the anniversary of Balfour's Declaration, they threatened 'breaking up the proceedings by a counter procession'.[61] Storrs threatened that any Arab who dared do such a thing would be arrested and instantly put in jail. The Military Governor of Jerusalem advised the Zionists to break their processions before they reached the Jaffa Gate where the Arabs assemble daily in numbers. Two school processions disregarded these instructions and a scuffle with two Palestinian Arabs, one Muslim and the other Christian, developed, and both received four months jail sentences which Storrs described as severe. The result was the first Arab demonstration led by the Mayor, Musa Kazem Pasha al-Husseini, who submitted written protestations to the Government. Another petition of protest was addressed to the American Government.[62]

New Tactics

One week after the War was brought to an end, Clayton detected an incipient transformation in the Palestinian Arab methods of opposition to Zionism:

> Christian and Moslem antipathy to Zionism has been displayed much more openly since Armistice. The recent Anglo-French declaration has encouraged all parties to make known their wishes by every available means in view of approaching Peace Conference.[63]

On the occasion of the first anniversary of Allenby's victory over the Turks, the Muslim-Christian Committee of Jaffa submitted a memorandum to the Military Governor which testified to the accuracy of Clayton's report and mirrored the prevailing Palestinian reactions to Zionism and their arguments against the Balfour Declaration. The memorandum started out by paying tribute to Great Britain and reiterated the Committee's faith in Mr Lloyd George's declaration regarding 'self-government for the Arabs' and President Wilson's declarations regarding 'national self-determination'. The memorandum then proceeded to affirm that Palestine was an Arab country in the full meaning of the word and expounded a full refutation of the possible Zionist arguments:

> If the country be the pretext, we should hasten to say that the country as well as the inhabitants are Arabs. If the numbers be the pretext, it should not be forgotten that the Arab are 30 times more numerous than the Jews. If majority of the land be the pretext, the Jews must be warned that the portion they possess in Palestine is nothing more than 1/500 comparatively to the possessions of

Moslems and Christians. Is it for the language? Then it is fairly well known that the language of this country is pure Arab.[64]

The Zionist claim to Palestine, the Committee argued, 'suggests the impracticable necessity of drawing up quite a new map of the world'. In any case the Palestinian Arabs

> can never support to be subjugated, on the contrary try to hold fast in our National right up to death.
>
> We, Arabs, are not hostile to the others, and never entertain the least idea to expel other elements from our country wherein we cannot agree to see that our guests the Jews are going to frustrate us from political rights as we are unwilling to consider as native the people who come from outside our country.
>
> We refuse to see millions of Jews coming into Palestine, for they will engross and monopolise all the product of Palestine, as it should not be forgotten to state the Jew likes only the Jew, help the Jew and nobody else.
>
> Undoubtedly, such deeds will be the cause of successive revolutions which will ruin the country and be the misfortune of the inhabitants.
>
> ... Then the Jews be informed, that Palestine belongs to us, and will never part with it; they must also know that we are born in Palestine wherein we hope to die and be buried in its holy grounds.

The memorandum was conciliatory towards Britain and uncompromising towards the Zionists in conformity with the general policy adopted by the Arab political notability in Palestine. However, it was not unlikely that the members of the Jaffa Muslim-Christian Committee were more friendly to the British than other Committees in view of their trading and citrus interests which depended to a great extent on the goodwill and policies of the Government. Another factor in the (Jaffa) Committee's attitude towards the British Government may be attributed to the relatively friendly disposition of Colonel Hubbard, the ·Military Governor, who was in favour of a more even-handed British policy in Palestine.[65]

Following a visit to Jerusalem, Sykes observed that there were two Arab complaints:

(I) The Zionists are aggressive, demonstrative and provocative, and threaten them with a Jewish Government. (II) The British Home

Government is acting in such a way that the Palestinian Arabs will sooner or later become subject to Jewish rule.[66]

However, Sykes detected

a feeling among the Arabs that the declaration really does not amount to much and that the Arabs have only to agitate in order to get it shelved or rendered nugatory.

Nevertheless, Sykes genuinely feared 'that non-Jews may think best demonstration is violent outbreak'.

Contemplated violence was not the only problem which faced British officials in Palestine. To the embarrassment of the British authorities the Palestinians raised the issue of the unity of Syria and Palestine. During the second half of November, eighteen copies of the Anglo-French Declaration of 7 November were distributed. On the following day a deputation of Muslims and Christians called on Storrs. After offering to the Allies their sincere thanks for the Declaration, they asked Storrs formally:

(a) Whether Palestine formed or did not form part of Syria.
(b) Whether, if so, Palestine came under the category of those inhabitants of the liberated countries who were invited to choose their own futures; and
(c) If, not, why the notices had been sent to them at all.[67]

In his report of the incident, Storr also spoke about the solidarity between the Muslim and Christian Arabs and their united stand regarding 'their acceptance of the Anglo-French Declaration and their desire for a Sherifian Government'.[68] Days later Storrs reported that, in addition to the formation of a Christian-Muslim Arab Committee in Jerusalem,

daily meetings were reported to me at the Muktaaf al-Drus School, the name of which has now been changed to the Arab Club. Two main decisions were taken at these meetings (1) that a signed petition should be sent to the French Commissariat begging that Palestine might be formally included in Syria, and (2) that on Friday last the 22nd the name of the Sherif should be pronounced as Caliph.[69]

The Traditional Leaderhip's Dilemma

Storrs lost no time in sending for the Mufti to instruct him to dissuade those under his influence from adopting the second decision. He also sought to break the new organisation by calling on the Mayor and other leading figures of the Christian-Muslim Arab Committee who held official posts in the Administration

> to opt for an administrative or political career, the two being for the present incompatible. The Mayor seemed grateful for this warning, which enabled him to say that he thought he would be more useful to his country as President of the Municipality.[70]

The efficacy of Storrs' threats demonstrated the inadequacy of the traditional political notability to lead the populace in situations of conflict. When faced with a choice between a salaried government career and an uncertain future as popular political leaders, the elderly notables opted for the safer and more remunerative alternative.

In 1919 the realities of a long-term pro-Zionist British policy in Palestine became undeniably clear, and Palestinian political circles were confronted with a grave choice that could not be sidestepped or ignored. The alternatives were acquiescence or defiance.

Although the opposition to Zionism was virtually universal among the Palestinian Arabs, an important sector (class or group) of elderly notables took the course of acquiescence, and new forces began to compete with the propertied notables for political leadership. These comprised the active and vocal members of the educated middle classes in addition to the 'young bloods' some of whom were members of the urban and rural upper classes. In January 1919, the first Scout organisation and the first Arab Women's Club were founded.[71]

The struggle between the quiescent elderly propertied notables and the activist young educated members of the middle classes became apparent in the Palestine Arab Conference which met in Jerusalem between 27 January and 10 February 1919. The Conference, which comprised delegates from Muslim-Christian Societies from various parts of Palestine, was called to discuss the presentation of Palestinian demands for self-determination before the Peace Conference and to voice Palestinian Arab fears regarding Zionism and the prospect of Jewish domination.

According to a report on the Conference filed by Captain J.N. Camp of the British Intelligence, eleven out of the twenty-seven delegates were pro-British, two pro-French, two delegates with uncertain political sympathies and the remaining twelve were pan-Arab or pro-Arab.[72] The conference was presided over by Aref Pasha Dahudi Dajani and dominated by the notables of Palestinian towns mostly representing the propertied classes and vested political and economic interests. The most outstanding members of the Pan-Arab group were two young intellectuals belonging to the urban middle classes, 'Izzat Darwaza and Yusuf al-'Isa, editor of *Falastin.*

Camp reported that, from the outset, the Conference was subject to strong pressure from outside. 'The pan-Arab influence of certain members of the Muntada al-Adabi and Nadi el-Arabi was very persistent'. The struggle inside the Conference was between the pro-British bloc and the pan-Arab bloc, and the split owed its origins to economic factors as well as to a generation gap:

Young Moslems, members of the various Arab Societies agitate for an independent Palestine, which would form part of a great independent Arab State. Moslem villagers and Moslems who own any considerable amount of property are nearly all pro-British.

Camp asserted that the fear of Zionism was

the main reason that leads the young pan-Arab element to favour its union with an independent Arab Syria, for with Palestine joined to an Arab Syria the people of Palestine with the help of other Arabs would be able successfully to resist Jewish immigration.[73]

Herein lay the dilemma of the pro-British Palestinian Arabs: although they were opposed to Zionism (the report spoke of 'the unalterable opposition of all non-Jewish elements in Palestine to Zionism'), they were actually helping the Zionist cause by being loyal to a pro-Zionist Britain. They adopted the Zionist position: namely British rule and separation of Syria and Palestine.[74]

In view of this dilemma it was not surprising that Camp should have reported:

I have personally heard many Arabs, both Christians and Moslems, declare that they will forcibly resist any attempt to set up in this land a Jewish State or anything resembling it. The pan-Arab young bloods, very bold in speech, say so openly, the elderly declare that they will sell out and leave the country. I do not think the threat of the young Arabs is to be taken lightly, as they might cause much trouble by appealing to the fanaticism of the villagers and as they would certainly be supported by Arabs outside Palestine.[75]

It was under the influence of the 'young bloods' that the Conference passed some strong-worded resolutions. The delegations held that the resolutions expressed the wishes and demands of the people of 'Southern Syria known as Palestine'. They communicated these resolutions to the Peace Conference 'being convinced that it will admit our rights, comply with our demands and grant our requests'. The Palestinians' wishes and demands submitted to the Peace Conference opened by a reference to 'the fact that the Declaration of President Wilson is considered to be one of the fundamental principles on which the Peace Conference is based for the freedom of nations liberated from the Turkish yoke, the cancellation of all secret treaties concluded during the war and the promise to nations to choose the kind of government they desire for themselves'.[76]

The decisions are worth quoting in full:[77]

1. We consider Palestine as part of Arab Syria as it has never been separated from it at any time. We are connected with it by national, religious, linguistic, natural, economic and geographical bonds.

2. The Declaration made by M. Pichon, Minister for Foreign Affairs for France, that France had rights in our country based on the desires and aspirations of the inhabitants has no foundation and we reject all the declarations made in his speech of 29th December, 1918, as our wishes and aspirations are only in Arab unity and complete independence.

3. In view of the above we desire that one district Southern Syria or Palestine should not be separated from the Independent Arab Syrian Government and to be free from all foreign influence and protection.

4. In accordance with the rule laid down by President Wilson and approved by most of the Great Powers we consider that every promise or treaty concluded in respect of our country and its future as null and void and reject the same.

5. The Government of the country will apply for help to its friend Great Britain in case of need for the improvement and development of the country provided that this will not affect its independence and Arab unity in any way and will keep good relations with the Allied Powers.[78]

The Palestine Conference also decided to send a delegation to Damascus 'to inform Arab patriots there of the decision to call Palestine Southern Syria and unite it with Northern Syria'.[79] Another delegation of three was named 'as possible representatives to go to Paris'.[80] The decisions of the Conference were presented in writing to the British, French, Italian and Spanish representatives in Jerusalem. It was apparent that the young elements, with the help of Palestinian pressure from outside, prevailed on the Conference. Before adjourning, the Conference agreed to meet again at Nablus three months hence, but failed to elect an executive Committee to the Conference.

Camp's observations and remarks were upheld by a paper written by Weizmann based on reports supplied by a nascent Zionist intelligence department. The paper, which was forwarded by Sykes to the F.O., added new dimensions to the possibilities of Arab action against Zionism:

> The pro-Arabic and the absolute annexation of Palestine to the Cherif is the opinion of the greatest intellectual and agitating part of the youth. . .
>
> The moderate class of opinion belongs to the notability of the elder age are for a local autonomy. They are much more materialistic than idealist. Though being hostile to the Jews they do not show their hostility and will not oppose themselves to a political entente with the Jew. Youth fighting very much against them.[81]

In a 'Postscriptum to the note concerning the Arab question', dated 8 January 1919, Weizmann disclosed that the Palestinian moderates, aged men, Muslims and Christians belonging to the rich and influential families of Palestine, especially of Jerusalem, had organised themselves under the name of 'Moslem and Christian Association'. This Association advocated

> the necessity of sending delegates to Europe who will reclaim 'Palestine for the Palestinians'. They said that it was impossible for the Christians as well as for the Jews to accept the rule of the Cheriff over Palestine as asked by the youth.[82]

Britain's Weak Point

As Arab agitation against Zionism mounted,[83] the relations between the Palestinian Arabs and the British Administration became increasingly precarious. The failure of the British Government to respond to the

Palestinian Arab demands for self-determination and to their appeals against Zionism was bound to lead to friction. One reason why Palestine was denied self-determination was explained in a letter from the Foreign Minister, Balfour, to the Prime Minister which no amount of Arab petitions against Zionism could alter.

> The weak point of our position of course is that in the case of Palestine we deliberately and rightly decline to accept the principle of self-determination. If the present inhabitants were consulted they would unquestionably give an anti-Jewish verdict. Our justification for our policy is that we regard Palestine as being absolutely exceptional, that we consider the question of the Jews outside Palestine as one of world importance.[84]

As the Peace Conference dragged on the Palestinians became more restless as their worst fears were confirmed by Zionist public statements. Towards the end of March Clayton reported:

> Anti-Zionist propaganda has increased considerably in Palestine lately and feeling is now running very high among Moslems and Christians who fear that political and economic advantages may be given to Jews in peace settlement. This feeling is increased by the rash actions and words of the Jews themselves and by pronouncements which appear by leading Zionists in the Press in England and America and elsewhere. There are considerable grounds for belief that anti-Jewish riots are being prepared in Jerusalem, Jaffa and elsewhere. Precautions are being taken but an announcement that Jews will be given any special privileges might precipitate outbreaks.[85]

On the 28 March, the Muslim-Christian Committee of Jerusalem proposed to hold a demonstration on 1 April to protest against the Zionist Programme. When permission was denied, the Mufti and the three ex-deputies of Jerusalem acquiesced but elaborate precautionary schemes were prepared to provide against trouble in the cities and the more exposed Jewish colonies lest the more extreme Arab elements decide to act on their own. Towards the end of April the Zionist Organisation informed the Foreign Office that 'they were perturbed by the most recent advice they had had from Palestine which represented the Arabs as preparing to make trouble and as secretly arming'.[86]

The Palestinian situation was aggravated by the confusion that dominated the discussions of the Paris Peace Conference on the future of the Near East. In April the Peace Conference decided to send an Inter-Allied Commission to Syria, Palestine and Mesopotamia to ascertain the sentiments of the people with regard to the future administration of their affairs. The departure of the Commission was delayed because the French were unwilling to name their members for the Commission. The British too were apprehensive lest the findings of the Commission prove detrimental to their plans and policies in Palestine.

London's worst fears were unequivocally confirmed by the Palestine Chief Administrator's report on the likely results of the findings of the Inter-Allied Commission, and on the potentially explosive situation in Palestine:

> In the present state of political feeling there is no doubt that if Zionism's programme is a necessary adjunct to a mandatory the people of Palestine will select in preference the United States or France as the mandatory, or as the protecting power of an Arab administration.
>
> . . . The Palestinians desire their country for themselves and will resist any general immigration of Jews however gradual, by every means in their power including active hostilities. . .recent events in Egypt have greatly impressed the people of Palestine.
>
> In conclusion, the idea that Great Britain is the main upholder of the Zionist programme will preclude any local request for a British Mandate and no mandatory power can carry through Zionist programme except by force.[87]

Clayton considered the report 'a true appreciation of the situation. Fear and distrust of Zionist aims grow daily and no amount of persuasion or propaganda will dispel it'. Furthermore, he reported that, 'There was recently a danger of serious disturbance in which Arabs from East of Jordan were to take part'.

In accordance with the Faisal-Weizmann agreement of January 1919,[88] Faisal tried to reconcile the Palestinian Arabs to Zionist policy. On 11 May 1919 Clayton reported that,

> "Faisal has. . .informed an Arab delegation in Damascus that he did not consider Arab and Zionist aims to be incompatible and delegation seemed favourably impressed. Members of Zionist Commission are being invited to visit Faisal who may also ask a few leading Palestinian Arabs to attend with a view to rapprochment.[89]

It Will Have to Be Coerced

Weizmann, however, was under no illusion as to the inevitable failure of all such efforts to bring about a reconciliation with the majority of the Arabs of Palestine.[90]

Nevertheless, the Zionist leader was determined to turn Palestine into a Jewish country. Alarmed by Zangwill's statement that the 'Arabs ought to be removed to Syria leaving their land to the Jews of Palestine', Herbert Samuel[91] remarked (in the course of a meeting of the Advisory Committee to the Palestine Office) that 'If we (Zionists) were to go to Palestine to oppress other people it would be an unspeakable disgrace'.[92] Weizmann then spoke with considerable frankness regarding the impending Inter-Allied Commission, and the unpleasant implications of a Zionist policy in Palestine:

> Will the British apply self-determination in Palestine which is five hours from Egypt or not? If not it will have to be coerced. . . Yes or no: it amounts to that.[93]

Weizmann then asked for preferential treatment and for state lands to settle 40,000 to 50,000 Jews per year. Ormsby-Gore accepted Weizmann's arguments and was in favour of granting his requests. He was in favour of encouraging non-Muslims, Europeans and Jews, to develop and stabilise the Near East in view of the fact that Islam was the main danger. Since the Zionist Organisation provided the required human element to man the Palestinian output in Europe's fight against Islam,

> It is in the interest of England to assist the Zionist Organisation and any other organisation which may cooperate with them in the practical development of Jewish colonisation in Palestine.[94]

To Ormsby-Gore, as well as other major British political figures, Zionism and the Balfour Declaration's policy of a Jewish national home in Palestine was a *chose jugée*.

A week before the Inter-Allied Commission arrived the Muslim-Christian Society of Jerusalem proposed to issue a circular regarding their views which they intended to put forward before the Commission. The circular stressed the unity of Syria and affirmed that Palestine — southern Syria — was an inseparable part of Syria. As far as the Zionist issue was concerned, an enlightened differentiation between native Jews and foreign incoming Zionists were made.

We completely refuse to allow Palestine to be turned into a national home for the Jews. We also do not admit any Jewish immigrant into our country and energetically protest against the Zionist movement. The native Jews who are previous inhabitants of the country, should be considered as native and possess privileges and misfortunes as we do.[95]

General Allenby, however, considered the circular undesirable and withheld permission to issue.

For reasons which go beyond the scope of the present study, the French and the British failed to participate in the Inter-Allied Commission. Eventually, it was decided that the American members of the Commission should proceed and make the necessary investigations on their own. The implications of the absence of the other powers that were to participate in the Commission could not have failed to leave an adverse reaction among the Arabs, but Clayton could have been right when he informed the FO that

It is conceivable that the leaders of the people may feel themselves more free to express their real feelings being unembarrassed by any fear of offending either Great Britain or France, both of whom are considered to be interested parties.[96]

The King Crane Commission

In his meticulous study[97] on the Inter-Allied Commission, known later as the King Crane Commission after the two American Commissioners, Harry Howard delved very deeply into the formation and findings of the American investigators, and there is no need to go over the same ground again. The Commission arrived on 19 June and lost no time in ascertaining the opinions and desires of the whole people. Before they left Palestine the Commission heard evidence and received petitions from all kinds of political groups in the country.[98]

Summarising their findings the Commission reported:

Judging from the evidence which had been presented to the Commission during its short visit to Palestine, June 10-25, only the Zionist Jews, about one-tenth of the total population favoured the establishment of a Jewish National home in that country. The rest of the population Moslem and Christian Arabs alike, desired to preserve the unity of the country with Syria of which they considered Palestine to be both historically and geographically a part.[99]

The Moslem and Christian population were practically unanimous against Zionism, usually expressing themselves with great emphasis.[100]

The Commission also noted that

The feeling against the Zionist program is not confined to Palestine, but shared very generally by the people throughout Syria, as our conferences clearly showed. More than 72 per cent – 1350 – in all – of all the petitions in the whole of Syria were directed against the Zionist program. Only two requests – those for a united Syria and for independence – had a larger support.[101]

Before the Commission left Palestine they began to hear consistently about a forthcoming congress in Damascus. 'For the first time the Arab delegations were sounding the note that the problem of a mandatory power should be left to conference shortly to assemble in Damascus'.[102] The change from the insistence on independence to the acquiescence in a mandatory system was a significant one. Colonel Cornwallis, Deputy Political Officer at Damascus, attributed this change to

A letter received from Rustum Bey Haidar, the Arab representative in Paris, saying that it will be fatal to ask for complete independence, as the Powers have decided that there must be a mandate.[103]

Cornwallis further reported that Faisal had by that time dissolved both *Hizb al-Istiqlal* (The Independence Party) and *al-Ittihad as-Suri* (The Syrian Union) and had announced that there will be no more political societies in OET East. However, the Hashemite Prince began

to realise the difficulties which he will have in reconciling the Palestinians and Zionists, and no longer treats the question as a minor one... Meanwhile Palestinians here are vehement, and Mohamed-es-Saleh-al-Husseini of Nablus has been advocating the defence of Arab independence in Palestine by the sword.[104]

The Palestinians did not share Faisal's tendency to bow before the powers and their political schemes. According to Clayton the opposite was true.[105]

The General Syrian Congress

The General Syrian Congress finally held its meetings in Damascus during the first week of July,

> comprising representatives from the three zones viz. the Southern, Eastern and Western, provided with credentials and authority by the inhabitants of our various districts, Moslems, Christians and Jews.[106]

A delegation chosen by the Congress presented to the Commission a statement signed by the members of the Congress, known as the Damascus Programme, which called for 'immediate complete independence for Syria without protection or tutelage, under a civil constitutional monarchy'. As far as Palestine was concerned, the Damascus Programme voiced Palestinian feelings in the seventh, eighth and tenth resolutions of their statement:

> 7. We oppose the pretensions of the Zionists to create a Jewish commonwealth in the southern part of Syria known as Palestine and oppose Zionist migration to any part of our country, for we do not acknowledge their title but consider them a grave peril to our people from the national, economical and political point of view. Our Jewish compatriots shall enjoy our common rights and assume the common responsibilities.
>
> 8. We demand that there shall be no separation of the southern part of Syria known as Palestine...from the Syrian country, and desire the unity of the country to be guaranteed against partition under whatever circumstances.
>
> ...
>
> 10. The fundamental principles laid down by President Wilson in condemnation of secret treaties impel us to protest most emphatically against any treaty that stipulates the partition of our Syrian country, and against any private engagement aiming at establishing Zionism in the Southern part of Syria, thus we demand the annulment of these conventions and agreements absolutely.[107]

The Palestinian members of the Congress, who came from all the major towns of Palestine, played a conspicuous part in it and 'Iszat Darwaza was its secretary.

A report on the political situation by Colonel French, Chief Political Officer, EEF, in the wake of the departure of the King Crane Commission stated:

the whole country is now quiet from a political point of view, but it is the quiet resulting from exhaustion which followed the political orgy during the visit of the Commission, and partly from the tension caused by the belief that the decision of the Conference will be known shortly.[108]

In the same letter French replied to an allegation made by Weizmann regarding 'artificial agitation' in Palestine:

It is the considered opinion of British officers who know Palestine well that the opposition to Zionism, which is based to a certain extent on the national sentiment of the inhabitants, has grown stronger during the past months, and it is believed that is well known to the (Zionist) Commission, which has an efficient 'intelligence' service.

Colonel French's report was, in fact, a subdued version of what one of his staff at Haifa had to say about Weizmann's allegations:

The striking miscalculation of Weizmann's as to the general opposition to Zionism which he characterizes as 'artificial agitation that may still be prevalent' is startling. I found at Jerusalem the opposition still more strong than when I left there 4 months ago, and better organized, it is generally recognised that Jerusalem and Nablus are the political touchstones for Palestine, the latter place being if anything more fanatical and anti-Jew than Jerusalem. The Zionist Commission have in Jerusalem a very efficient counter-espionage service, and I suggest that their reports have either been sent home or ignored as alarmist.[109]

Preparing for Revolt

The Zionist Intelligence records of that period — The Hagana Archives — corroborate what British Intelligence Officers in Palestine were reporting to their superiors in Cairo and London. Before we deal with the interesting and detailed reports of the Zionist Intelligence, it is necessary to refer to a highly informative report by Major Camp about the 'Arab Movement and Zionism'.[110]

The report gave an account of the leading Arab societies in Jerusalem: *el-Muntada el-Adabi, el-Nadi el-Arabi, el-Akha we'l-Afaf, Muntada el-Dajjani* and *el-Feda'iyyeh,* the latter being a secret commando type body comprising many policemen and gendarmes.

The activities of these societies involved a comprehensive preparation for a revolt:

> Arming of members with small arms; preparation of lists of prominent Jews and pro-Zionists among non-Jews, with place of residence of each; propaganda among the Bedouin of the trans-Jordan. . . effort to concentrate Palestinian officers at Amman, so as to be ready in case pro-Zionist policy is announced, learning of Hebrew by a few agents so as to follow Hebrew papers and conversation; appointment of agents to watch everything going on; effort to effect agreement with police and gendarmes to hand over arms or at least to put no obstacles in the way in case a revolt takes place; teaching of pan-Arab ideals to children, especially those in Reshidieh and Rawdte el-Maarif Schools.

The activities of three of these societies were described earlier in Weizmann's 8 February report. According to that report members of these societies were to

> . . . try also to organise terrorists and secret corporations to fight later against the Jews by guerrillas. They try generally to create an 'etat d'esprit' very hostile against us. Many of them engage themselves in the Police service so that they might do much easier their work. Many of them are quite learned young men, having studied in Europe and several of them know perfectly well the Jewish question.[111]

An undercover agent of the Zionist Intelligence reported a meeting of sixteen members of *el-Feda'iyyeh* on 27 August 1919, presumably in preparation for a revolt. Members reported on successful contacts with the chiefs of Trans-Jordan, the availability of arms, and on all the villagers around Jerusalem who 'wait impatiently for the first signal'.[112]

A speech delivered at that meeting by one of the leaders of the secret commando organisation *Jawdat el-Halabi* illustrated the radical character of the *el-Feda'iyyeh* and the readiness of its members to draw the logical conclusions against the Anglo-Zionist alliance in Palestine:

> We purchase arms as much as we liked and we shall receive more. Our principal action must be against the Jews who want to take our land, but if the Government will help them we shall also be against the Government. Many of our members and friends are policemen

and gendarmes and that is very good for our future. We must all know the martyrs of the Fatherland and our honour.[113]

Another member reported that 'all the fellaheens and beduins are waiting for the first signals and are ready for everything'.

The Zionist informer did not fail to report the secretive manner of the *el-Feda'iyyeh* 'who decided to meet once or twice a week without mentioning the next meeting only a few hours before the meeting time'.

Another report covered a meeting at the *Muntada el-'Adabi* where Issaf Nashashibi, the well-known literary figure, stated that money was very much needed, and it was not a shame to collect the money either by representation or by lottery. He also advocated 'continuous troubles' with the Jews as a means of discouraging immigration.[114]

Mahmoud 'Aziz el-Khalidi, who belonged to many secret societies, advocated assassinating some Jewish leaders in Jaffa and Haifa as a means of intimidating potential Jewish immigrants. Furthermore, his speech revealed the existence of religious overtones and considerable agitation against the British:

The youth of this country are not afraid of anybody even the autocratic Government. They want to begin already and they will all receive death gladly. Most of them ask me always when we are going to rise against the unbelievers and know our strength and get rid of them once and for all.[115]

In the light of these activities and points of view, General H.D. Watson's warning shortly after taking over the Administration of OETA South, was both realistic and timely:

The antagonism to Zionism of the majority of the population is deep-rooted — it is fast leading to hatred of the British — and will result, if the Zionist programme is forced upon them, in an outbreak of a very serious character necessitating the employment of a much larger number of troops than at present located in the territory.[116]

From the available intelligence reports, British and Zionist, it was apparent that the peasants were more prone to action and to revolt entailing self-sacrifice than other groups of society. This was, in some instances, attributed to religious fanaticism. In addition to this relevant element, there were economic reasons for peasant resentment of Zionist schemes and ambitions: the boycott of Arab labour in Jewish colonies and Jewish enterprise, the prospect of being uprooted as the Zionists acquired more lands, and finally Zionist opposition to the Agricultural Loans Scheme.[117]

According to the report of the Court of Inquiry which investigated the circumstances that led to the disturbances of April 1920:

> The incident of the veto on the Agricultural Loans, however, had a far greater effect in inflaming the growing irritation of the population against the Zionists... The people at once came to the conclusion that the Zionists had interfered in order that they should be left in great straits and should ultimately have to sell their lands to the Zionists at any price.[118]

During September British Naval Intelligence reported that anti-Zionist feeling was becoming increasingly bitter and that 'a plot has been discovered by us by which it was proposed to assassinate Dr Weizmann on his arrival'.[119]

On announcing the separation of Palestine from Syria towards the end of September vehement protests were voiced in Jerusalem's *Suriyya al-Janubiyya* (Southern Syria), which was owned and edited by 'Aref al-'Aref, and in the Damascus press. The announcement inspired an article by 'Izzat Darwaza in *al-Urdun* (The Jordan), published in Damascus, appropriately entitled 'Now is the Time to Act':

> It is not for the representatives of English, French and Zionist affairs to do as they please with a country which has been liberated by the blood of its children, who are ready to shed more blood if necessary to attain their ends.[120]

Another Naval Intelligence report noted that by November 1919 the whole anti-Zionist movement in Palestine had taken a very anti-British turn. Four weeks later Naval Intelligence reported that anti-Zionist propaganda was spreading to small villages where the fellaheen

> are interested listeners when local and Damascus papers are read out to them... The possibility of active opposition to the Jews is being discussed. There are indications that a definite demonstration against the Zionists will be attempted, and an undoubted air of expectancy exists.[121]

By early 1920 it was evident to all parties in Palestine that an anti-Zionist outburst was imminent. In January British Naval Intelligence reported that emissaries from Damascus were frequently proceeding to Jaffa.

> These hasty visits are thought to foreshadow an attempt at simultaneous disturbances throughout Syria and Palestine on the lines of those organised in Egypt.[122]

The report further asserted that anti-Zionism was responsible for a decided rapprochment between Christians and Muslims. As for the *fellahin,*

> They allege that the Jewish colonists are subsidised from without and have been granted privileges by the Administration which were denied to others, and state that they cannot compete against such advantages, and would therefore be ultimately squeezed out of existence.

By February the process of polarisation had been accomplished. In a letter to Curzon, Weizmann pointed out that 'there is no doubt that anti-Zionist and anti-British propaganda amongst the Arabs run parallel'.[123]

On 27 February 1920 a big Arab political demonstration was held in Jerusalem with the knowledge of the authorities. Despite Zionist protestations, General Bols, the Chief Administrator, took the view that organised processions could be controlled and that they acted as a safety valve.[124] A second demonstration was held on 8 March amidst considerable excitement owing to the recent proclamation of Prince Faisal King of Syria and Palestine:

> The speeches were of a violently political character. . .There was an incident said to have been caused by a Jewish boy trying to force his way through the processes. This started a quarrel and there was some stone throwing. A few Jews were injured, but the police quickly regained control and the demonstration dispersed without further accident.[125]

On 1 March two Jewish settlements at Metulla and Tel Hai near the Syrian border were attacked by armed Palestinian bands[126] probably organised by the Palestinians in Damascus[127]. Captain Joseph

Trumpledor, a prominent Zionist soldier, and six other Jews were killed during the raid. The incident which was indicative of the Palestinian political mood, and a glimpse of coming events, failed to spark a general anti-Zionist uprising owing to the deteriorating political situation and the imminent collapse of the Arab regime in Damascus.

Describing the situation in Palestine on the eve of Easter 1920, the Palin Commission Report stated:

> The whole native population Arab and Christian, was in a condition of active hostility at once to the Zionists and the British Administration, their sentiment influenced by a sense of their own wrongs, their fears for the future, and the active propaganda of various anti-British and anti-Zionist elements working freely in their midst. The signs and warnings had not escaped either the Zionists or the Administration.[128]

The Spark

On 11 March as a result of Zionist pressure brought to bear on the Chief Administrator, demonstrations were prohibited, a measure which must have added to the already widespread Arab resentment. The approach of Easter week with its inevitable religious disorders and the coincidence of the Christian and Jewish festivals with the Muslim Nebi Musa Pilgrimage caused serious anxiety to the Jewish Community and the Administration. On that occasion Muslim pilgrims assembled bearing their local banners from the surrounding villages at Jerusalem. The Pilgrimage had always been officially recognised by the Government who used to provide the necessary troops and a band in honour of the ceremony. In view of the political excitement and the prevailing tension, it was not surprising that Palestinian Arab nationalist circles were determined to turn any Arab gathering into an occasion for protest and agitation against Zionism and the Administration. Thus, when the Hebron pilgrims arrived on 4 April, their procession was halted more than once, to hear speeches by 'Aref al-'Aref, Musa Kazem, the Mayor, Hajj Amin al-Husseini and other prominent Muslims. The Palin Commission report stated that the practice of delaying the procession to hear speeches was first introduced in 1919. In 1920, however, the speeches were of a flagrantly political character culminating in the exhibition of the portrait of the Emir Faisal, who was greeted as 'King of Syria and Palestine'. The crowd at this point was gradually worked up into a high inflammatory condition and it seems extremely probable that there were *agents provocateurs* intermingled with them here awaiting their opportunity.[129] According to Darwaza, anti-Zionist and anti-British slogans were shouted in the procession.[130] 'Isa as-Sifri, a Palestinian Christian, recorded that the Palestinian Christians participated in the procession calling for Arab unity and independence and declaring their opposition to Zionist immigration.[131]

After hearing the speeches and as the procession was passing through the Jaffa Gate, an explosion occurred:

> The exact incident which caused the explosion has not been clearly ascertained — possibly there were more than one. . .there is some evidence to show that the attitude of the Jewish spectators was in certain cases provocative, but it appears much more likely that the mine was deliberately fired by some *agents provocateurs* raising the cry of an insult to the banner by a Jew. . .It is quite evident, however, that in the excited condition to which the pilgrims round the Nadi el-Araby Club had been wrought by the speeches of the political orators and the exhibition of Emir Feisal's portrait, the most trivial incident would be sufficient to cause an outbreak.[132]

The explosion led to stone-throwing at the shops in the vicinity of the incident. Several Jews were also beaten and at least one stabbed. The crowd then passed down into the city looting Jewish shops and assaulting Jews. 'There is some evidence to show that a few of the Jews were armed and occasionally retaliated by firing on the mob'.[133]

The outbreak lasted sporadically from 4 to 10 April. Fighting and looting took place despite the declaration of Martial Law. This was partly due to the narrow alleys of the old city of Jerusalem as well as to the state of exasperation and excitement prevalent among the Arabs at that time. The total casualties reported amounted to 251, of which 9 died, 22 were seriously wounded and 220 slightly wounded. Of these casualties, the Jews sustained 5 killed, 18 seriously wounded and 193 slightly wounded, most of which resulted from Arab attacks with knives, sticks and stones. Seven British soldiers were reported wounded — all apparently at the hands of the Arab mob. The Arabs sustained 28 casualties, 4 of which were killed by firearms. The Court suspected that 'a number of fellahin suffering from slight wounds may have escaped to the country'.

From all the evidence available the Court concluded that 'the attack was entirely against the Jews'. Nevertheless, the Court admitted that, in

Palestine, the British were

> faced with a native population thoroughly exaperated by a sense of
> injustice and disappointed hopes, panic stricken as to their future
> and as to ninety per cent of their numbers in consequence bitterly
> hostile to the British Administration.[134]

Before coming to the Court's conclusions, two phenomena stand out
in the report under discussion relevant to the Anglo-Zionist convergence in Palestine and the nature of Arab opposition to that alliance
during the disturbances of 1920. The first was the emergence of Jewish
'Self-Defence' units, the Hagana, raised by V. Jabotinsky, who served as
a lieutenant in the British Army during the War, and Mr Rutenberg,
who was a prominent Russian official under Kerensky (1917). The
Court's report stated that these units were raised without the Administration's approval or knowledge, but nevertheless 'were openly drilling
at the back of Lemel School and on Mount Scopus',[135] a fact that was
familiar to the Arabs during the month of March. Of greater significance
was the Administration's decision to use the illegal Jewish units.[136]
   The other phenomenon was the divergence of views between the
Zionist leaders and some British officials, including the members of the
Court, as to the real causes of Arab unrest in Palestine.

> It has been said by the Zionists that the popular excitement is purely
> artificial and largely the result of propaganda by the effendi class,
> which fears to lose its position owing to Jewish competition. It is
> sufficient to quote the evidence of Major Waggett with which the
> Court finds itself in full accord, when he says: 'It is very important
> to realise that the opposition is by no means superficial or manu-
> factured, and I consider this a dangerous view to take of the
> situation'.[137]

In their final conclusions the members of the Court pointed out that
'The Administration was considerably hampered in its policy by the
direct interference of the Home Authorities'. They also found it
necessary to warn that 'the situation at present obtaining in Palestine is
exceedingly dangerous and demands firm and patient handling if a
serious catastrophe is to be avoided'.[138]
   Various prison sentences were passed against twenty-three individuals
for complicity in the Jerusalem disturbances.[139]
   The Easter troubles brought to a head the question of the Mayoralty

of Jerusalem; Musa Kazem was dismissed because of his participation in the demonstration against Zionist policies. Musa Kazem inforced Storrs that under these circumstances no Arab will dare take my place.[140] As it turned out, a rival notable Ragheb Bey Nashashibi accepted the post the moment it was offered to him, thus demonstrating a lack of solidarity and resolution among the notables *vis-à-vis* the British Administration.

The Palin Commission Report was suppressed and until recently (1968) treated confidentially. Violent Arab opposition failed to introduce any fundamental changes in the overall British policy in Palestine. Quite the contrary, His Majesty's Government were contemplating a switch from military administration to civil Mandatory Government incorporating in its provisions the Balfour Declaration, despite the delay in concluding the peace treaty with Turkey. Moreover, the British Government proposed to appoint Herbert Samuel, a well-known Jewish politician, as the first British High Commissioner in Palestine.[141] The risks involved in appointing a well-known Zionist Jew were promptly pointed out by the British Authorities in the area. Both Samuel and the Cabinet were well aware of the nature of these risks. In a letter to Lord Curzon, Samuel reported the gist of a conversation with a deputation from the Council of Jews of Jerusalem:

I told them that the Government had received a grave warning. . . that the appointment of any Jew as the first Governor of Palestine would likely to the signal for an outbreak of serious disorder, that there was a danger of widespread attacks upon the Jewish colonies and upon individual Jews; that raids might take place across the border; and further, that important Christian elements in the population, whose co-operation was necessary for the effective conduct of the Government, might withdraw their support. It had been represented that Mohammedan opinion was already in an excitable state, owing to the inclusion of the Balfour Declaration in the Turkish Treaty, and that such an appointment would be regarded as the transfer of the whole country to the Jews.[142]

In his published memoirs, Samuel contended that he had been appointed 'With full knowledge on the part of His Majesty's Government of my Zionist sympathies, and no doubt largely because of them'.[143]

On 31 May following the announcement of the Palestine Mandate, the inclusion of the Balfour Declaration in its articles, and the appointment of Samuel as the first High Commissioner for Palestine, a number of leading Palestinian political personalities met at the *Nadi-al-'Arabi* in Damascus where they resolved to form 'The Palestinian Arab Society'. The officers of the Society were Haj Amin Husseini, 'Izzat Darwaza and 'Aref al-'Aref. The society urged all Palestinian societies and clubs to work together for the common good. Moreover, the Society protested against the San Remo Conference's decision to grant Britain a mandate over Palestine and against Samuel's appointment. It also appealed to the Muslims of India and to the Pope, drawing attention to the Jewish danger in Palestine.[144]

The appointment of Samuel came as a severe blow to the Palestinian Arab masses, who, nevertheless, seemed determined to resist Zionism and the Balfour Declaration as their struggle against them entered a new stage.

Notes

1. *Memorandum of the Jewish Palestinian Question,* Arab Bureau, 5 February 1917, FO 822/14, p.16.
2. He played an important role in Palestinian affairs later on when he assumed the post of Secretary of State for the Colonies.
3. Ormsby-Gore, 'Palestine Political', 12 January 1917, FO 822/14.
4. See Antonius, p.187. Also see 'al-Thawra al-'Arabiyya al-Kubra' ('The Great Arab Revolt'), Mulhaq *al-Hayat,* Beirut, 22 November 1966, p.41.
5. For the Hussein-McMahon correspondence see *Correspondence between Sir Henry McMahon and the Sharif Hussein of Mecca, July 1916-March 1917,* Cmd. 5957 (Miscellaneous No.3) 1939, HMSO London.
6. For an early confidential discussion of the subject asserting the inclusion of Palestine in the proposed Arab state see *Memorandum on British Commitments to King Hussein,* Political Intelligence Department, 5 November 1918, FO 371/3384. For other documents written at the time the McMahon pledge was given, see McMahon to FO, 26 October 1915, FO 371/2486. Also see Grey to Buchanan, 30 November 1915, FO 371/2767. Also see Grey to McMahon 20 October 1915, FO 371/6237 and FO 141/461.
7. See FO 371/4368. The text of the Agreement also appears in E.L. Woodward and R. Butler (eds.) *Documents on British Foreign Policy, 1919-1939.* 1st ser., vol.IV, p.241-51.
8. The original letter deposited by Lord Rothschild in the British Museum: addl. Ms.41178 folios 1 and 3; for a reproduction of the letter and a full discussion of the efforts and negotiations leading to the Declaration, see Leonard Stein, *The Balfour Declaration,* London 1961, *passim*; J.M.N. Jeffries, *Palestine: The Reality,* London, 1939, pp.88-186 *passim;* and Chaim Weizman, *Trial and Error,* London 1950, pp.223-52, *passim.*
9. As early as March 1916 Sir Mark Sykes of the FO reported that: 'When in Cairo Dr Feris Nimr and (Major) Faruki, poles asunder on the political question, both told me that Arabs, Christians and Moslems alike would fight in the matter to the last man against Jewish Dominion in Palestine'. See Sykes to Buchanan, 14 March 1916, FO 371/2767.

10. MacDonogh to Clayton, 21 November 1916, FO 882/14.
11. HMSO, *Palestine Royal Commission Report* Cmd. 5479 of 1937 (London, 1937 edition), p.153. Hereafter referred to as the Peel Commission Report. Also see Colonel A.P. Wavell, *The Palestine Campaigns* (London, 1928), p.13; Jeffries, op.cit., pp.210-11; and T.E. Lawrence, *Revolt in the Desert*, London, 1927 p.208.
12. Deedes to H.Cr. of Egypt, 16 December 1917, FO 141/803. Also see Clayton to FO December 1917, FO 141/803.
13. Deedes to General Headquarters, EEF, 19 December 1917, FO 141/803.
14. Clayton to FO, 30 December 1917, FO 141/803.
15. Clayton to Sykes, 15 December 1917, Clayton Papers, Durham University, 147/1.
16. Sir Mark Sykes, 'The Palestine and West Arabian Situation', War Cabinet, 1 January 1918, FO 371/3388.
17. Ibid.
18. Between December 1917, and the summer of 1920, Palestine was governed according to the rules of military administration of occupied enemy territory. This meant that the Occupied Enemy Territory Administration (OETA) was bound by military law to preserve the *status quo,* to avoid the introduction of marked change in the laws of the country or their manner of application and to carry on with the least disturbance of public life pending the appointment of a permanent government. The Administration in Palestine was a military organisation acting under a chief Administrator who received his orders from the Commander-in-Chief (General Allenby) through the General Officer Commanding. There were thirteen Military Governors of Districts, reduced in 1919 to ten, with fifty-nine military officers as assistants. See Peel Commission Report, op.cit., pp.153-4.
18, Ronald Storrs, *Orientations,* London, 1937, p.353.
20. A letter from Mr Joseph Cohen, *The Times,* 19 September 1919; and Weizmann, op.cit., p.305.
21. Weizmann to Eder, 17 December 1918, FO 371/4170.
22. 'Note on the Interview with Mr. Balfour, 4 December 1918, FO 371/3385.
23. FO to Wingate, 4 January 1918, FO 371/3054. Also see Commander Hogarth's interview with King Hussein, 15 January 1918, FO 371/3383.
24. Clayton to FO, 25 February 1918, FO 371/3391. For manifestations of anti-Zionism among Arabs outside Palestine see same to same, 5 March 1918, FO 371/3391.
25. FO to Wingate, 13 February 1918, Durham 148/5, No.218.
26. Clayton to FO, 10 March 1918, FO 371/3391.
27. Clayton was not altogether happy at the complete identification of Britain with the Zionist aims and hoped that the Zionist Commission would rectify the situation. See same to same, 14 March 1918, FO 371/3391.
28. Clayton to FO, 30 March 1918, FO 371/3391.
29. Clayton to Sykes, 31 March 1918, FO 371/3383.
30. Weizman, op.cit., p.272.
31. Clayton to FO, 9 April 1918, FO 371/3391.
32. Ormsby-Gore to Balfour, 19 April 1918, FO 371/3395.
33. Ibid.
34. Ibid.
35. *The Palestine News,* 25 April 1918, British Museum, author's translation.
36. Weizmann to Ormsby-Gore, 16 April 1918, FO 371/3398.
37. Storrs to OETA, GHQ, 22 April 1918, FO 371/3398. Clayton too found it necessary to sound a vote of caution to Sykes, see Clayton to Sykes, 18 April 1918, Durham 148/8.

38. See 22 April 1918, FO 371/3398.
39. A letter from Weizmann to Brandeis, 25 April 1918, FO 371/3395.
40. 'Future of Palestine', May 1918, FO 371/3383.
41. Weizmann to Balfour, 30 May 1918, FO 371/3395.
42. Ibid. Clayton was the one who encouraged Weizmann to befriend the Hashemites. See 13 June 1918, Durham 148/10.
43. P.C. Joyce, 'Interview between Dr Weizmann and Sharif Faisal', 5 June 1918, FO 883/14.
44. 27 August 1918, FO 271/3389, Annex 2.
45. Clayton to Wingate, 2 August 1918, Durham 149/3.
46. Albina to Sykes, n.d., FO 800/221.
47. *The Palestine News*, 27 June 1918.
48. Clayton to FO, 31 August 1918, FO 371/3395.
49. See 1 October 1918, FO 371/3395.
50. Clayton to Balfour, 16 June 1918, FO 371/3395. It is not unlikely that Ormsby-Gore included agricultural workers in the category of 'Arab labour'.
52. Clayton to FO 17 July 1918, FO 371/3391.
53. 27 August 1918, FO 371/3389.
54. 'Report of the Arab Movement', Arab Bureau, Cairo, July 1918, FO 882/3391.
55. Clayton to FO, 25 August 1918, FO 371/3391.
56. Colonel T.E. Lawrence saw 'Zionist ambitions in Palestine as a counter to the Sykes-Picot agreement and a way of 'hiffing' the French out of the Middle East' and it was not surprising that the French were willing to condone Arab anti-Zionist articles in 1918. See Philip Knightly and Colin Simpson, *The Secret Lives of Lawrence of Arabia*, London, 1969, p.102.
57. Sykes to Picot, 7 September 1918, FO 371/3388.
58. See Clayton to Wingate, 21 September 1918, Durham 148/8.
59. Amery, L.S. 'The Future of Palestine', 18 October 1918, FO 371/3384.
60. 'The Strategic Importance of Syria to the British Empire', General Staff, War Office, 9 December 1918, FO 371/4178.
61. Clayton to Foreign secretary, 8 November 1918, FO 371/3385. Also see 4 November 1919 FO 141/803.
62. Ibid.
63. Clayton to FO, 19 November 1918, FO 371/3395. The Anglo-French Declaration referred to is that of November 1918, addressed to the Arab provinces of the Ottoman Empire, which was instrumental in fostering the rising hopes for freedom and independence: 'The object aimed at by France and Great Britain in prosecuting the War in the East. . .is the complete and definite emancipation of the peoples so long oppressed by the Turks and establishment of national governments and administrations deriving their authority from the initiative and free choice of the indigenous populations'. See 25 March 1919, FO 371/4179; also see Great Britain, Parliamentary Papers, Cmd. 5974 of 1939, p.51 and Jacob Hurewitz, *Diplomacy in the Near and Middle East*, vol.II, Princeton 1958 (first published 1956), p.30.
64. 16 November 1918, FO 371/3386.
65. See Hubbard to H.Q., OETA South, 20 November 1918, FO 371/3386.
66. 15 November 1919, FO 371/3386.
67. Storrs to OETA South, HQ, 19 November 1918, FO 371/3386.
68. The Muslim Arabs consistently backed the struggle of the Christian Orthodox Arabs against the Greek hierarchy in their Church. Storrs thought that 'this solidarity has been very greatly increased by the menace of Zionism'. See Storrs to HQ, OETA South, 16 November 1918, FO 371/3386.
69. Same to same, 24 November 1918, FO 371/3386.
70. Ibid.

71. *The Palestine News*, 6 February 1919.
72. J.N. Camp, 'The Palestine Conference', 15 February 1919, FO 371/4153.
73. Ibid., p.3.
74. See 5 February 1919, FO 371/4153.
75. Camp, op.cit.
76. Ibid.
77. Ibid.
78. Ibid.
79. According to Darwaza the delegation was prevented from proceeding to Damascus by the British authorities. See 'Izzat Darwaza, *al-Qadiyya al-Falastiniyya* (The Palestinian Question) (Saida, 1959), p.36.
81. A report by Weizmann, 8 February 1919, FO 371/4170.
82. Ibid. The Catholics, however, were in favour of a united Syria on account of their anti-Zionist leanings as well as their pro-French sympathies. See 18 March 1919, FO 371/4180.
83. The presence of three Jewish battalions Royal Fusiliers (British Army) augmented Arab unrest; a complete file on the history, formation and record of these units is available at the Public Record office, War Office, 32/1539.
84. 19 February 1919, FO 371/4179.
85. Clayton to FO, 26 March 1919, FO 371/4153.
86. See 30 April 1919, FO 371/4180.
87. 2 May 1919, FO 371/4180.
88. For the text of the Agreement and Faisal's hand-written reservation see St Anthony's Private Papers, Middle East Library, Oxford; and Weizmann, op.cit., pp.308-9.
89. Clayton to FO, 11 May 1919, FO 371/4180.
90. See Weizmann to Aaron and Felix, 8 May 1919, FO 371/4181.
91. A prominent British Zionist who had assumed the post of Home Secretary and who later became First High Commissioner in Palestine.
92. 10 May 1919, CZA Z/16009.
93. Ibid.
94. Ibid.
95. Clayton to FO, 2 May 1919, FO 371/4181.
96. Ibid.
97. See Harry Howard, *The King Crane Commission*, Beirut, 1963, pp.9-34 *passim*.
98. In Palestine itself 260 petitions in all were submitted and out of these 222 (85.3 per cent) declared against the Zionist programme. This was the largest percentage in the district of any one point. For some of the original Arabic petitions see King Papers, Oberlin College Library, Oberlin, Ohio.
99. Howard, op.cit., p.100.
100. Ibid., p.102.
101. Charles R. Crane and Henry C. King, *Report of the American Section of of the Inter-Allied Commission of Mandates in Turkey, Section One, Report upon Syria*, Paris, 28 August 1919, National Archives, Department of State, 181.9102/9, hereafter referred to as the *Syrian Report*. Also see Department of State, *Papers Relating to the Foreign Relations of the United States. The Paris Peace Conference 1919*, US Government Printing Office, 1947. Also see Howard, op.cit., pp.345-56.
101. Howard, op.cit., p.98.
103. Clayton to Curzon, Enclosure no.1, 5 June 1919, FO 371/4181.
104. Ibid.
105. Clayton to Foreign Secretary, 19 June 1919, FO 371/4181.

106. Memorandum of the General Syrian Congress to the American Section of the
      Inter-Allied Commission, 3 July 1919, FO 371/4182.
107. Ibid.
108. French to Curzon, 30 August 1919, FO 371/4182.
109. 12 August 1919, FO 371/4226.
110. Camp to CPO, GHQ, Cairo, 12 August 1919, FO 371/4182.
111. Weizmann, op.cit., 8 February 1919. These societies were *el-Muntada
      el-Arabi, et-Nadi el Arabi and el-Akha we 'l-Afaf.*
112. Hagana Archives, Jerusalem, 27 August 1919.
113. Ibid.
114. Ibid., 2 September 1919.
115. Ibid.
116. Watson to CPO, EEF, 16 August 1919, FO 371/4171.
117. The Scheme would have provided much-needed loans for the Arab farmers.
      For Zionist objections against the scheme see Weizmann to Sir Ronald Graham,
      14 July 1919, FO 371/4225.
118. 'Report of the Court of Inquiry convened by order of H.E. The High
      Commissioner and Commander-In-Chief dated the 12th Day of April 1920',
      1 July 1920, FO 371/5121, hereafter referred to as the Palin Commission
      Report.
119. 'Zionism', Naval Intelligence, 19 September 1919, FO 371/4238.
120. 18 October 1919, FO 371/4185.
121. 'Situation in Syria and Palestine', Naval Intelligence, 12 December 1919,
      FO 371/4238.
122 'Situation in Syria and Palestine', Naval Intelligence, 9 January 1920,
      FO 371/4238.
123. 7 February 1920, FO 371/4181.
124. Palin Commission Report, op.cit., p.56.
125. Ibid., p.57.
126. See Weizmann, op.cit., pp.317-18; Christopher Sykes, *Crossroads to Israel,*
      London, 1965, p.21.
127. See Darwaza, op.cit., p.37.
128. Palin Commission Report, op.cit., p.53.
129. Ibid., p.62.
130. Darwaza, op.cit., p.37.
131. 'Isa Sifri, *Falastin al-'Arabiyya bayn al-Intidab wa al-Sahyuniyya,* Jerusalem,
      1937, p.47.
132. Palin Commission Report, op.cit., pp.63-4.
133. Ibid., p.65.
134. Ibid., pp.75-8.
135. Ibid., p.68.
136. Ibid., p.70.
137. Ibid., p.79.
138. Ibid., pp.81-2.
139. Long prison sentences were passed against 'Aref al-'Aref and Haj Amin
      Husseini, but both were able to escape to Trans-Jordan.
140. Storrs, op.cit., p.391.
141. See Elie Kedourie, 'Sir Herbert Samuel and the Government of Palestine',
      Middle Eastern Studies, vol.V, no.1, January 1969.
142. A letter from Herbert Samuel to Lord Curzon, 14 May 1920, FO 800/156.
143. Herbert Samuel, Memoirs, London, 1945, p.168.
144. Sifri, op.cit., pp.34-5.

4 DEADLOCK: 1920-1923

The Jerusalem outbreak of April 1920 attracted the attention of the San Remo Conference to the Arab-Zionist conflict in Palestine. Far from bringing about a review of Britain's JNH policies, the Conference nominated Great Britain as Mandatory in Palestine whose duties were defined by a verbatim repetition of the Balfour Declaration.

It was not until April 1920 (three days after the Mandate nomination), that the Declaration itself was officially disclosed by the Military Administration to the people of Palestine.[1] Five days later, the San Remo decisions were announced to the notables of Nablus. Despite Allenby's grave warnings[2] and despite legal considerations arising from the delay in the ratification of the Peace Treaty, the Prime Minister and the Cabinet approved a Zionist suggestion that Herbert Samuel be the first High Commissioner in Palestine[3].

Between the San Remo nomination in April 1920 and September 1923 when the Palestine Mandate was brought into full operation, the respective attitudes of the three parties to the Palestine problem hardened and crystallised. The Mandate provisions transferred the British-Zionist accord — as embodied in the Balfour Declaration — from a love affair built on mutual interest into an internationally sanctioned Catholic marriage, where Britain was committed to a JNH policy in return for Zionist cooperation and backing in Palestine.

Following the official announcement of the Balfour Declaration and the San Remo decision, a wave of Palestinian Arab protests against these policies and against the separation of Palestine from Syria swept Palestine[4] and manifestations of anxiety and restiveness abounded. Several major clashes between Arab tribes and the British garrisons along the Beisan-Samakh frontier with Syria took place, where heavy casualties on both sides were inflicted.

On 6 May *Fata al-'Arab* of Damascus, reported that 'Muslims and Christians are convening more political meetings which may result in protestations against the British policy that helped divide Syria'.

Four days later *al-Karmal* reported that 'delegates were sent to Galilee and Acre to urge the inhabitants to assist in the Jerusalem Conference'.

Indignant as the Palestinians were at British pro-Zionist policies, the Palestinian political notability sought with energy and determination to avoid a head-on collision with the British authorities in the course of the fight against Zionism. The Palestinian leadership aimed at bringing about a change of British policy (in Palestine) through a show of (peaceful) determination and friendly persuasion.

In an article on the composition and purpose of the proposed Congress, *al-Karmal* reflected the prevalent strategy of the Muslim-Christian Associations' leadership *vis-à-vis* the Anglo-Zionist convergence in Palestine: 'The British Government is strong and therefore it is difficult to fight it. We must confine our revolt against our opponents'.[5]

Conciliatory gestures notwithstanding, the British authorities prohibited the convention of the Palestine Second Congress for security reasons.

A minority of the political notability went to the length of co-operating with the Zionists. In accordance with a secret Zionist programme drawn up by Weizmann,[6] Dr Eder of the Zionist Commission concluded a deal with the editor of *al-Akhbar* for £P 125. He also concluded deals for larger sums of money with Sa'id Bey Nablusi and Rashid Abu Khadra of Jaffa and Haidar Bey Tuqan of Nablus. This particular Zionist drive failed and Palestinian protests against the collaborators were reported by Eder's liaison officer.[7] It was this episode that prompted *al-Karmal's* call on 14 May 1920, for national unity 'in order to influence public opinion to see that landowners do not sell their land to the Jews'.

The announcement of Samuel's appointment as High Commissioner came as a severe shock to the Palestinians. Following a comprehensive tour in May, General Bols recorded:

They are convinced that he will be a partisan Zionist and that he represents a Jewish and not a British Government.[8]

In the same report Bols spoke of 'definite signs of Bolshevik propaganda and ideas'. However, neither the *Poale Zion* (Workers of Zion) nor the Socialist Workers' Party (Communist Party) had any great following among the Arab proletariat workers and peasants. A pamphlet by the Poale Zion accused the Zionist leaders of 'poisoning the soul of the Jewish workers against the uncultured fellah and of waging economic war against those who have nothing'.[9] The Socialist Workers' Party 'remained exclusively Jewish up to late 1920 and the Communists had great difficulty in finding, not only Arab candidates for party membership but even sympathisers and potential allies'.[10]

As the date for the introduction of civil government drew nearer, Palestinian Arab protests against the Sam Remo decisions and the appointment of Herbert Samuel as High Commissioner became more vehement. Faisal begged Allenby to urge the British Government 'to reverse a decision which vitally affects both interests and *amour propre* of Arab population'.[11]

Opposition to Samuel's appointment was not confined to diplomatic notes: 'rumours of intended Arab raids on June 30th, with intention of impressing Sir Herbert Samuel. Further reports that attempts to assassinate him are intended'.[12] The Zionists gave information regarding an alleged impending outbreak at the end of Ramadan.[13] When Samuel arrived on 30 June 1920, he found the Military Authorities nervous 'and had made the most formidable preparations against any possible eventuality'.[14]

Samuel's Two-pronged Policy

Prior to his arrival Samuel had decided to adopt a two-pronged policy devised to bring about Palestinian Arab acquiescence to Britain's JNH policy in Palestine. On the one hand he intended to bring home to the Arabs that the gradual establishment of the national home for the Jews in Palestine was a *chose jugée* as far as HM Government were concerned.[15] On the other hand Samuel intended to win over the moderate Palestinians, i.e. vested interests, by a display of personal friendliness, political liberalism and impartiality within the framework of the Balfour Declaration.

Soon after his arrival, Samuel summoned the notables of Jerusalem and the neighbouring districts to a meeting on 7 July and those of Haifa on the following day. The Palestinian national movement, which had earlier declared that the Palestinians cannot recognise Herbert Samuel whom they regarded as a Zionist leader,[16] called for a boycott:

> for a few days, and in certain districts some of the leading men were wavering as to the course they would pursue, in the end with exceedingly few exceptions they all attended.[17]

The failure of the boycott exposed the timidity of the political notability in Palestine. At both of these assemblies, Samuel read a message from the King to the people of Palestine and delivered speeches promising freedom and equality for all religions, good administration and economic development, and declared an amnesty for all who were in prison on account of the Easter disturbances in Jerusalem. Furthermore, Samuel disclosed his plans for a 'first stage in the development of self-governing institutions'.

The 'Advisory Council' was a step calculated to permeate a feeling of participation in the government, and a channel of peaceful expression of feelings that would help avert sudden and violent political explosions. In his report to the Foreign Secretary, Samuel expressed his satisfaction at the favourable effect of his pronouncements throughout the country: '...the extremists will no doubt continue their criticisms'.[18]

In reply to Samuel's seemingly moderate announcements, *al-Karmal* pointed out the basic irreconcilability of the two injunctions of the Balfour Declaration and the Mandate:

We do not understand how the making of a national home for strangers in our country can be without prejudice to our religious and civil rights. . .

We strongly protest against separating Palestine from its mother, Syria, and making it a national home for Jews and we appeal to the British Government and to the liberal British Nation for Justice.[19]

The Advisory Council foreshadowed in Samuel's inaugural address had its first meeting on 6 October 1920. It consisted of twenty members, with Samuel as Chairman, of whom half were British officials and half nominated Palestinians – seven Palestinian Arabs (four Muslims and three Christians) and three Jews.[20] The Arab members were pro-British notables with entrenched vested interests. Deedes described the first meeting of the Advisory Council as a great success in spite of the criticisms voiced by the non-official members. Furthermore, Deedes reported the presence of 'a feeling amongst a section (notably Moslem) of the population that members of the Council should be elected and not nominated'.[21]

Three weeks later the optimistic outlook of the Administration gave way to a more solemn mood. Deedes explained that the reasons for this change included a new initiative by the 'so-called Intelligentsia': 'In the East this Class is almost impossible to compete with', and 'the existence of such movements, as Arab Nationalism, Pan Islamism etc.,'[22] and the necessity of dealing with certain practical questions arising out of the Zionist programme.

The Third Palestine Arab Congress

Another factor was the prospect of a Third Palestine Conference. The fall of the 'Arab regime' in Damascus in July 1920 was a severe blow to the Palestinian Arab national movement that had repercussions on the orientation and outlook of that movement. The sense of identity was irreparably damaged, and an important source of backing was suddenly cut. The Palestinians were left alone in an arena where the balance of power was hopelessly tipped in favour of their determined enemies. The proposed Conference was charged with the arduous task of devising a strategy for the new situation.

The Third Palestine Arab Congress was held in Haifa on 13 December 1920, and was attended by representatives of the Muslim-Christian Associations and Societies from almost every part of Palestine, under the presidency of Musa Kazem Husseini. In the resolutions of the Congress the participants affirmed that Palestine was included in the Arab Kingdom which Britain promised to recognise in the Hussein-McMahon correspondence. They declared their dissatisfaction with 'the present form of government in that it does not satisfy their wishes and fails to safeguard their interests'. The manifesto of the Congress pointed out, in a somewhat circumspect manner, that the Government was illegal since it exercised 'the power of legislation without a representative Council and before the final decision of the League of Nations is given'.[23] They objected to the Government's recognition of the Zionist Organisation as an official body, of Hebrew as an official language and of the use of the Zionist flag, and to admitting Zionist immigrants. The Advisory Council was condemned as 'a false attempt to show that there exists in Palestine a council with legislative powers representing the population'. Furthermore, the Congress contended that too many Zionists were appointed to various offices of Government. The manifesto concluded by spelling out the three 'doctrines' or 'National Charter' of the Arab National Movement in Palestine:

(i) The condemnation of the Zionist policy which embodies the establishment of a National Home for the Jews, based upon the Balfour Declaration.

(ii) The non-acceptance of the principle of Jewish immigration.

(iii) The establishment of a National representative Government.

The Congress elected an Executive Committee of moderate Palestinian notables, headed by Musa Kazem, and entrusted it with the execution of the resolutions until the following Congress was convened.

The Congress, although clearly anti-Zionist, was quite moderate *vis-à-vis* the British government. The three 'doctrines' did not challenge the Mandate outrightly, but rather concentrated on objecting against the inclusion of the Balfour Declaration in its articles.

A state of excitement and agitation in Palestine prevailed during December and early January. As a Congress of the Muslim-Christian Societies it was representative of the elements that had assumed the leadership of these Societies from 1918 onwards; namely, town and village propertied notables,[24] merchants and a minority of middle class intellectuals. National unity meant the lowest common denominator in the anti-Zionist camp, and the. composition of the Executive Committee was bound to reflect that. The absence of any mention of independence and unity with Syria was a significant omission that can only be explained in the light of the French occupation of Syria.

The demands of the Congress were not spared criticism by the younger and more vigorous elements. An article by 'Isa al-'Isa on the Haifa Congress concluded by saying that the demands of the Congress were not radical enough.[25]

Moderate as the resolutions and the leadership of the Haifa Congress were, the government maintained that the delegates were appointed by small groups of people and refused to acknowledge them as being representative of the population. Thereupon, the organisers of the Congress felt compelled to vindicate their representative character and launched a wide-spread successful campaign to demonstrate general endorsement of the resolutions and leadership of the Congress.[26] The agitation which ensued, with public meetings and leaflets, etc., helped stimulate renewed daily interest in politics and concern for the future among the Palestinians, which inevitably resulted in the revival of tension in the country.

In an attempt to allay growing apprehensions, as well as to establish personal relations with the leaders of the opposition, Samuel invited Musa Kazem and five of his political associates to Government House to discuss with him — in a private capacity — 'the questions about which their minds were exercised'. Musa Kazem 'mentioned the fears of the community in regard to Mr Balfour's statement and Jewish immigration. He also raised the question of representative government'. In the course of his reply Samuel made it clear that it was not within his competence to discuss the policy laid down by HM Government and the Balfour Declaration, but rather it was his duty to carry out these policies. However, Samuel pointed out, it was within his competence to give effect to the second part of the Balfour Declaration. The question of the election of municipalities was already receiving his close attention. Furthermore, Samuel declared that he was prepared to recognise any body of 'gentlemen' representing any important section of the community, in the same manner as he had already given recognition to the Jewish National Assembly and under the same conditions, namely, that no resolutions should be adopted or submitted that were contrary to the conditions of the Mandate.[27] While the Palestinian leaders refrained from accepting Samuel's proposals, they responded favourably to the prospect of a friendly personal relationship with the High Commissioner and the political implications thereof.

A Feeling of Unsettlement

The revival of political agitation in the wake of the Haifa Congress owed much to a prevalent feeling of unsettlement in the area. The victories of Mustafa Kemal (Ataturk) inspired the belief that Turkey would probably refuse to ratify the Peace Treaty thus bringing the issue of the Mandate under fresh consideration. Then, there was the feeling that an attempt will be made by the Arabs to expel the French from Syria. In mid-January 1921 Deedes reported that even 'responsible' Palestinian Arabs firmly believed 'that there is still a chance of getting the Mandate changed and that many British Statesmen and a portion of the British Public desires that change'.[28] In view of the many imponderables and the ample room for agitation Deedes expressed his apprehensions regarding the immediate political prospects:

> I do not feel that there is much reason to fear the responsible members of the discontented party; but the words and actions of the irresponsible members are apt to be dangerous in an atmosphere always more or less charged with electricity, especially at this time of the year when we are approaching Easter.[29]

This same feeling persisted after the text of the draft mandate was reported in the local newspapers.[30]

The February Report gave an account of a movement to collect signatures as a protest against the separation of Palestine from the rest of a region to which, it was contended, the country belongs geographically as well as ethnographically and historically. This movement, among other things, reflected, 'a renewed effort on the part of Arab Nationalists in Egypt, in Palestine and in Syria to achieve their ends by cooperation'. The Report also gave accounts of increased interest in the question of Jewish immigration into Galilee brought about by the attempts of the Haifa Congress to gain support for their resolutions.

In the neighbourhood of Beisan some anxiety and apprehension have recently been expressed by the Arab population owing to an unfortunate and unfounded impression having gained ground that the Government intends to further the settlement of Jews in a manner detrimental to the interests of the Arab population.[31]

The ownership of the *Jiftlik* (Imperial) Beisan lands issue had a direct bearing on the involvement of the *fellahin* in the political fight against the pro-Zionist policy of the Government. The fears of the *fellahin* were genuine in view of the complications involved in their rights to ownership and tenancy of the lands under question.

Churchill's Cairo Conference

On assuming responsibility for the Middle East Department,[32] the Secretary of State for the Colonies, Winston Churchill,[33] summoned his lieutenants and key British military, political and administrative staff in the area to a Conference in Cairo.

The Conference's main aim was to review the British position and lay plans for future policy in the Middle East in the light of the French occupation of Syria and the unsettled conditions of Trans-Jordan and Mesopotamia.

As far as Palestine was concerned the Conference considered that HMG was responsible under the terms of the Mandate for establishing a national home for the Jewish people. In a 'Memorandum drawn up by Middle East Department' presented to the Cairo Conference, it was observed that the Palestine Administration was being conducted 'in strict accordance with the terms of the Mandate, and has been attended by the happiest results'.[34]

The Conference recommended that Trans-Jordan should be constituted an Arab province of Palestine under Prince 'Abdullah, Faisal's brother, responsible to the High Commissioner. It would not be included in the administrative system of Palestine, and therefore the Zionist clauses of the Mandate would not apply. In return for all this and the promise of financial assistance, 'Abdullah pledged – after interviews with Churchill in Jerusalem – to respect British international commitments: to the French in Syria and to the Zionists in Palestine.[35]

Soon after Churchill's intention to visit Egypt, and perhaps Palestine, became known, the Executive Committee of the Haifa Congress announced the appointment of a deputation that would proceed to Egypt and lay before Churchill the grievances of the Palestinian Arabs. Despite the Administration's advice to await the arrival of Churchill in Jerusalem the deputation — headed by Musa Kazem — left Palestine 12 March and returned two weeks later. Churchill, reluctantly, received the deputation but refused to discus political questions on that occasion but said he would be pleased to see them in Jerusalem on 28 March. During their stay in Egypt the Palestinian leaders were invited by Syrian-Lebanese political figures to banquets and gatherings where speeches in favour of Arab unity were delivered:

> On the evening of the 19th the Syrian Union Party held a meeting where the possibility of joining forces with the Arab Palestinians was discussed in the interests of the complete independence of Syria.[36]

While in Cairo Muza Kazem saw Dr Ismail Bey Sidki, of the Watani Party, who advised him to form a national party in Palestine to work for complete independence. Muza Kazem's reported reply revealed the basic strategy of the Muslim-Christian Association's leadership at that stage:

> Musa Kazem said that the intentions of the Palestine Delegation included complete independence, but they desire, if this were not possible, that the real power should be with the English and not with the Jews; they desired also their own parliament.[37]

When Churchill visited Palestine, he found that the Palestinians were eager to convey to him their strong feelings against Zionism wherever he went. Although no official intimation of the hour of the arrival of the special train bringing the Colonial Secretary and the High Commissioner to Gaza had been received,

> Large and expectant crowds of people assembled and many persons came in from outlying villages.
>
> During the visit cries of 'Long Live the High Commissioner and Mr. Churchill', 'Down with Balfour', and 'we won't have the Jews' were heard.[38]

When the Governor of Haifa prohibited demonstrations on 25 March and issued warnings regarding the risks and penalties attendant upon joining in a demonstration forbidden by the Government, the demonstrators defied his orders and a collision occured with the police, one Christian boy and a Muslim were killed, one Christian injured by a bullet wound, and ten Jews injured by knives or stones and five policemen were slightly injured.

Three days later the Governor of Jaffa refused to grant permission for a peaceful demonstration. As a consequence all Muslim shops were closed in protest. On the same day in Jerusalem, a large but orderly demonstration was held to protest against the Balfour Declaration.

On 28 March, the deputation of the Executive Committee of the Haifa Congress met Churchill at Government House, Jerusalem. A comprehensive memorandum, which Churchill described as a 'very able paper', on Palestinian Arab grievances and demands was presented to the Colonial Secretary. The memorandum accused the British Government of creating the national home idea and of putting life into it and carrying it into execution even before the ratification of the Mandate by the League of Nations. It dealt with the Palestine problem from legal, historical, moral, economic and political points of view and concluded by putting forth five Palestinian Arab demands calling for the abolition of the JNH, stoppage of immigration and land sales, the establishment of a national Palestinian government, responsible to a parliament, and the non-separation of Palestine from her sister states .[39]

In his reply Churchill informed the Palestinian leaders that it was not in his power to repudiate the Balfour Declaration and to veto Jewish immigration to Palestine, which the JNH policy inevitably involved. The Balfour Declaration was a *fait accompli* brought about by the War that the Arabs in Palestine could do nothing about but accept.[40]

He assured his visitors that the Government fully intended to stand by the second part of the Balfour Declaration which in fact imposed a dual obligation on the Government, 'if one promise stands so does the other'.[41]

In the light of Churchill's offhand treatment of the Palestinian leaders, it was not surprising that the Monthly Political Report for April should have started by stating that 'The visit of the Secretary of State gave satisfaction to the Jews and brought disappointment to the Arabs'.[42]

Captain Brunton of the General Staff Intelligence in Palestine reported that Churchill's visit had added to the anxiety of the Palestinians because the Colonial Secretary 'upheld the Zionist cause and treated the Arab demands like those of a negligible opposition to be put off by a few political phrases and treated like bad children'.[43]

The heavy-handedness of the troops and the killings that took place during the Haifa demonstrations on 28 March increased hostility to the

Government and strengthened unity between Christians and Muslims not only in Haifa but in other districts as well. In Beisan demonstrators protested against Zionism and Jewish immigration during Samuel's visit to the town. In Samaria the Governor reported 'increasing influence of anti-Zionist leaders over the peasantry'.[44]

Hajj Amin as Mufti

The report also made reference to an important and controversial issue:

> In Jerusalem the chief topic of interest has been the election of the New Mufti; opinion has been divided as to who should succeed Kamel Eff al Husseini, members of whose family (one of the most influential and respected in Palestine) have held this office for several generations. Learned opinion, represented by the Law Courts, has not favoured the popular candidate al Hajj Amin al Husseini, brother of the late Mufti and the elections that were held returned to the latter at the bottom of the poll causing indignation to the Husseini family (to which somewhat clamorous expression has been given) to a very large section of the inhabitants of all the districts. The Government, the Jews and the Mayor of Jerusalem were all suspected of having influenced the election. Technical flaws in the constitution of the electorate have delayed the settlement of this question.[45]

Settled or not, Hajj Amin soon assumed the role of the Mufti, and it was he who invited Samuel to a luncheon on the occasion of the celebration of the carrying of the standard to Nebi Musa on 25 April. Samuel's acceptance of the invitation implied Government's recognition of Hajj Amin as Mufti, while the latter's friendliness and courtesy to Samuel on that occasion proved that he was willing to come to terms with the Government. It soon became clear that the election was to be disregarded and Hajj Amin allowed to become Mufti. Thus Samuel avoided alienating the Husseinis in a balancing act in accordance with recognisable traditional imperial policy.

The question of the Muftiship was an important one in view of the fact that the Mufti of Jerusalem was regarded by the Administration as the head of the Muslim community in Palestine. Furthermore, Hajj Amin was elected as *Ra'is al-'Ulama'* and President of the Supreme Muslim Council which provided him with a solid power-base through the effective control over the management of religious endowments *awqaf* and the expenditure of income therefrom, the appointment and dismissal of all *shari'a* (Islamic) Courts and *waqf* officials, as well as the nomination of *qadis* (Judges).

The Administration's efforts to conciliate Arab public opinion in Palestine could not possibly do away with the two grounds on which Arab opposition stood, namely, the political and the constitutional grounds. On the political level the Administration was not in a position to nullify the Balfour Declaration and the JNH policy. On the constitutional side the Palestine Administration could do nothing to hasten the final settlement of the Mandate at the Peace Conference, nor could it change its autocratic and bureaucratic character to a representative and popular one. For whereas the purpose of other mandates was preparing the natives for self-government, the Palestine Administration was committed to a policy of 'immobilism' since self-government for the Arab majority in Palestine was inconsistent with the JNH policy.

Jaffa's Revolt

Shortly after the collision between the Haifa demonstrators and the police, an Arab was found dead in the neighbourhood of a camp of Jewish immigrants, and the situation became exceedingly explosive. The expected outburst eventually took place in Jaffa during the first two weeks of May. This was not surprising in view of unemployment and widespread resentment against Zionist immigration and the quality of the immigrants who abounded in the Arab port.[45]

On the evening of 30 April, Communist pamphlets and leaflets in Hebrew, Yiddish and Arabic were distributed calling for a May Day cessation of work, a proletarian rising against the British and the establishment of a Soviet Palestine.[47]

On the morning of 1 May an authorised Zionist socialist (Poale Zion) demonstration clashed with an unauthorised demonstration by some fifty Communists carrying a red flag in Tel-Aviv, the Jewish quarter of Jaffa. The Communists (Bolsheviks) were eventually forced out of Tel-Aviv into the mixed Muslim and Jewish quarter of Menshiah. When the police attempted to disperse the Bolsheviks, the Muslims became involved and a general disturbance occurred, which soon spread to the other parts of the town. Wild rumours of Jewish attacks enraged the Arabs.

According to Brunton, 'It is stated that the Jews first began by firing on the Arab passers-by' and that the Arabs attacked a house for the reception of Jewish immigrants. On this occasion the Muslims and Christians demonstrated their solidarity and unity in the fight against Zionism.[48]

Of greater significance was Brunton's reference to several incidents that occurred on the first day's rioting which caused the Arabs to suspect the impartiality of the troops and the Authorities. The instances cited by Brunton included 'the placing of Jewish guides on the armoured cars'; 'a Jewish civilian being seen and heard ordering British soldiers to fire on the crowd'; and 'the searching of Arabs by Jews in front of British soldiers'.[49] These incidents precipitated what Brunton described as a monster demonstration on 2 May, where Palestinian Arabs demanded the replacement of British troops by Indians and demanded arms to defend themselves against the armed Jews.

Troubles continued on 3 May and killing on both sides occurred, considerable damage being done to Jewish shops. Women played 'a considerable part in urging on the Arabs to attack Jews',[50] while the notables were trying to calm the population and had a very 'good effect'.[51]

The events that took place in Jaffa during the first three days of May galvanised the villagers in other Palestinian districts into a truculent mood. Samuel reported to Churchill that several Jewish colonies were attacked in various districts:

> It has been necessary to send detachments of troops, armoured cars, aeroplanes, and police to a number of different places, and to request the naval authorities to send warships to Jaffa and Haifa as a precautionary measure.[52]

The more serious clashes however occurred in the district of Jaffa. On hearing that Arabs were being killed by Jews in Jaffa, the neighbouring peasants and beduins were immediately drawn into the foray.

> On the 5th May some 3,000 Arabs (according to reports) had assembled to the north of the Jewish colony of Petah Tkvah (Mulebbis) about 10 miles north of Jaffa. Another force of Arabs several hundred strong was preparing to attack from the south.[53]

Government forces repulsed the attackers and pursued them with a loss of sixty killed and many wounded. The Haycraft Commission estimated the number of killed during the Jaffa outbreak at 95, of whom 48 were Arab and 47 Jewish, and 219 wounded of whom 75 were Arab and 146 Jewish.[54] These statistics exclude some of the casualties of the 5 May attack.

Brunton informed his superiors that the Zionists were trying to substantiate a theory to the effect that the outbreak of 1 May 'was premeditated by the Arabs and that it was arranged by a few notables, encouraged by French intrigue'. In his opinion:

> Nothing could be farther from the truth. I have carefully gone into the case, and there is not a vestige of proof of French or other intrigue. On the contrary, the attitude of the French consul appears to have been all that could have been desired. There is no evidence of premeditation on the part of the Arabs.[55]

In view of his opinion that the Jaffa disturbances were not a simple outbreak of mob violence but rather an expression of a 'deep seated and widely spread popular resentment at the present British policy', Brunton found it inescapable to recommend concessions to the Arabs on Jewish immigration, or failing that increasing the garrison in order to enforce British support for Zionism in Palestine.

The Haycraft Commission were impressed by the level of crude political interest and consciousness in the Palestinian towns and villages like Tulkarem:

> In a small Moslem centre of this sort the people are more politically minded than a small English country town, and the discussion of politics is their chief, if not their only, intellectual occupation.[56]

The Role of the Notables

In a report to Churchill, Samuel attributed the outbreaks to political and economic considerations aggravated by the increase of Zionist immigration. The Arabs, Samuel added, demanded representative institutions and regarded the Administration as unduly autocratic.[57] Furthermore, the delay in the ratification of the Mandate 'has been an important factor in preventing the quiet settlement of the country.[58]

Samuel conveyed his feeling of gratitude for the leaders of the 'Arab Nationalist Movement', i.e. leaders of the Haifa Congress and of the Muslim-Christian Associations, who

> used their best efforts to calm agitation. . .If the political leaders had set themselves to foster, instead of to check, the present agitation, the whole country could have been thrown into a state of turmoil, and order would have been reestablished only with the greatest

difficulty.[59]

Another indication of the role played by the notables was their attitude towards the reactions of the Palestinian populace against the Jewish boycott of Arab traders in May 1921. The notables were bound to be discredited in view of their failure to play the role the majority of Palestinians demanded of them:

> During the month a boycott of all Jewish goods broke out. The notables are stated to have done their best to stop it but met with much difficulty; such a step being interpreted by the people as having been prompted by the Jews and tended consequently to decrease the prestige of the notables in the eyes of the public.[60]

Samuel proposed to deport Bolsheviks, to suspend Jewish immigration temporarily,[61] to regulate immigration on stricter grounds, and to look into 'the very early establishment of representative institutions'.[62] Lastly, Samuel informed Churchill that he viewed with favour the impending visit of a Palestinian delegation to Europe and London and thought that efforts should be made to promote an understanding between them and the Zionist organisation. In another report Samuel recommended to Churchill that Article 4 of the Palestine Mandate, which recognised the Zionist Organisation as an advisory body to the Administration, should be watered down or rendered unobjectionable to the Arabs by the insertion of a similar article providing for the parallel recognition of a non-Jewish body.[63]

Who Opposed Democracy?

Unlike Samuel, Churchill was not willing to conciliate the Palestinian leaders by means of political concessions, even after they had demonstrated a cooperative attitude under tense conditions and trying circumstances. He was particularly averse to giving way to Palestinian Arab demands regarding elected representative institutions.[64] When the Zionists got wind of what Samuel was contemplating, they hastened to convey their strong opposition to any form of representative institutions, stressing once more the identity of British and Zionist interests.

> Such a body as appears to be contemplated would at the present time in all probability prove to be unfriendly to British policy in general and the Jewish National home in particular.[65]

The events of the spring of 1921 demonstrated that the notables were in need of reestablishing their leadership in the country. A show of political solidarity on a wide scale was necessary, and the Fourth Palestine Arab Congress was convened in Jerusalem in May 1921, under the traditional chairmanship of Musa Kazem. About a hundred delegates attended and reaffirmed the resolutions passed by the Haifa Congress and nominated a Palestine Arab Delegation to plead the Palestine Arab case in Europe and London. 'Pending the departure of this Delegation and its discussions in London, instructions have been given that all disorderly movements are to be avoided'.[66]

During June 1921, a more peaceful mood in Palestine prevailed. There were two major reasons for this change, although, as Samuel observed, the 'causes of unrest remain'.[67]

The first reason was Samuel's important speech at an Assembly of notables on the occasion of the King's Birthday, 3 June, when he reinterpreted the meaning of the Balfour Declaration in a way designed to allay the fears of the Palestinian Arabs and promote tranquillity in Palestine. Samuel promised the Palestinians that Britain 'would never impose upon them a policy which that people had reason to think was contrary to their religious, their political and their economic interest'.[68]

Samuel's pronouncement had an unfavourable reception in Zionist circles. Its effect on the Palestinian Arabs was more difficult to gauge. The 'extremists' were not appeased, as nothing less than the withdrawal of the Balfour Declaration or even the abolition of the British Mandate would satisfy them. The greater public, though reassured, 'feel very suspicious of the Administration's intention or ability to carry them out'.[69] Samuel admitted that the Palestinians had expected a declaration more far-reaching and more specific in its terms.

The second factor was the impending departure of the Delegation to Europe, and the deliberate cooling-off policy adopted by the political leadership of the Palestine Congress:

> ...if the leaders of the opposition to Zionism were at any time to set themselves to fan the ambers, they would soon begin to glow, and perhaps burst into flame. Their influence is being exerted, for the time being at least on the side of tranquility.[70]

The Weapon of Passive Resistance

Samuel was aware of the precarious position of the Palestinian political leadership. He pointed out to Churchill that latest events revealed the great interest in public affairs in the minds of the population in general

— peasants, beduins and the uneducated — and their discovery of their power to resist and obstruct the Government was an important new factor to consider. Furthermore, the Arabs possessed another weapon against the Government, namely, that of passive resistance. Should the British Government snub the Delegation, Samuel warned that the turbanned class — the Muslim religious leaders, who had hitherto been 'mere spectators' — would step in to take the place of the politicians in leading agitation and rebellion against the Government's policy.

> The conclusion is that a serious attempt must be made to arrive at an understanding with the opponents to the Zionist policy, even at the cost of considerable sacrifices. The only alternative is a policy of coercion, which is wrong in principle and likely to prove unsuccessful in practice.[71]

An understanding with the Delegation was not only urgent and necessary, Samuel added, but was also possible. Speaking of the members of the Delegation, he reassured the Colonial Secretary, 'I am informed that their present attitude is by no means uncompromising'.[72]

Despite the upholding of Martial Law in the district of Jaffa and the arming of the Jewish Colonies, the resumption of immigration produced some effervescence 'and the boatmen at the Port (of Jaffa) have given much trouble in connection with the landing of Jewish travellers'.[73] Nonetheless, Samuel expected the country to remain quiet so long as the Delegation was in England.

> Meantime certain sections are proceeding with the formation of a more moderate party which, while not concealing its dislike of the Zionist Policy, emphasises rather the need for domestic reform, particularly, in the interests of the population of the villages.[74]

The idea of co-operating with a Government committed to a JNH policy was not altogether new among a section of the political notability. In May 1921, the Mayors of Jerusalem, Tulkarem and Jaffa, the Muftis of Acre and Safad and the *Qadi* of Jerusalem received British decorations 'for services rendered in Palestine'. Furthermore, the battle over the Muftiship renewed and intensified old family feuds, particularly between the Nashashibis and the Husseinis. Zionist efforts and money to promote discord and disunity among the Palestinian political leaders constituted a contributing factor to the idea of a 'moderate party'. In a letter to the Zionist Executive, Eder had the following to report;

> Arabs. I am still in negotiation with Arabs. There are various moves
> on. If I had money something might still be done. . . There is just a
> possibility of being able to send a second delegation in opposition
> to the first.[75]

Neither a moderate party nor a second delegation were necessary
at that stage, from the British point of view. The delegates were
showing signs of eagerness to come to an agreement with the
Government and hinted that they may even agree to an implicit acceptance of the Balfour Declaration in principle.[76]

The Delegation's moderation, however, did not represent the
political mood of the population. A confidential Government report
assessing the political atmosphere in July 1921 spoke at length about
waning Government prestige, public insecurity and the explosiveness of
the whole situation:

> There is a consensus of opinion that a rising cannot be postponed
> much beyond the return of the Delegation from Europe should they
> come back empty handed.[77]

The report concluded that 'nothing short of a modification of the
Jewish policy and the establishment of some form of proportional
representation will ease the situation'.

After a short visit to Cairo, the Delegation went to Rome where they
were received in audience by the Pope who expressed sympathy with
their cause. They then proceeded to London where they found out that
Parliament was not in session. Three members of the Delegation
returned to Geneva to put the Palestine Arab case before the League
of Nations and protest against the Zionists clauses in the draft Mandate.
These delegates also participated in a coordinated general Arab
propaganda effort in Geneva.[78] On their return to England they
launched a general propaganda campaign and engaged 'the services of an
Advertising and Press Agency'.[79]

One day before Churchill received the first memorandum from the
Arab Delegation, he raised the Palestine Question before the Cabinet.

> The situation in Palestine causes me perplexity and anxiety. The
> whole country is in a ferment. The Zionist policy is profoundly
> unpopular with all except the Zionists. Both Arabs and Jews are

armed and arming, ready to spring at each other's throats. . . In the interests of the Zionist policy, all elective institutions have so far been refused to the Arabs, and they naturally contrast their treatment with that of their fellows in Mesopotamia.

It seems to me that the whole situation should be reviewed by the Cabinet.[80]

In their first memorandum to Churchill the Delegation reiterated the Palestinian national demands[81] and during the second half of August, the Delegation had two lengthy interviews with Churchill and Major Young of the ME Department. Churchill stressed that he was receiving them as an unofficial body and that as long as they insisted that the Balfour Declaration should be repudiated there was nothing to say. The Declaration, he argued, had to be carried out, and the Arabs must accept the fact.

But they could see that it was not carried out in a manner to injure the Arabs, and try and find some basis for a friendly arrangement for the next few years.[82]

The Delegation submitted that while they still had confidence in the British Government and their sense of justice, they felt that Palestinian rights were being carried away. They had to come to London to discuss the root of the problem – the Balfour Declaration – with those who could bring about a change of policy. When the Delegation entered into a discussion of ways and means of protecting Arab rights and interests, Churchill made it quite evident that any representative elective assembly or council would have no power over the control of immigration or any other matter that was vital to the implementation of the JNH policy. Thereupon, the Delegation declared that the two parts of the Balfour Declaration were irreconcilable as Zionism was incompatible with Arab rights.

On the following day the same stumbling blocks were encountered, and Churchill pressed on the Delegation to meet Weizmann and other Zionist leaders, to see if they could work out an agreement under the auspices of the Colonial Office. The Delegation were unwilling to accept this particular suggestion as they did not recognise Weizmann and the Zionist Organisation. Besides, 'The people of the country do not wish us to parley with them. They sent us to the Government'.[83] Churchill insisted that the Delegation should take up his suggestion and convince him that they were making an effort to come to an agreement as a preliminary condition to arranging an interview with the Prime Minister. The Delegation asked that they be given the opportunity to consult with each other before answering Churchill's request.

Before the Delegation could decide on its course of action in London, the High Commissioner summoned twenty-nine members of the 'Moslem and Christian Consultative Committee' to a meeting in Jerusalem in an apparent effort to undermine the position of the Delegation in London. The declared aim of the meeting was to invite the Palestinian Arabs to express their views on the terms of the impending Constitution being prepared by the British Government. The spokesman for those present replied that it was premature to consider a constitution at all since the status of the country had not been settled, that they could not in any case approve a constitution embodying the Balfour Declaration, and that the Delegation then in London was the body to be consulted on these matters.[84]

Apart from informal conversations between Shuckburgh, Head of the ME Department and individual members of the Delegation, there were no formal contacts between the Delegation and the Colonial Office from 1 September to 15 October. In the course of these conversations Shuckburgh found the Delegates agreeable but non-committal. Although offended by Churchill's suggestion that they should get into communication with the Zionist Organisation, Shuckburgh gathered the impression that they would not be unwilling to meet the Zionists under official auspices at the Colonial Office.[85]

On 24 October, the Delegation addressed a letter to Churchill which they wanted put before the Cabinet. In this letter they reiterated the fears of 93 per cent of the People of Palestine regarding Zionist policies and maintained that

> The very serious and growing unrest among the Palestinians arises from their absolute conviction that the present policy of the British Government is directed towards evicting them from their country in order to make it a national state for immigrant Jews. . . The Balfour Declaration was made without (us) being consulted and we cannot accept it as deciding our destinies.

What they suggested, or demanded, among other things, was that

> The Declaration should be superseded by an Agreement which would safeguard the rights, interests and liberties of the People of Palestine, and at the same time make provision for reasonable

Jewish religious aspirations, but precluding any exclusive political advantages to them which must necessarily interfere with Arab rights.[86]

Should their suggestions and views be favourably received by the Cabinet, the Delegation were ready to enter into negotiations with HMG regarding the details of the scheme which would subsequently be submitted to the people of Palestine.

After much hesitation[87] and as a result of discussion with Churchill, the Delegation agreed to attend a meeting in the Colonial Office where the Zionists would be present. In a telegram to Samuel, Churchill claimed that the accepted aim of the meeting was 'to discuss the possibility of making working arrangements,[88] between the Delegation and the Zionists. In contradistinction to that version, Weizmann wrote Deedes that the Arabs 'had come, not to discuss practical details, but to hear a statement of policy as promised'. The meeting was a failure. 'They entrenched themselves behind this position and Mr Shuckburgh was unable to dislodge them.[89]

As the negotiations dragged on in London, the Palestinians lost hope of obtaining any decisive gain through diplomatic efforts. In December Weizmann passed reports, which he considered accurate, to Shuckburgh on secret Arab political meetings that took place in Palestine during September 1921. These reports revealed a number of facts about the composition, aims and tactics of the anti-Zionist Palestinian Arab national movement at that particular period.

Political and Economic Factors

These reports covered meetings that took place in Hebron, Ramleh, Loubie and Tulkarem where delegates from the neighbouring villages and towns participated. The meetings provided an opportunity for coordination and cooperation between the national leadership in the cities and political activists in the rural areas. The reports indicate that the direct reason for convening the secret meetings of September 1921 was the realisation that the Arab Delegation in London stood no chance of obtaining their demands and that necessary action should be taken in Palestine. As the Arabs were too weak to confront the British troops in Palestine, there seemed to be 'only one effective method to stop immigration and to destroy the Balfour Declaration, and that is a systematic series of attacks on the Jews in Palestine'.[90] The neighbouring nationalist committees in the towns had convened the respective assemblies attended by 30 to 50 delegates to decide whether it would be possible to prepare in the next three or four months a systematic series of attacks upon the Jewish colonies in their vicinity. These attacks were designed to frighten Jewish immigration, to convince the British that the Arabs were stubborn and meant to stick to their demands and to show the world that the Palestinian demands were just, and 'As a result of this the League of Nations will not sign the Mandate'.[91]

These reports revealed the basis of agitation and the grounds for resentment against the Jews. We have seen how the political factor was considered important, but the economic factor, closely connected with the political one, was equally relevant:

> We must not allow a Mandate over us, as then all the rich Jews would grab everything in their hands, our commerce will be destroyed, we shall not be able to stand competition, they have many banks, and these banks assist only Jews, they are looking for concessions which will ruin us.[92]

In another meeting a similar line of argument stood out, this time with greater emphasis on aspects which explain the tough opposition of educated and semi-educated Arab middle classes to Zionism, who provided a high percentage of the leadership of the militant wing of the anti-Zionist Movement in Palestine:

> We must get rid of Jewish domination over us. The Jews are occupying important Government posts all over the land, and the Arabs are forced out everywhere. There is a general attempt by the Jewish intelligentsia to seize all the official Government positions. We must not allow this to continue. If the Balfour Declaration will be signed, we shall remain slaves to the Jews for ever.[93]

At the meeting at Loubie (near Tiberias) the incompatibility of the Balfour Declaration with Arab political rights was stressed, and the generation gap clearly spelt out as the old Sheikhs, i.e. elderly people, were opposed to the younger generation's violent tactics. 'These old Sheikhs do not understand that they are playing with out future, but fortunately they do not have much influence.'[94]

Although the *fellahin* were reported to be rather 'tired of politics', the activists were sure of their participation in attacks on Jewish colonies if they were assured that the Jews were not as well-armed as they say they were.

The participants in those meetings agreed to prepare the population for future attacks, to collect information on the amount of arms the Jews possess, and to propagate among the military officers (British) that they should remain passive during future attacks.

The Zionists endeavoured to counter the activists by a concerted effort to divide the Palestinian ranks by establishing 'Moslem National Societies' and, later, 'National Christian Societies'.

The object of these Societies is stated to be to work with the Government and promote good relations between the different sections of the community.[95]

Zionist efforts in this direction failed to achieve the desired results as all Arabs who were associated with these Societies were considered by the Arab Press and the Palestinians as traitors.[96]

Samuel viewed these Societies with misgivings, as it was public knowledge 'that these Societies have been established largely owing to Jewish influence',[97] and to the influence of Mr Kalvarisky (a Jewish member of the Advisory Council) in particular.

Sensing a resurgent fighting mood among the Palestinians owing to an accumulation of political and economic frustrations, the High Commissioner resumed his efforts to gain political advantage by conciliating Muslim opinion through relegating Muslim control over Muslim Religious Affairs (*Awqaf, Shari'a Courts,* etc.).[98]

Towards the end of October the 'Palestine Committee in Egypt', issued a leaflet calling upon the people of Palestine to desist from work, to close their shops and to mourn the anniversary of the Balfour Declaration. Although orders were given for the seizure of the leaflet where found, it had obtained a wide circulation in Palestine whereupon strict security measures were taken to prevent disturbances throughout Palestine. Arab notables in Jerusalem and Jaffa undertook, as far as lay in their power, to prevent protestations. In spite of these precautions and undertakings a disturbance took place in Jerusalem on the morning of the Declaration's anniversary.

When 'Arab roughs' appeared in the Jaffa road, they were dispersed by the police but soon after gathered for an attack on the Jewish quarter which was averted by the police. Shots were exchanged between the Arab crowd and a crowd of Jews inside the Jewish quarter. Thereafter troops patrolled the city and the Governor, accompanied by the 'principal Moslem notables walked through the streets and restored order'.[99] Five Jews and three Arabs were killed and thirty-six persons were wounded. Although there were no disturbances in other cities, the atmosphere was tense throughout Palestine. On the following day the political notables of Jerusalem publicly disassociated themselves from the 'unseemly and illadvised' behaviour of irresponsible youths on 2 November. However, these notables found themselves compelled to protest against the nature of the Court set up to deal with the disturbances, and the unduly harsh sentences passed against the Arabs by it, in contrast with the lenient sentences against the Jews.

A show of mild defiance to the Government by the notables was staged at a meeting held in Jerusalem on 11 November. The Muslim-Christian Society unanimously decided not to obey the Ordinance conferring upon Governors the power to exact a bond of security for good behaviour from those suspected of political or other offences.

These protestations notwithstanding, the political notables appeared in the eyes of the Palestinian public as failing their duty to lead opposition to Zionism and British Zionist policies. In the aftermath of the November disturbances the Government's Intelligence Service had reported that, 'A somewhat disquieting feature is a tendency of the populace to act apart from the notables and to disregard their advice' [100]

All Classes Suffer

The events of November stimulated Samuel and his assistants to bring about the settlement of the Beisan Land Question and that of the *Awqaf* and Muslim Religious Affairs in order to create a good impression in the country. This favourable impression was shortlived owing to the seizure of 300 revolvers and a quantity of ammunition at Haifa consigned to Isaac Rosenberg, which revealed Zionist efforts to smuggle arms on a wide-scale. This event was the cause of considerable excitement and agitation in the press and elsewhere. Further attempts, albeit on a smaller scale, to procure arms and ammunition were resumed in the following month. The continued presence of unemployed immigrants in Jaffa and Haifa was considered by the Arabs as proof that the Administration did not intend to carry out the undertaking given on 3 June 1921, that only such immigrants for whom work can be found or who can support themselves should be allowed to enter the country. 'It is reported that the formation of a society to be known as the "Palestine Youths Society" has been mooted. The promoters are stated to be extremely Pan Arab'.[101]

Jewish immigration and British policies were augmenting Arab distress and anxiety in an economic as well as a political sense. A report by the Governor of Haifa, G.S. Symes, on the reasons for discontent and disaffection amongst the Arab population of his district was circulated to the Cabinet by Churchill. Symes rightly noted that economic conditions have a powerful influence on politics and that the former were most unsatisfactory in his district. The villagers were responsive to incitements and anti-Government agitation from the towns and the mass of the 'non-Jewish' population was thoroughly disgruntled:

At Acre and Shefa Amr business is at a standstill. At Haifa nearly all trades which are profitable to the Arabs show a decline. . .The Customs barrier with Syria is evidently killing transit trade. . .the non-Jewish shopkeeper is being 'frozen out' of the retail business. Even porters and other casual labour are beginning to be affected by the preference shown by Jewish firms and employers towards immigrant labour. . .all classes of townspeople suffer from the high cost of living. . .Higher up in the social scale the merchants and the effendi class are in a state of mind bordering on despair; they find it increasingly difficult to live by the proceeds of trade or other employment. . .many of them are faced with the alternatives of bankruptcy or emigration. The case of the large landed proprietor is little better; he is heavily in debt, and can obtain no more credit; the price of cereals is low; foreign markets, for one reason or another, are practically closed to him, he is even finding it difficult to dispose at a fair price of lands he may have to sell.

To the Arab dweller in a town, his disabilities and distress appear to be the direct consequence of the present British policy and its corollary the Jewish immigration.

The bedouin, of course, will have either to become fellahin or quit the country as it becomes settled and populated.[102]

The only hope for the Administration, in Symes's opinion, was to show practical concern for the welfare of the fellahin which may enable the Administration to prevent their 'total alienation' and thus secure the fulfillment of British policy in Palestine. British policy, Symes admitted,was 'anathema to the large majority — including the most enlightened elements'. Even then, 'only [by] a wonderful combination of firmness, tact and good luck, can we hope to execute it by pacific means'.

Jewish immigration and Jewish smuggling of arms brought forth a general protest from the Muslim-Christian Societies in the early months of 1922. An additional cause for Arab protest against the Administration's policies was the loan it extended for the construction of the

Richon-Rehoboth Road. The exclusive employment on the road of Jewish immigrants — at higher wages than corresponding Arab labour — coupled with the fact that the road would mainly benefit Jewish colonies were a source of bitter criticism and accusations of clear discrimination in favour of the Zionists.

According to Deedes,

> The terms of the proposed Constitution have been very unfavourably received by Moslems and Christians throughout the country. The main points of their objection are the recognition in the Constitution of the Balfour Declaration, the official and nominated majority in the Legislative Council, the excessive centralisation of power in the Hands of the High Commissioner and the exclusion of the people of the country and their representatives from, as is alleged, any real power either administrative or legislative in matters which profoundly affect the destinies of Palestine and its people.[103]

A more positive note was struck by the visit of Lord Northcliffe the powerful newspaper magnate, to Palestine which gave the Palestinians an opportunity to gain a sympathiser with influence at the right place in London. In a further effort to gain the sympathy of foreign visitors the Muslim-Christian Society were distributing copies of their propaganda publications in English. Samuel viewed Arab public relations and propaganda efforts as an alternative to the use of violence and as a means of drawing attention to their cause. He informed Churchill that

> The principal leaders in the country cooperate in this policy, and are not slow to use their influence whenever necessary to prevent or suppress disorder.[104]

Absence of a Revolutionary Organisation

The inclination to resort to disorder and violence, Samuel added, was characteristic of the lower strata of the population in the towns and villages.[105]

During March, a feeling of nervousness throughout Palestine was reported, and rumours of impending trouble were widely discussed. The growth of political consciousness in various districts, and in the relatively inarticulate districts of Beersheba and Gaza in particular, become more marked and a belief that the Administration has broken faith in the matter of immigration. . .that justice is subject to coercion from political Zionism and that the British Government will only yield to violence.[106]

But violence was not possible without an organisation which aimed at rebellion and had the necessary means to carry it out, 'All available information confirms the impression that there is no organisation which exists to cause it'.[107] Clearly this was a case of failure of leadership; the traditional leadership was anti-revolutionary, and the forces advocating revolutionary tactics failed to produce the required leaders.

There is no doubt whatsoever that the Administration's attitude regarding the Muftiship and the Supreme Muslim Council and the friendly relations with Hajj Amin played an important role in preventing outbreaks and rebellions at a time when the state of public opinion and popular sentiments were conducive to upheavals and violence.

A number of 'responsible' Muslims were involved in constructive work which included educational work for the formation of a Muslim college and development of a Boy Scout Movement — religious and economic projects. An Arab Economic Society was founded and discussions were taking place on the possibility of forming an Arab National Bank and of establishing Bonded Stores. These activities, Deedes reported, stimulated efforts towards the attainment of an increased measure of cohesion and solidarity particularly among the Muslims.[108]

The beneficial outcome of this rapprochement with Hajj Amin and his associates on the one hand, and the fear that this positive development might be wrecked by the complete failure of the Arab Delegation's mission, on the other hand, spurred Samuel to visit London. Samuel's departure engendered a mood of expectancy and among many, of anxiety. Apart from Arab protestations against the Government's condonation of the existence of the Jewish Defence Force (Haganah), and the installation of benches for the accommodation of Jews wailing before the walls of the Sanctuary (Muslim shrine), no major developments took place during the month of May.

Churchill's White Paper

As pressure against Britain's pro-Zionist policies mounted, Churchill sought to bring about an end to unrest in Palestine, and to criticism in the British Press and House of Lords, by publishing an authoritative statement on British policy in Palestine. In his 1922 White Paper, Churchill maintained that the Balfour Declaration, which the Government intended to uphold, did not aim at subordination of the Arab population or culture. The Jews, however, were in Palestine 'as of right and not on sufferance'[109] and would be able to increase their number by immigration subject to the 'economic absorptive capacity' of the country. The White Paper declared that it was the intention of HM Government to foster the gradual establishment of full measure of self-government. A legislative council with a majority of elected members would be set up immediately, and a committee of elected members of the legislative council would confer with the Administration upon matters relating to regulation of immigration. In case of differences between the committee and the Administration, HMG were to be the final judge.

The Churchill White Paper was accepted by the Zionists and rejected by the Arabs.[110] The Delegation was simply not empowered to accept any British policy based on the Balfour Declaration. Regulated Jewish immigration would still entail the prospect of eventual Jewish majority and thus Jewish domination in Palestine. Furthermore, the promise of elected majority did not provide for the Arabs who constituted the majority of the people, an elected majority in the legislative council as a whole.

While the White Paper failed to reconcile the Arabs to Jewish immigration and to slower development of the JNH, it was necessary for the purpose of defeating the opposition which had developed in the British Parliament to accepting the Mandate with the inclusion of the Balfour Declaration. During the latter part of June, Lord Islington had raised the question of Palestine in the House of Lords and obtained the passage of a resolution which declared the Palestine Mandate unacceptable. However, an attempt ro bring the Palestine Mandate before the House of Commons for parliamentary examination failed.

A Turning Point

Shortly afterwards, the League of Nations approved the Palestine Mandate, and the British Government made it clear that the Mandate would be carried out in the light of the 1922 Statement of Policy.[111]

As it became decisively clear that the British Government did not intend to rescind the Balfour Declaration, the Executive Committee of the Fourth Congress met between 23 and 27 June to decide upon the steps to be taken in the event of the expected ratification of the Mandate. The resolution adopted at that meeting included the organisation of peaceful demonstrations and the closing of shops in all Palestine on 13-14 July against the British policy, and the communication of protests to the League of Nations from all societies and representative bodies in Palestine. In case the Mandate was ratified, it was resolved to call the Delegation back 'for work in Palestine and among the Eastern nations'.[112] Delegations were to be despatched to Mecca and to the Vatican to obtain the sympathy of the Christian and Muslim worlds. 'Secret' resolutions called for hoarding some funds, dissemination of anti-Zionist propaganda and keeping a close eye on the Government.

An incipient change of an important character in the Palestinian strategy become discernible at that point:

> Hirtherto their opposition has been confined to the National Home policy and the terms of the Mandate but now that it is realised that the Mandate is likely to go through, there is a tendency to believe that the only way of successfully opposing the obnoxious clauses is to oppose the British Mandate as a whole and to move for the total independence for a united Syria and Palestine.[113]

As a corollary to this reluctant shift from anti-Zionist to anti-British orientation in the Palestinian national movement's strategy, it was reported that the number of people prepared to run greater risks in their effort to promote disorders and conflict against the Government's authority was on the increase. Furthermore, Palestinian students issued an appeal to fellow students in England to support the Palestinian struggle against the Zionist clauses in the Mandate which could only lead to revolution in Palestine. Villagers and Mukhtars refused to accompany government commissioners for the demarcation of *mewat* (waste) lands as a demonstration of their lack of confidence in the Administration and its intentions. Protests against land concessions granted to the Jews in Beisan, Birah and Caesarea, and against the dismissal of Arab and pro-Arab officials in the Government were lodged.[114] The tone of the press was also becoming more and more anti-British.

During 13 and 14 July a general strike was observed in the large towns throughout Syria and Palestine as a protest against the British Mandate based upon the Balfour Declaration. The Arab Executive Committee was occupied with organising the collection of funds through the local Muslim-Christian Societies.[115]

As the Palestinians were becoming more militant in their anti-British attitude, a growing solidarity between the nationalist bodies of Syria,

Palestine and Egypt developed and the agitation for the complete independence of Syria and Palestine was renewed. The villagers were urged not to pay tithes to a non-Muslim Government and prayers declaring Palestine to be in danger introduced in the Friday prayers at Jaffa.

The Governors of the various districts reported during July that there were two schools of thought, the one favouring a non-violent negative and obstructionist attitude towards the Government, the other favouring rebellions methods and advocating 'enlisting Beduin assistance to promote guerilla warfare'.[116] The latter were encouraged by Mustapha Kemal as an example of how recognition was to be obtained at the hands of the European Powers. The Arab Executive Committee preferred non-violent methods, and the High Commissioner even reported that they were actually cooperating with the Government in maintaining order.[117]

The Fifth Congress

The Delegation left England at the request of the Arab Executive Committee in Jerusalem, arrived at Haifa on 21 August 1922 and proceeded to Nablus the same day to attend the Fifth Palestinian Congress. The Delegation was met with popular enthusiasm at Haifa, Nasra (Nazareth), Jenin, Silet al-Daher, Burka and Nablus. In his first speech at Haifa, Musa Kazem assured his audience that the doors of England were still open for negotiations and that there were many supporters of the Arab cause in England and France prepared to further the Arab cause at any time.[118] The H.Cr. reported that the cry of 'Long Live Palestine', down with the Mandate, the Balfour Declaration and Zionism' was repeated by many of those present, but Musa Kazem refrained from agitating against Britain and discouraged any tendency to resort to violence as a means of fighting Britain's Zionist policies, in spite of the fact that the Declaration was, in his opinion, incompatible with independence.

The sessions of the Congress commenced on the following day, 22 August, and continued until 25 August. The report of the Delegation to the Congress summarised the accomplishments of the lengthy visit and recommended that greater cooperation between the Arabs of Palestine and the rest of the Arabs by practical means of economical and educational movements and 'to send Delegates to Arab Amirs and potentates to inform them of the real situation and injustices in Palestine and to discuss means of agreement and of an understanding'.[119]

Eighteen resolutions were adopted, the most important of which were: to reject the New Palestine Constitution and boycott the coming elections of the Legislative Council, to establish a Palestine Arab Bureau in London, to provide means for enlightening the *fellah* on national affairs, to boycott Jewish goods and the Rutenberg (electricity) Scheme, to prevent the sales of immovable property to Jews and to carry out a 'finance scheme' for the collection of funds. A 'Palestine Covenant' was adopted and the oath committed the delegates to a certain line of policy:

> We, the representatives of the Palestine Arab Nation in the Fifth Palestine Arab Congress held at Nablus, pledge ourselves to God, History and the Nation that we shall continue our endeavours for the independence of our country, and for achieving Arab unity by all legal methods, and that we shall not accept the establishing of a Jewish National Home nor Jewish immigration.[120]

The efforts of the Palestinian political notability to prevent violence as a means of expressing opposition to the Mandate and Jewish immigration were not a total success. During August it was reported that

> The recent murderous attacks on Jews at Jaffa by small groups of Arabs together with the retaliatory assaults on Arabs by Jewish mobs, has resulted in a decided increase of racial animosity in the Jaffa District.[121]

A very illuminating and interesting letter from Deedes to Shuckburgh sought to describe the political situation in clear and intelligible terms. The members of the Delegation, Deedes reported, 'seem to have come back very pro-British',[122] and all with the exception of Tawfiq Hammad were moderate and reasonable. They would not have approved of the resolutions of the Fifth Congress had they not been rushed into it by their local organisation. Since the attitude of the Congress was one of boycott to the elections, there were signs that a new party would gradually emerge and which would be willing to cooperate with the Government and to put up candidates for election. The emergence of the moderate party was not only influenced by political considerations but also by very acute and generation-long family antagonisms, between the Husseinis and the Nashashibis.

The difference in the attitude of the two parties towards the Government was demonstrated on the occasion of the Ceremony for

Taking the Oath, i.e. when Samuel was sworn in as High Commissioner, on 11 September. The Husseinis, the Hajj Amin included, and the Muslim-Christian Societies called for a strike in the country at large and boycotted the Ceremony while 'Abdullah and the Nashashibis attended.[123]

During September and October the Governors of some Districts reported a growing belief among the peasants that the causes of their numerous disabilities were chiefly political. Police severity during a series of operations conducted in certain villages of the Samaria District in search of arms was strongly resented by the people. In the Hebron villages the peasants' anti-Government attitude was reinforced by 'their difficulty in disposing of their crops at a reasonable figure and their consequent embarrassment when called upon to pay the tithe redemption price'.[124] The agitation against the proposed Government census and the Administration's counter-measures and arrests strengthened the prevalent anti-Government feeling. The Arabs later modified their attitude and the census proceeded without further obstruction.

In September 1922, news of the Kemalist victories were 'received with jubilation by the Moslem population'.[125] Turkish victories raised the prospect of the revision of the Treaty of Sevres which covered the Palestine Mandate and encouraged fresh hopes that a radical change in the situation in Palestine would result from such a revision. A delegation was nominated to attend the forthcoming Lausanne Peace Conference and relatively big sums of money were collected for the Red Crescent to help the Turks of Anatolia.

The idea of contacting the Turks to obtain support for the anti-Zionist movement in Palestine gathered momentum. It received added impetus when 'Abdul Kader al-Muzaffar' returned from Turkey in the middle of December and reported that the Turkish leaders promised to back the Palestinian National aspirations and Arab independence. A group of Palestinians cabled Mustapha Kemal pleading support for Palestinian independence under a Turkish Mandate.[126]

A further strong stimulant to Palestinian hopes for a change of policy was provided by the news of the resignation of Lloyd George's coalition Government.

While external factors gave rise to fresh hopes, the agitation against the proposed new Constitution and the proposed Legislative elections — stipulating acceptance of the JNH policy — encouraged bolder tactics inside Palestine.[127] The Executive Committee occupied itself with protests and representations over land concessions to the Jews and the necessity of safeguarding the interests of the Muslim fellahin who lived on these lands. Arab nationalists directed their efforts towards reconciling partisan and family differences. More important still, it was reported that

> At a meeting of the Nadi al Arabi the possible advantages of an insurrectionary movement at the present juncture were referred to; Jemil el Shehabi considered that news from the Delegation should be awaited.[128]

The Idea of a 'Moderate Party'

At this stage Samuel adopted a new attitude toward the Palestinian opposition, when he advocated encouraging the emergence of the Moderate Party. In a comprehensive survey of the political and economic conditions in Palestine, Samuel urged the Duke of Devonshire, the new Colonial Secretary, to maintain his predecessor's Palestine policy as a means of bringing about political stability, in addition to strengthening the hands of the pro-Government elements among Arab ranks.[129]

When Devonshire received the Palestinian Delegation in January 1923, he informed them that the new Conservative Government did not propose to repudiate the Balfour Declaration or to change the policy enunciated in Churchill's White Paper.

Back in Palestine the Arab National Movement energetically campaigned in favour of the boycott of the Legislative Council elections. At the instigation of the preachers, Palestinians swore an oath in their places of devotion to boycott the elections,[130] and numerous meetings harped on the theme that accepting a Constitution based on the Balfour Declaration was tantamount to national suicide.

Beside boycotting the Legislative Council the Palestinian national movement was engaged in an effort for economic self-betterment and for the protection of the Arab agriculturalists. On 1 February 1923, the Arab Economic Agricultural Conference held its first meeting. An Executive Committee was elected and attached to the Executive Committee of the Arab Congress with which it was charged to cooperate in economic and political matters. It was resolved to demand the abolition of certain agricultural taxes and dues, to encourage the plantation of tobacco and trees, and to request the Government to institute an agricultural school. However, the most important resolution was

To demand from the Government the enactment of a law forbidding the Fallah to sell his land if it is less than 200 dunoms in order that it provides means of livelihood on the lines of the Egyptian Law of the 5 feddans.

As the boycott campaign gathered momentum both Samuel and the pro-Government forces found themselves in a tight spot. The pro-Government party sought to extract certain concessions as a means of justifying its inclination to work with the Government. Samuel favoured the granting of some concessions to the Moderates as a means of strengthening their hand and mitigating public opinion in Palestine. On 11 February, Samuel reported to Devonshire that he had received an overture on behalf of important sections of Arabs who would be prepared to abandon opposition to the Balfour Declaration and come forward to cooperate with the Government at elections on certain conditions:

(One) annual immigration to be limited numerically.

(Two) Election to Legislative Council of Arab members by High Commissioner from lists submitted by local bodies in such number as to constitute a majority with elected members.

(Three) British officials to retain the substance of executive authority but number of Palestinians in important positions in the Administration to be largely increased.

(Four) An Arab Emir to be appointed in Palestine the High Commissioner remaining with present functions.[131]

While Samuel found that last condition objectionable and had other reservations to make he proposed to carry on with the conversations awaiting a positive decision by the Colonial Secretary.

Devonshire's reply was discouraging and nothing could be done to save the patriotic pretences of the pro-Government Party. The boycott of the elections by the overwhelming majority of the Palestinians provided a clear victory for the Arab Executive Committee over the Government's policies and the pro-Government elements who dared nominate themselves. It bolstered the Committee's position in the country. On 12 March 1923 it issued a proclamation advising stoppage of work and closing of shops on 14 March in honour of the attitude adopted by the 'Arab Nation' at the elections.[132] It was also decided to extend a popular welcome for the returning Arab Delegation. During the processions the police came in contact with the crowds when attempting to arrest a number of marchers who were shouting provocative slogans.

Many were wounded, others were arrested, and the incident was looked upon as an example of police brutality. Protests were received from all parts of Palestine, and the incident gave rise to a fresh wave of ill-feeling against the Government.

The approaching Nebi Musa celebrations provided an opportunity for the Executive Committee to force the hand of the Government by a display of militancy. Instead they devised 'general arrangements for the control of the crowds and of the processions'. Earlier on Jamal Husseini, Secretary of the Executive Committee, was reported to have told Deedes, in a private interview, that there were two alternative methods for the attainment of full political rights in Palestine:

> either by constitutional means or by revolution; that the first was to be preferred though the second would give them what they justly claimed in six months. [133]

In the following month Jamal Husseini had an interview with a member of the Administration during which he reported that pressure from many quarters was being exerted with the object of convening the Arab Congress and of defining and laying down the attitude to be adopted by the country at large towards the Government. Furthermore,

> A strong body of opinion was in favour of non-payment of taxes as the next step to be taken without making any more appeals to England and the British Government. He himself, he said, was not in favour of plunging into a non-payment policy. He preferred to make another appeal to England. [134]

Following the successful Arab boycott of the elections Samuel announced the suspension of the Legislative Council clauses of the Constitution and proposed to establish a new Advisory Council. [135] The Executive Committee took strong exception to the new measure and maintained that nothing but more chaos without the least benefit could result from it.

During the month of May, pressure by the Executive Committee was exerted on the nominees for the Advisory Council to refuse to serve. The Arab members were faced with popular agitation and after hesitation had to resign before Samuel's set date for the Council's first sitting.

A telegram from King Hussein to the Arab Executive Committee dated 17 May caused the circulation of rumours that the Balfour Declaration had been revoked. The telegram was paraphrased and published by the Arab Executive accompanied by advice to the people to avoid anything that might disturb peace and transquility in Palestine. A weekly later the Arab Executive Committee resolved to postpone convening the Sixth Arab Palestine· Congress until after the publication of Hussein's treaty with Britain, better known as the Anglo-Hijaz Treaty.

The Sixth Congress

The Sixth Palestine Arab Congress was held in Jaffa between 16 and 20 June 1923, under the chairmanship of Musa Kazem. The Anglo-Arab Treaty, one of the major topics of the Congress, was rejected and declared to be contrary to the rights and interests of the Arabs of Palestine. Furthermore, it was resolved that a new Arab Delegation, again headed by Musa Kazem, proceed to London immediately and contact members of Parliament and the Colonial Office before the new Treaty was definitely signed.

The other major issue that preoccupied the Congress was the question of non-payment of taxes to the Government. The discussion on this vital issue, which preoccupied public opinion before the Congress was convened, was opened by Jamal Husseini, who argued in a lengthy and well reasoned speech for the adoption of a policy of non-payment of taxes. The Government he said obtained taxes and distributed them to Zionist Societies and Jewish immigrants. Owing to Zionist pressure the Government refrained from extending agricultural loans to the Arabs thereby causing the economic death of the *fellah.* The High Commissioner was granting lands and concessions to the Jews without consulting the Arabs. He concluded by specifying that the Economic Committee should consider the non-payment of taxes on the basis of the principle 'No taxation without representation'.

In the Economic Committee sharp differences of opinion arose, and and it was decided to refer the matter to the Executive Committee who 'should study the question of refusing to pay taxes to the Government and put it into force when the occasion arises'.[136] Opposition to this resolution was expressed in the general meeting on the basis that it was impossible to implement this measure without causing a revolution and in a country as small and poor as Palestine it was futile to hope that a revolution against the British Government would succeed.[137]

No definite decision was reached on this cardinal issue. However, certain conclusions may be drawn from the respective backgrounds of the supporters and the opponents of the motion for non-payment. Jamal Husseini was mainly supported by 'Isa al'Isa and 'Isa Bandak, both educated middle-class Christian journalists, while his opposite number was mainly supported by Amin Bey Tamini and Hafez Bey Tuqan, both of whom were rich effendis, the latter on friendly terms with the Zionists.

An authoritative explanation of the motives of those who opposed the idea of non-payment of taxes was provided by the Governor of Samaria:

> Before the meeting (Congress) was held I had the Mayor's assurance that resolutions to refuse to pay taxes would not be adopted. He told me that Hajj Said Shawa was very anxious that the resolution to refuse to pay taxes should not be adopted because he was a large landowner and would be the first to suffer from whatever action the Government would take.[138]

It should be further noted that the political leadership failed to use the powerful weapon of non-payment of taxes at a time when such a measure stood a good chance of being adhered to by large sections of the population. According to the Administration's reports Jamal Husseini's speech advocating non-payment of taxes 'has given satisfaction to the Arab population'.[139] In Northern Palestine an attack on British gendarmes took place on 10 June. In the Southern District the inhabitants were discontented:

> Their state of mind is such that anti-Government propaganda and in particular non-payment of tithes and taxes propaganda would be sympathetically received.[140]

After electing a new Executive Committee the Congress adopted twenty-four resolutions, and charged the new Executive with carrying out the boycott of the Rutenberg Scheme and of Jewish goods and activities in general. Money was collected for the departing Delegation and for the London pro-Arab British Bureau.

No Change of Policy

Stimulated by news from England that a Cabinet Committee was sitting to report on the Palestine question the new Arab Delegation left Palestine on 15 July. The Cabinet Committee, however, refused to grant an interview to the Delegation, which 'caused disgust and disappointment in Arab nationalist circles'. [141] Instead of recalling the Delegation and convening a Congress to study the attitude of the British Government and draw the logical conclusions as to the line of action the Arabs should adopt, the Executive Committee resolved to instruct the Delegation to remain in England and visit America for propaganda and fund-raising purposes.

An explanation of the attitude was provided by Gilbert Clayton, an experienced old hand in Arab and Palestinian affairs, who replaced Deedes as Civil Secretary in the spring of 1923. In a letter to Devonshire, Clayton reported the gist of a conversation he had with 'some of the more advanced members of the Moslem Christian Association', who revealed to him the line of action the Association proposed to follow in the event of the return of the Delegation empty-handed. Far from contemplating a revolutionary course of action the Palestinian opposition to the Government intended to stick to constitutional and legal methods. They were particularly encouraged by the growing support for their cause in the House of Commons, and they

> seem confident enough that their influence over their followers is sufficiently strong to prevent any violent or unconstitutional action as long as they can show that their present policy is giving good results. [142]

Clayton shrewdly recommended to the Colonial Secretary not to dash these hopes to the ground too suddenly, and that the Arabs

> . . .should have some grounds for maintaining their present policy which at least has the merit of causing them to refrain from other and more undesirable methods, thus giving time for wise counsels to prevail.

Soon afterwards Clayton's hopes for 'wise counsels to prevail' were taking their speedy course towards realisation:

> A party which first termed itself the Liberal Moderate Party, and subsequently the National Party, is in process of formation. Its avowed policy, although nationalistic, is opposed to that of the Moslem-Christian Association inasmuch as it proposes to attain its

ends through cooperation with the Government instead of by opposition.[143]

The hand of the new Party was strengthened following the refusal of the Executive Committee to accept the recommendations of a Cabinet Committee formed during the summer of 1923 to review British policy in Palestine. Although some of the Committee's members thought that the Balfour Declaration was both unnecessary and unwise, the Committee found it impossible for any Government to extricate itself from the Declaration without a substantial sacrifice of consistency and self-respect.

By the time the Palestine Mandate was brought into full operation by the League's Council Resolution of 29 September 1923, the attitude of the three parties of the Palestinian Triangle had already crystallised.

The British Government stood firmly by the Balfour Declaration and the JNH policy, guided by the theory of 'dual obligation', and the principle of the 'economic absorptive capacity' on immigration policy. The final settlement of the Mandate removed all shades of uncertainty' and precluded any possibility of drastic change of British policy in Palestine for the foreseeable future.

The Zionists were satisfied that the articles of the Palestine Mandate and British policies in Palestine were conducive to the achievement of their immediate basic aim; namely, the attainment of a Jewish majority, and thus political supremacy, through immigration and land settlement. They were opposed to representative institution and the application of the principle of self-determination in Palestine on the grounds that the Arab majority would use such institutions to fight Zionism and revoke the Mandate. The Anglo-Zionist convergence was demonstrated by the Zionist acceptance of Churchill's White Paper and embodied in the person of Herbert Samuel himself.

The Arab position was accurately assessed by Samuel in a perceptive report submitted during January 1924. He said:

The large majority of the population of Palestine are Moslem Arabs, and among them, a majority possibly equally large, favour the general views of what may be termed the local opposition to the Palestine policy of His Majesty's Government as applied by this Administration.[144]

Samuel described the motives of the cyrstallising pro-Government minority party in the following terms:

They are anxious for a quiet life, and do not want to engage in political struggles. They wish to grow richer, and think that British control and guidance for the time being at all events, are best calculated to make the country more prosperous and themselves with it. Some as I have mentioned, are more largely animated by antagonisms in the Opposition camp. Some think that they may obtain advantages, direct or indirect, by standing well with the Government.[145]

The Christian Arabs were prominent in the ranks of the anti-Zionist movement in Palestine as well as in the ranks of the Moderate Party. In general they were inclined to take a less rigid anti-Government attitude after the Kemalist victories and the revival of Pan-Islamic ideas. The fact that they occupied a high proportion of Government posts in Palestine also contributed to their moderation *vis-à-vis* Britain. Nevertheless, a number of Christian-Arab intellectuals were among the most active and eloquent anti-Zionists in Palestine.

Three Currents of Thought

Samuel attributed Palestinian opposition to Britain to three currents of thought: Arab Nationalism, anti-Zionism and Pan-Islamism. These currents attracted men of varying standards of sincerity and zeal.

There is a nucleus of genuine patriots, who would be willing to make considerable sacrifices for their cause. There are a number of young men who take pleasure in the excitement and interest of a political movement. There is a large fringe, who sympathises in general with Arab and Oriental views. . .they are ready to close their shops, if they are shop-keepers, when asked to do so by the Central Committee on some occasion of political protest, and they are willing to join a crowd in the street to speed a parting delegation or to welcome its return.[146]

By the end of 1923 there was a growing belief among the Palestinian Arab majority that Britain and the Mandate were the real protectors of Zionism, and that the JNH policy represented the convergence of British imperial interests with Zionist colonialism in Palestine which was bound to lead to a Jewish majority and supremacy and the eventual eviction of the Palestinian Arabs from their country. The Husseini and the Muslim-Christian leadership, consistently and consciously, refused to commit themselves to any platform which would imply the acceptance of the Balfour Declaration on the one hand, but also refused to promote or condone any revolutionary course against the Anglo-Zionist convergence on the other. The latter stand could be attributed to the dread of British military might, as well as to belief that revolution would inevitably be detrimental to their own interests. Their failure to adhere to a revolutionary platform did not lead to the emergence of a revolutionary leadership from among the middle-class militant nationalists. Thus, the 'lower strata' of the Palestinian society, which was potentially willing to revolt was left leaderless and a long period of stagnation ensued.

Notes

1. Palin Commission Report, 1 July 1920, FO 371/5121, p.37.
2. Allenby to Lloyd George, 6 May 1920, Lloyd George Papers, Beaverbrook Library.
3. Weizmann, op.cit., p.352.
4. See 'Petitions of Protest', between 2 and 10 May 1920, FO 371/5120 and FO 371/5114.
5. *Al-Karmal*, 13 May 1920.
6. See Memorandum by Eder, 5 May 1920, Hagana Archives (HA).
7. A report addressed to Eder, 30 May 1920, Hagana-Archives (HA).
8. Bols to FO, 1 June 1920, FO 371/5114, p.2. In an effort to counter the advantages enjoyed by the Zionists through their accessibility to the British public, the Palestinian Arabs published a paper in English in *The Times*, under the name of the *Jerusalem Gazette*. Its first number on 22 June was full of bitter attacks on Zionism and Sir Herbert Samuel. See Paper submitted to the FO, 26 June 1920, FO 371/5120.
9. See Bols to FO, 7 June 1920, FO 371/5114.
10. Walter Laqueur, *Communism and Nationalism in the Middle East,* London, 1961, p.79. The author covers communism in Palestine throughout the Mandate period, pp.73-119.
11. Allenby, Cairo, to FO, 9 June 1920, FO 371/5120.
12. GHQ, Egypt, to WO, 23 June 1920, FO 371/5120. Also see Bols to FO, 24 June 1920, FO 371/5120 and 25 June 1920, FO 371/5114.
13. Situation in Palestine', FO Minute, 31 May 1920, FO 371/5119.
14. Samuel, *Memoirs*, p.154.
15. In order to make sure that the Palestine Government was in sympathy with the JNH policy Samuel asked Syndham Deedes, of Allenby's Intelligence Staff, to become Civil (later Chief) Secretary and Norman Bentwich to become Legal Secretary, both of whom were pro-Zionist. Ibid., p.155.
16. See Bols to FO, 25 June 1920, FO 371/5114.
17. Samuel to Curzon, 12 July 1920, FO 371/5121, p.1.
18. Ibid., pp.1-3, *passim.*
19. See 'Report on the Arabic Press', July 1920, FO 371/5188.
20. Edwin Montague, who was a minister and head of the India Office, protested vehemently to Lord Curzon against the placing of the Muslims in a minority position on the Council. See Montague to Curzon, 26 November 1920, FO 381/5124.
21. Deedes to Tilley, 10 October 1920, FO 371/5124.
22. Same to same, 1 November 1920, FO 371/5124.

23. For the English text of the resolutions see Matiel E.T. Mogannam. *The Arab Woman and the Palestine Problem*, London, 1937, pp.125-7.

24. According to the political report for December 1920, there were forty-three Muslim-Christian Societies with a membership of around 3,000 by June 1920. See Samuel to Curzon, 1 January 1920, Enclosure, FO 371/6374.

25. See *Falastin*, 20 and 27 March 1920.

26. Monthly Political Report, January 1921, Samuel to Curzon, Enclosure in No.1, 1 February 1921, FO 371/6374.

27. Ibid.

28. Deedes to Tilley, 14 January 1921, CO 733/17A.

29. Ibid.

30. Monthly Political Report, February 1921, H.Cr. to Curzon, 1 March 1921, FO 371/6375.

31. Ibid., also see Samuel to FO, 19 February 1921, FO 371/6375.

32. Until then Palestine's affairs were the responsibility of the Foreign Office.

33. For a general study on Churchill's favourable view of Zionism see Oskar Rabinowicz, *Winston Churchill on Jewish Problems*, London, 1956. Also see an article by Winston Churchill 'Zionism versus Bolshevism', *Illustrated Sunday Herald*, 8 February 1920.

34. For a general account of the Conference see CAB 24/126.

35. Ibid., p.108.

36. Monthly Political Report, March 1921, Deedes to Churchill, 8 April 1921, CO 733/2, p.6.

37. Ibid.

38. Ibid., p.2.

39. Cairo Conference, CAB 24/126, p.150. For another copy of the memorandum see 'official Report' attached to the Monthly Political Report, March 1921, op.cit.

40. Ibid.

41. Ibid., p.151.

42. Monthly Political Report, April 1921, Deedes to Churchill, CO 733/3, p.1.

43. Report by C.D. Brunton, 13 May 1921, presented to the Cabinet in a memorandum by the Secretary of State for the Colonies, 'The Situation in Palestine', 9 June 1921 CO 733/13.

44. Ibid., p.5.

45. Ibid., p.3. For a critical account of Samuel's attitude on the appointment of Hajj Amin to the Muftiship of Jerusalem see Kedourie, *Sir Herbert Samuel*, op.cit., pp.48-59.

46. On 7 May 1921, Samuel appointed a Commission of Enquiry headed by Sir Thomas Haycraft, Chief Justice of Palestine. For the findings of the Haycraft Commission see 'Palestine Disturbances in May 1921. Report of the Commission of Inquiry with Correspondence relating thereto'. Cmd. 1540. 1921.

47. Brunton, 9 June 1921, op.cit., The text of the original Arabic leaflet is quoted in my documentary, *Watha'iq al Muqawama al-Falastiniyya al-'Arabiyya dida al-Ihtilal al-Baritani wa al-Sahyuniyya (Documents of the Palestinian Arab Resistance Against British Occupation and Zionism)*, Beirut, 1968, pp.22-5, hereafter referred to as Documents.

48. Brunton, 9 June 1921, op.cit.

49. Ibid., pp.2-3.

50. Ibid.

51. See 'Interim Report of the Commission of Enquiry' (Haycraft), forwarded by Deedes to Churchill, 16 August 1921, CO 733/5, p.24.

52. Samuel to Churchill, 8 May 1921, CO 733/3, p.1. For other reports on the

reaction to the Jaffa disturbances, see Monthly Political Report, May 1921, Samuel to Churchill, 6 June 1921, FO 371/6375.
53. Brunton, 9 June 1921, op.cit., p.3.
54. Interim Report, October 1921, Appendix B, p.1.
55. Brunton, 9 June 1921, op.cit., The Haycraft Commission confirmed Brunton's conclusions; see Interim Report, October 1921, Appendix A, pp.1-3.
56. Interim Report, October 1921.
57. Samuel to Churchill, 8 May 1921, op.cit.
58. Ibid.
59. Ibid., p.4.
60. Monthly Political Report, May 1921, op.cit., p.2.
61. By 10 May 1921, this had been enforced. See Commander-in-Chief to Secretary of the Admiralty, 10 May 1921, CO 733/9.
62. Monthly Political Report, May 1921, op.cit., p.2.
63. Samuel to Churchill, 24 May 1921, CO 733/3.
64. Churchill to Samuel, 14 May 1921, CO 733/3.
65. Zionist Organisation, Central Office to CO, 1 June 1921, CO 733/16.
66. Monthly Political Report, June 1921, Samuel to Churchill, 7 July 1921, CO 733/4.
67. Ibid.
68. 'Sir Herbert Samuel's speech delivered at Jerusalem, June 3, 1921', CO to FO 28 June 1921, FO 371/6375.
69. Samuel to Churchill, 13 May 1921, CO 733/3.
70. Monthly Political Report, June 1921, op.cit.
71. ibid., p.6.
72. Ibid.
73. Monthly Political Report, June 1921, Samuel to Churchill, 7 July 1921, CO 733/4, p.2.
74. Ibid., p.1.
75. Eder to Zionist Executive, 4 June 1921, CZA, Z4/16151, p.5.
76. See 'Interviews between four members of the Haifa Congress Delegation and His Excellency the High Commissioner', 23 June 1921, CO 733/4. The Delegation however maintained that they rejected any institution that should imply the acceptance of the Declaration. See 'A Manifesto from the Arab Delegation', 29 July 1921, CO 733/16.
77. 'Situation in Palestine', July 1921, CO 733/13, p.1.
78. For these joint efforts see *A 'amal al-Wafd al-Suri al-Falastini (The Activities of the Syrian-Palestinian Delegation)*, Cairo, 1923.
79. Letter from Shibli Jamal (London) to Dr Shatara, 24 August 1921, Lloyd George Papers.
80. Palestine, 'Memorandum by the Secretary of State for the Colonies' 11 August 1921, CO 733/14. The Cabinet reviewed the memorandum but decided not to give in to Arab demands; see *Cabinet* 70(21). 18 August 1921, CO 733/14.
81. 'A Brief Statement of Demands of the Arab people of Palestine. . . Arab Palestine Delegation in London, 12 August 1921, CO 733/14, p.2.
82. 'Notes of a Conversation between the Secretary of State and Members of the Palestine Arab Delegation', 22 August 1921, CO 733/14, p.2.
83. 'Shorthand Writer's Report of the Conversation between the Right Hon. Winston Churchill and Members of the Palestine Arab Delegation', 23 August 1921, CO 733/17B, p.15.
84. Samuel to Churchill, 26 August 1921, CO 733/5.
85. 'Arab-Zionist relation', Inter-Departmental note, Shuckburgh to Sir J. Masterton Smith, 15 October 1921, CO 733/6. Later Shuckburgh complained

of the difficulties encountered by the Middle East Department and the lack of consistency in the British Government's attitudes. The roots of those difficulties was Weizmann's direct access to high political personages outside the Colonial Office. Long after Samuel's speech of 3 June the Prime Minister, Weizmann informed Shuckburgh, stated in the presence of Balfour that by the phrase 'Jewish national home' in the Declaration 'we meant a Jewish State'. On hearing this Shuckburgh wrote to his colleagues that 'it is clearly useless for us to endeavour to lead Dr Weizmann in one Direction, and to reconcile him to a more limited view of the Balfour pledge if he is told quite a different story by the head of the Government. Nothing but confusion can result if His Majesty's Government do not speak with a single voice'. See Shuckburgh to Masterton Smith, 7 November 1921, CO 733/15.

86. A letter addressed to Churchill, 24 October 1921, CO 733/16, pp.1-4.
87. At this point Riyad Bey as-Sulh, a Syrian-Lebanese politician who was involved in preliminary negotiations with the Zionists in Cairo, was invited by the Zionists to negotiate a proposed 'Arab-Jewish Entente'. For these negotiations and 'Draft Basis of Discussion' see 'Proposed Arab-Jewish Entente', 7 November 1921, CO 733/16.
88. Churchill to Samuel, 26 November 1921, CO 733/15.
89. Weizmann to Deeds, 13 December 1921, CO 733/16.
90. Weizmann to Shuckburgh, 2 December 1921, CO 733/17B, Jaffa Report, p.1.
91. Ibid., Jerusalem report, pp.2-3.
92. Ibid., p.1.
93. Ibid., Jaffa report, p.2.
94. Ibid., Tiberias report, p.3.
95. Monthly Political Report, October 1921, Samuel to Churchill, 4 November 1921, CO 733/7.
96. See Monthly Political Report, April 1922, Deedes to Churchill, 10 May 1922, CO 733/21, p.2. Also see Darwaza, op.cit., p.41.
97. Samuel to Churchill, 18 November 1921, CO 733/7.
98. See Samuel to Churchill, 8 October 1921, CO 733/6.
99. Samuel to Churchill, 2 November 1921, CO 733/7. For a full report on these disturbances see Deedes to Churchill, 29 December 1921, CO 733/8.
100. 'Summary of Intelligence', No.31, November 1921, CO 733/17B.
101. Monthly Political Report, January 1922, op.cit., p.2.
102. 'The Situation in Phoenicia', Cabinet Paper 3921, 3 April 1922, CO 733/38, p.1.
103. Monthly Political Report, February 1922, 9 March 1922, CO 733/19, p.1.
104. Samuel to Churchill, 9 March 1922, CO 733/19, p.6.
105. Ibid., p.5. In the same despatch Samuel described the high level of political consciousness in these towns and villages where newspapers and translations of the Hebrew and British press were read and discussed in every coffeehouse in the towns, p.2.
106. Monthly Political Report, March 1922, Samuel to Churchill, 11 April 1922, CO 733/20, p.2.
107. Ibid.
108. Monthly Political Report, April 1922, op.cit., p.2.
109. See a Memorandum by Churchill, 'British Policy in Palestine', June 1922, CO 733/34.
110. See Great Britain, 'Correspondence with the Palestine Arab Commission and the Zionist Organisation', Cmd. 1700, June 1922, pp.21-3.
111. Communicated by the British Government to the Council of the League of Nations under date of 1 July 1922, Cmd.1708, 1922.

112. Monthly Political Report, June 1922, Deedes to Churchill, 7 July 1922, CO 733/23, p.1.
113. Ibid.
114. See Memorandum to the H.Cr. from the Executive Committee of the 4th Arab Palestinian Congress, 28 June 1922, CO 733/23.
115. Monthly Political Report, June 1922, op.cit., The Executive Committee attempted to levy certain taxes on the adult Palestinian population through the 'Two Piasters Scheme' but later depended on the easier scheme of selling National Movement in Stamps to defray the expenses of the Arab National Movement. Palestine was engraved on each stamp together with a representation of the Dome of the Rock. 'Palestine for the Arabs' was written in English and Arabic on them. They were sold at one, two and five millims each.
116. Ibid.
117. Ibid., p.1.
118. Monthly Political Report, August 1922, Samuel to Churchill, 8 September 1922, CO 733/25, p.1.
119. Ibid., Appendix C, p.2.
120. Monthly Political Report, August 1922, op.cit., For the Arabic text of these resolutions see Documents, op.cit., p.53.
121. Ibid., p.3.
122. 15 September 1922, CO 733/38, p.2.
123. Monthly Political Report, September 1922, Samuel to Churchill, 6 October 1922, CO 733/26, p.3.
124. Monthly Political Report, October 1922, Samuel to Devonshire, 10 November 1922, CO 733/27, p.1.
125. See Monthly Political Report, September 1922, op.cit., p.3.
126. Documents, op.cit., pp.66-7.
127. See Monthly Political Report, November 1922, Samuel to Devonshire, 10 December 1922, CO 733/28, Appendix A.
128. Monthly Political Report, November 1922, Samuel to Devonshire, 8 January 1923, CO 733/41, p.3.
129. Mosques and occasionally churches were used as an effective political platform by the Arab national movement in Palestine, and the Administration protested against the use of places of devotion for purposes of political propaganda. Ibid., p.6.
130. Ibid., Appendix C. For arrangements made for boycotting the elections, see Appendix D.
131. Samuel to Devonshire, 11 February 1923, CO 733/42.
132. Monthly Political Report, March 1923, Samuel to Devonshire, 13 April 1923, CO 733/44, Appendix E.
133. Ibid., p.6.
134. Monthly Political Report, April 1923, Samuel to Devonshire, 15 May 1923, CO 733/45, p.4.
135. For details of the developments and the complications of the Advisory Council, see Samuel to Devonshire, 15 june 1923, CO 733/35.
136. For a comprehensive 'Summary of the proceedings of the Sixth Palestine Arab Congress', see Clayton to Devonshire, 22 June 1923, CO 733/46.
137. Ibid.
138. Monthly Political Report, June 1923, op.cit., pp.8-9.
139. Ibid.
140. Ibid., p.10.
141. Monthly Political Report, August 1923, Clayton to Devonshire, 13 September 1923, CO 733/49, p.1.

142. Clayton to Devonshire, 24 August 1923, CO 733/48.
143. Monthly Political Report, September 1923, Samuel to Devonshire, 19 October, 1923, CO 733/50.
144. Samuel to Thomas, 25 January 1924, CO 733/63, p.1.
145. Ibid., p.2.
146. Samuel to Shuckburgh, 6 October 1922, CO 733/38.

5 THE LULL: 1923-1929

Between 1924 and 1928 the Palestinian political scene witnessed a unique period of stagnation and paralysis. There were many factors accounting for this lull in the Palestinian Arab struggle against Zionism and the British Mandate, the most important of which was the final settlement of the Mandate in the League and the decline of the fortunes of the Jewish National Home in Palestine.

It should not, nevertheless, be assumed that this period was entirely uneventful. In any case it is worthwhile examining the actions and interactions of the Palestinian political forces in a period of political decline.

During October 1923, the Executive Committee of the Palestine Arab Congress held two important meetings in the course of which a clear political line emerged. At the first, which took place on 2 October, the proceedings were taken up by a report on the activities of the Delegation whilst in London and the results obtained thereby.[1] Far from resorting to a revolutionary or extra legal course of action now that the Mandate was brought into full operation Musa Kazem suggested that the Delegation should return to London when Parliament next reassembled.

The second meeting took place on the 26 October, at which Hajj Amin and Muhammad 'Ali at-Taher, secretary of the Palestine Committee in Egypt, were present. At-Taher declared himself in favour of a revolt as the only means of attaining Palestinian demands. Musa Kazem mentioned that one of the British supporters of the Arab cause in England had also advised this course: 'Musa Kazim Pasha, however, deprecated any action at the present juncture, being satisfied with the progress made by the Arab cause'.[2]

The Palestine Arab Executive adhered to their policy of non-cooperation with the Government and rejected an offer to establish an Arab Agency in Palestine which was to occupy a position analogous to that accorded to the Jewish Agency under Article 4 of the Mandate. The Executive Committee derived very little credit or prestige from its rejection since 'public opinion was so unanimous against the project'.[3]

The political impasse which blocked the way of the Executive Committee strengthened the position of the increasingly active advocates of the (Moderate) National Party. The first Congress of the

National Party was held in Jerusalem on 9 and 10 November and was attended by a number of notables led by 'Aref Dajani, who was notoriously opposed to the Muslim Christian Association. There were also a number of villagers present mainly from the Ramallah sub-district. Sheikh Suleiman al-Taji al-Farouki was elected President and a Central Executive of eight members with a supervising Committee of twenty persons, appointed. The High Commissioner reported that their declared policy 'gave great disappointment to the Jews who had hoped for something approaching an acceptance of the Balfour Declaration'.[4]

The calibre of the Central Executive of the National Party was unimpressive and politically timid. A number of them were mayors, e.g. Ragheb Nashashibi, and therefore ostensibly 'non-political'.

The new party was vehemently attacked by the supporters of the Arab Executive and both parties were soon involved in mutual condemnation in the press.

Furthermore, the Governor of Samaria reported during the same month the foundation of a new party mainly composed of villagers with a program very similar to that of the National Party.

In Jaffa, an attempt to incite the people against the Government in the wake of the municipality's acceptance of the Rutenberg Scheme, was unsuccessful. This brought the municipality (dominated by notables and merchants) strongly on the side of the Government, and the temporary collapse of the Muslim-Christian Society in Jaffa.

Towards the end of December the Governor of Samaria reported that the political atmosphere had become less tense in the last few months, and that the people were losing confidence in their leaders: 'The leaders in consequence, feeling that their power has decreased, are inclined to be much more friendly with the Government'.[5]

Simultaneous with the decline of the prestige of the leadership of the Palestinian National Movement was the emergence of the Supreme Muslim Council as a political force. The visit of King Hussein to Amman preoccupied the Palestinian political leadership as it touched on two important issues: the Caliphate and the proposed accord between Hussein and the British known as the Anglo-Arab Treaty. The Palestinians urged the Arab King to reject the Balfour Declaration and to veto Jewish immigration. They also asked that he should confirm the rejection of the mandatory governments, to demand the independence of Syria, Palestine and the other Arab countries and to endeavour to realise Arab unity.[6]

King Hussein's visit, however, failed to introduce a greater measure of cohesion among the various Arab political forces in Palestine. A new party emerged at this point, the Peasants' Party which was regarded in Arab nationalist circles as a Zionist creation, a result of Kalvarisky's efforts in particular. When the leaders of the National Party left the Palace where King Hussein had received them 'some youths and small boys shouted at them, "down with the traitors, down with the Zionists" and began to stone them'.[8]

The political platform of the nationalist movement was increasingly stressing the demand for a national government: 'This idea is given priority even to the abolition of the Balfour Declaration. Cabinets have been discussed and ministerial candidates nominated'.[9]

The inability of the traditional leadership to articulate the demands of the Palestinians in any effective manner gave rise to criticism of 'the obsolete methods and interested motives of the old school'.[10] The old school, however, were determined not to lose power. The Husseinis took precautionary measures to preserve their hegemony over the two most important Muslim positions in Palestine, namely, the Muftiship and the Presidency of the Supreme Muslim Council, in the event of protests being raised against the union of the two posts in the person of Hajj Amin.

Despite the continued supremacy of the traditional leadership, the educated 'young bloods' were reported to be gaining ground. In a meeting of the Executive Committee, held with a view to issuing a summons for a fresh Arab Congress, the political inactivity of the Committee was severely criticised:

> The dominating note of the debates appears to have been dissatisfaction with the 'old' party, whose maintenance of family interests and general incapacity were held up to ridicule by the 'intellectuals'. These in their turn were characterised by Ismail Bey al-Husseini as Bolsheviks but, nevertheless, succeeded in obtaining the lead.

The proposed Congress failed to materialise despite the efforts of the visiting Tunisian leader, 'Abdul-'Aziz al-Tha' 'alibi to promote unity among the ranks of the Palestinian political leadership. Family dissensions and personal interests predominated:

> In both Jerusalem and Jaffa family jealously is aiding political opposition in starting a campaign against the respective Municipalities for their chief support of Government policy.[12]

The disputes between the parties persisted leading to the indefinite postponement of the Arab Congress. The Arab Executive's attempt to meet Jamal Husseini's condition for resuming office — i.e. adequate funds — was not a total success. The (Agricultural) Peasants' Party, though inconsequential, was reported to be negotiating for Zionist support and the National Party was reported 'busy with village propaganda'.[13]

A Bone of Contention

Jamal Husseini's activities, and the efforts of the Supreme Muslim Council failed to put an end to internal divisions or to enhance the standing of the Arab Executive. What brought a flicker of nationalist activity was a proposed transfer of large areas of land, including villages, from the Sursuq family (absentee Lebanese landlords) to Jewish groups, and the backfiring of the activities of the Peasants' Party. As a reaction to the latter's efforts a Muslim-Christian Society branch was established at Beisan. The Acting District Governor of Haifa deplored the fact

> that Colonel Kisch and Mr. Kalvarisky should imagine that the future of the policy lies in the hands of those who attempt to create a favourable attitude of mind through the agency of promises of financial help.[14]

Land sales continued to be the main political issue and it was expressly suggested that the proposed Congress should devote all its attention to the formation of a company for buying Arab lands, which would otherwise be sold to the Jews. The sale of five villages, during September 1924, roused public feeling and 'every effort, is being made to prevent it becoming effective'.[15]

The departure of the High Commissioner for Geneva spurred the Arab Executive into submitting a comprehensive memorandum to the League of Nations attacking the policy of Government. The final sentence of the long memorandum summed up the Arab demand in the following words:

> The establishment in Palestine of a National Constitutional Government in which the two Communities, Arab and Jewish, will be represented in proportion to their number as they existed before the application of the Zionist Policy.[16]

A proposal to send a delegation to Geneva fell to the ground for lack of funds. A press campaign, however, urging reconciliation between the National Party and the Executive Committee brought about a meeting between delegates from the two parties, but failed to create national unity. An offer made by the leaders of the Muslim Christian Association to the National Party to send five representatives to sit on the Executive Committee, and also that its leader Sheikh Suleiman al-Taji be appointed Vice-President of the Committee, in return for the dissolution of the National Party was rejected.[17] No progress was made in the reconciliation of the conflicting parties until the presence of a prominent foreign visitor reminded them of their common interests.

Balfour's Visit

During the first two months of 1925, the prospect of Lord Balfour's visit to Palestine, with the object of opening the Hebrew University, became the dominating political topic.[18] Numerous articles appeared in the Press and several meetings were held by the Executive Committee to decide upon a course of action during Balfour's tour. The Executive Committee declared Balfour's day of arrival a day of mourning and called for a general strike throughout Palestine on this occasion. Furthermore, a complete boycott of the British statesman, who epitomised the Anglo-Zionist convergence, was to be observed throughout his visit. 'The Arabs see in Lord Balfour the personification of British interest in Zionism and consider him not only the initiator but the faithful supporter of the policy'.[19]

The day Lord Balfour set foot in Palestine, a general strike (shops, schools, cabs etc.,) was observed by Muslims and Christians throughout Palestine. Black flags were raised and *Falastin* published a special English edition. Khalil Sakakini, an educated Christian, delivered a patriotic speech from the platform of the *Haram-ash-Sharif*, where

> A motion, none too politely phrased, inviting Lord Balfour to leave the country which he had entered against the wishes of the inhabitants, was passed and communicated through the District Governor to the High Commissioner.[20]

The only Palestinian Arabs who failed to observe Balfour's boycott were the Mayor of Jerusalem and three officials in addition to few Beduin Sheikhs who were present at the inaugural ceremonies at the Hebrew University. The Mayor's attitude on this occasion was a subject of adverse comment and protest among Arab nationalist circles in Palestine.[21]

The Mayor's defiance of the generally observed instructions to boycott Lord Balfour did not, *prima facie,* aggravate the antagonisms between the Executive Committee and the National Party. When the new Colonial Secretary, L.S. Amery, visited Palestine, he received a Palestinian Arab deputation which comprised representatives of the Executive Committee, the National Party and the Peasants' Party. After introducing the members of the deputation, Musa Kazem requested the Colonial Secretary to allow the President of the National Party to speak on their behalf. The central theme of Sheikh Suleiman al-Taji al-Farouki's speech was the willingness of the Palestinians to cooperate loyally with the British on the basis of friendship and mutual interest.[22] Arab hopes and aspirations, Farouki stressed, were not incompatible with British interests, but were in fact the *sine qua non* of the achievement of British interests and influence in the area.

Eventually, Farouki predicted, Britain would reach the conclusion that the Zionist policy is 'inapplicable'. He then went into the specific Palestinian Arab grievances such as excessive taxation, which to some Arabs seemed to be a deliberate measure calculated to force the inhabitants to sell their lands and leave the country, lack of participation in the legislative process, and being forced by the Government to build roads leading to Jewish colonies in the interests of Jewish colonisation. He concluded by reiterating the demand for a National Government 'representative of all elements in the country and responsible to the inhabitants. . .as the Mandate provides that the civil rights of the people of the country be safeguarded'.[23]

Signs of Weakness

The Executive Committee's unprecedented acquiescence in allowing a member of a rival party to speak on behalf of all the Palestinians on an important official occasion was indicative of their weakened position and thus their desire to cover that weakness by a semblance of national unity before the public and the Government. When Field Marshal Lord Plumer of Messina came to Palestine to take over as High Commissioner from Samuel, the Palestinian political mood was totally different from that which prevailed in the summer of 1920:

> The various Arab parties would like to present to the new High Commissioner a united but friendly front, and appear to be convinced that the time for a purely negative policy is over.[24]

This more conciliatory approach to Government was reinforced by two factors that played a dominant role throughout Plumer's tenure of office. The first was the sharp decline in Jewish immigration and the temporary inability of the Zionists to overcome the difficulties thereof. In 1927 immigration was represented by a negative figure and in 1928 immigration and emigration balanced one another.

The second factor was the overriding predominance of factionalism, the ascendancy of personal rivalries and self-interest among the Palestinian political notability in the period under discussion.

Political factionalism found its greatest scope in the fight for the control of the Supreme Muslim Council between the Husseinis and the Nashashibis. The Council attracted universal attention and interest among the Muslims of Palestine as it appealed to their eagerness for participation in the process of self-government,[25] which the Mandatory government denied them to prevent obstruction to its Zionist policies.

In the heat of the electoral battles for the Council, the struggle against Zionism was overshadowed by the determination to acquire power within the Muslim community. As a result the contenders for power sought the favour of the Government, and consequently the Arab National Movement throughout Palestine was considerably weakened. Although Hajj Amin's grip on the Council was not seriously shaken, the ferocity of the campaign and the reluctance of the Government to antagonise him, must have reinforced his resistance to any call for a direct confrontation with the British Government as a means of fighting Zionism in the early thirties.

Hajj Amin's national leadership and his direct appeal to the populace threatened the position of the local notables and their intermediary role. It was this factor that enabled the 'Moderates' to score their success at the Municipal elections in 1927, where local vested interests had the upper hand.

The weakness of the Arab position was conducive to a conciliatory Arab attitude towards the Government. In July 1926, a group of Arab politicians from the two major parties entered into negotiations with one of the major British officials in Palestine with the purpose of working out an arrangement that would facilitate Arab participation in the Government. These politicians pointed out that the basic source of difficulty was the insertion of the Balfour Declaration in the Mandate. The Palestinians were eager to see that this international obligation did not frustrate the Arabs' civil, religious and political rights, including their participation in the administrative and legislative setup in the country: an elected Constitutional National Government. Furthermore, they requested that the Mandate should include a statement to the effect that HM Government did not consult the Palestinians when it accepted the Mandate and the Zionist clauses thereof.[26]

However, nothing came out of these overtures, and two years later Plumer had no intention of raising the issue of a democratic parliamentary system before the end of his tour of duty in Palestine.[27]

Despite the decline in Zionist activities between 1925 and 1928 the Zionist Organisation was anxious to acquire more agricultural and State lands for Jewish settlement. The Colonial Secretary regarded the Zionist Organisation as having first claims on the lands suitable for agriculture, and the Palestine Government were active in procuring these for them.[28] Another bone of contention between Arabs and Jews, which came to the fore once more towards the end of 1927, was Jewish labour's organised opposition to the employment of Arab workers in Jewish-owned enterprises. An attempt to prevent Arab workmen from proceeding to the groves at Petah-Tikvah to pick oranges bought by Arab merchants led to clashes and racial conflict.[29]

A religious grievance was added to the political and economic ones, when the International Missionary Council held its first Conference at Jerusalem during the first two weeks of April, 1928. Protests from various districts and bodies were lodged against the Missionary Conference, expressing fear of 'Evangelising Moslems on a large scale'. In Gaza the police fired at the excited crowds wounding three persons, and 'all telephonic and telegraphic communications with Gaza were cut off to prevent repercussion in Jerusalem and elsewhere during the Nebi Musa processions'.[30]

It was not until June 1928, that the Seventh Palestine Arab Congress was convened. The flagging (Arab) Executive Committee succumbed to pressure brought to bear by other political forces to make it an all-embracing hodge-podge of a Conference comprising every shade of opinion and interest in the country. It was the weakest of all Congresses and came near to passing a resolution demanding a National Government under the existing Mandate system, had it not been for the efforts of a few members who advocated the appealing alternative of adopting the resolutions of all previous Congresses. The composition of the Congress was inevitably reflected in the Executive Committee which had to be enlarged to forty-eight members in order to accommodate the various groups, districts and interests represented in the Congress. Disunity and personal rivalries reduced the new Executive Committee to complete impotence.

Renewed Zionist Initiative

Before the end of 1928 there were indications that the period of political stagnation was giving way to renewed Zionist initiative and correspondingly renewed Palestinian Arab agitation and counter-measures. The Zionist Organisation pressed for a loan of two million sterling to be raised under the auspices of the League and guaranteed by HM Government, for more State lands to be given to Jewish colonisation and agricultural bodies.[30] and concluded a pact with non-Zionist Jewish Organisations in America which aimed at raising funds and supporting the building of the Jewish National Home in Palestine.[31]

Even as early as April 1928, the Chief Secretary, sounded a well-timed note of caution in a memorandum to Lord Plumer on the necessity of instituting a Legislative Council containing popular representatives in spite of Jewish opposition. The memorandum warned of the political influence of the 'Intelligentsia' and their desire for popular representation in the Government which was prompted, apart from motives of personal interest:

> by a sense of National preservation. Their fear is that our system of administration and our laws may create general conditions prejudicial to what they conceive to be their political rights and material advantage. This fear is the chief ingredient in the quasi-Nationalist sentiment which is common to Palestinian Arabs as to other Oriental peoples at the present time and which can be quickened into popular agitation by any disaffected minority.[32]

Wailing Wall or Buraq?

The issue of political representation and the economic grievances of the Arabs constituted the underlying factors of renewed tension and Arab-Jewish animosity on the eve of the fateful year of 1929.[33] Yet, it was a religious issue, that of the *Buraq* or Wailing Wall, that triggered off the disturbances of 1929.

An incident which occured in Jerusalem on 24 September 1928, the Jewish Day of Atonement, proved to be the starting point of a series of events which culminated in the first and only religious clash in August 1929.

The incident was triggered by a Jewish attempt to introduce screens to divide the men from the women worshippers while praying before the Wailing Wall, a Holy Muslim property, which constituted the Western face of the platform of the *Haram-ash-Sarif*.[34] In accordance with their duty to maintain the *status quo* the Government ordered the removal of the screen, and when the order was not complied with the screen was forcibly removed by the police.

A widespread campaign of protest against Jewish intentions and designs to take possession of the Al-Aqsa Mosque swept Palestine. A 'Society for the Protection of the Muslim Holy Places' was established, and secret messages were despatched to the Muslims of India. In the course of the following months Muslim building operations in the neighbourhood of the Wall were instituted which the Jews believed to be intended to interfere with their devotions. 'An attempt by the Government to settle the various questions in dispute by mutual agreement between the two communities were baffled as much as Jewish reluctance as by Arab'.[35]

An examination of the respective attitudes of the parties involved in the dispute — Arabs, Zionists and the Government reveals that the various leaderships availed themselves of the opportunities provided by the turn of events.

To begin with the Government stood to profit from the diversion of an increasingly anti-Government oriented Palestinian Arab nationalist movement to an anti-Jewish Muslim movement. As for the Zionists the incident of 24 September 1928, came at a critical moment when Weizmann was touring America trying to stir enthusiasm and elicit funds for the stagnant fortunes of the JNH in Palestine. It is not unlikely that the incident helped bring about a partnership between the Zionists and the non-Zionists in the United States during the latter part of 1928. Writing to Shuckburgh from New York on the lucrative new partnership Weizmann stated that the incident at the Wailing Wall 'has stirred the feelings of the Jewish Community throughout this country'.[36] A religious conflict in Palestine could be used as a major propaganda weapon for a successful money-raising campaign. Jewish apathy in the Diaspora was among Zionism's greatest enemies and the Wailing Wall dispute was guaranteed to overcome lack of interest and funds.

The Peel Commission observed that until 1929, the

. . .highly incendiary element of religion had had little to do with the growth of Arab antagonism to the National Home. In Palestine, as elsewhere in the Moslem world, nationalism had been more political than religious. But, if the religious cry raised, if it were widely and genuinely believed that the coming of the Jews to the country would mean not merely their economic and political ascendancy but also the full re-establishment of ancient Judaism, the invasion and desecration of the Holy places and the rebuilding of the Temple on its original site, then there could be little doubt that Arab hostility would be more unanimous, more fanatical, and more desperate than it had ever been.[37]

Moreover, Jewish encroachments against the third most sacred shrine in Islam was bound to elicit solidarity and backing to the cause of the Palestinian Arabs from all Muslim quarters in the world, which the Palestinians hoped to use as a countervailing force *vis-à-vis* Jewish and Western backing enjoyed by their adversaries.

Nevertheless, the Arab religious and political notability continued to show restraint in order to avoid trouble with the Government. The Muslim Conference which was held on the first of November passed off quietly,[38] as did the Balfour Declaration's anniversary on the second of November.

A few days earlier Hajj Amin expressed his readiness to comply with the Government's request to restrain the Palestine Arab press, despite his belief that the alarm felt by all classes of Muslims at Jewish encroachments and propaganda in connection with the Wall was genuine.[39]

Early in 1929, the Palestine Government decided to conduct a closer examination of the principal question in the Wailing Wall dispute, namely, the rights of the Jewish worshippers to bring appurtenances to the Wall. Accordingly, both the Supreme Muslim Council and the Chief Rabbinate were requested to produce documentary evidence of rulings given under the Turkish regime and any other evidence in regard to the bringing of various appurtenances of worship to the Wall. The Supreme Muslim Council

returned an early reply to this request and in part supported their statement of the case by documents deriving from the time of the Turkish regime. On the other hand, repeated reminders to the Chief Rabbinate failed to elicit any response to the request which had been made to them by the Government.[40]

Four months after the issue of the Government's White Paper which called — to the Muslim's satisfaction — for the maintenance of the *status quo,* Hajj Amin complained to Chancellor that

Jews were bringing benches and tables in increased numbers to the Wall, and driving nails into the Wall and hanging lamps on them.

This constituted an infringement of the status quo on which the White Paper was so explicit.[41]

Hajj Amin added that the situation 'was getting serious and might even become critical', since there was 'a widespread fear amongst the Muslim masses that the surrender of any right relating to the Wall might endanger their exclusive title to the Haram'. The Muslim authorities were thus motivated to lower one of the walls in the *Haram* area in order to check any Jewish attempt to contravene the *status quo*. The Muslim structural alterations in the neighbourhood of the Wall were suspended by the Hajj Amin, as an act of courtesy, at the request of the High Commissioner, while the matter was referred to the Law Offices of the British Crown.[42]

Anti-British Agitation Revived

Although the Mufti's relations with the British Authorities were friendly it was reported that in the course of his travels abroad to collect funds for the restoration of the *Haram* building he was agitating in favour of the Arab cause in Palestine. During May, Hajj Amin was

Reported to have said to King Fuad (of Egypt) that he would be happy to place his services at the King's disposal in Palestine for the purpose of his ambitions regarding the Khalifate, and that Palestine was the one place under British rule where Moslems could without difficulty carry out anti-British agitation.[43]

Anti-British propaganda, however, was not Hajj Amin's preoccupation, despite the fact that the task of agitating against the British was becoming increasingly easier in view of the economic situation and the gradual resurgence of Zionist immigration and land acquisition.

Reflecting the exasperated mood, the Secretaries of the Executive Committee submitted during June 1929, a strongly worded memorandum demanding Parliamentary Government, and repudiating the Government's policy of 'Legislation without Representation'. Moreover, the Arabs believed that the economic crisis was a natural result of the Government's policies:

The inhabitants of Palestine can no longer tolerate any injustices in addition to the injustices done to them up till now as an outcome of the present system of Administration. In fact this Administration has placed the country in great economic crisis which compelled a not inappreciable number of the inhabitants to sell their lands to foreigners who only buy lands for political purposes i.e. to create a foreign nationality on the remains of Arab Nationality.[44]

The Wailing Wall dispute, however, continued to provide the focus of political interest and concern in Palestine. Cables of protests against 'Jewish acts of aggression on Holy Buraq' were despatched to London during the first week of August. Muslim religious authorities charged that the Government's hesitation to effect application of the White Paper encouraged Jewish encroachment on the *Buraq*. Moreover, the Palestinian Muslims protested vehemently 'against political interest under cover of Buraq religious futile pretensions'.[45]

The immediate incident that led to the clashes of 23 August was a Jewish demonstration at the Wailing Wall during the preceding week. On 14 August 1929, a demonstration took place in Tel-Aviv in commemoration of the destruction of the Temple, and on the following day a crowd of Jewish young men led by a minority of Zionist extremists from Tel-Aviv 'anxious to create trouble',[46] staged a hitherto unprecedented procession through the streets of Jerusalem to the foot of the Wailing Wall. There they raised the Jewish flag and sang the Zionist anthem – Hatikvah – against the specific instructions of the Acting High Commissioner.[47]

The incident provoked the Muslims[48] to stage a counter demonstration on the following day which was not only a Friday, but the Prophet's Birthday as well. After midday prayers at the *Haram* a demonstration estimated at some two thousand, including villagers who had come to celebrate the Prophet's Birthday, proceeded to the Wall where an inflammatory speech was made by Hasan Abu as-Sa'ud, one of the Sheikhs of the Al-Aqsa and a confidante of Hajj Amin. A table belonging to Jews which was standing on the pavement was broken and some pieces of paper containing Jewish prayers and petitions placed in crevices of the Wall were burnt.

As the High Commissioner was absent, it fell on the OAG to guide th excited Muslims and Jews 'into channels of prudence', but his task was rendered difficult by 'the absence of all responsible Jewish leaders from the country'.[49]

A quarrel which arose between an Arab and a Jewish youth in Jerusalem on 17 August ended in bloodshed, when the Jewish youth was stabbed. A serious affray between Arabs and Jews followed during which eleven Jews and fifteen Arabs were wounded:

Upon the arrival of the police, who arrested the Arab guilty of the initial wounding, they were attacked by the Jewish crowd. The prisoner and one of the British police were injured, the injuries sustained by the policeman being of a severe character. The Jewish crowd also attacked Arab houses in the neighbourhood and wounded some of the inmates.[50]

Several arrests of Arabs and Jews within Jerusalem and outside it took place within the next four days. When the stabbed Jewish youth died on 20 August, his funeral was turned into a political demonstration against the Government and the Arabs.

Anticipating trouble the Government ordered a section of armoured-cars to come from Transjordan to stand by in Ramlah, on the Jerusalem -Jaffa road. A meeting between three prominent Jews and three prominent Arabs took place on 22 August at Mr Luke's house. The meeting was friendly, and it was agreed that it should be resumed again on 26 August.

While prominent Arabs were ready to confer with the Government officials and reason with their Jewish counterparts, the Arab villagers and the man in the street were excited and worked up by the resurgence of the Zionist menace in general and by the Wailing Wall dispute and the events of the third week of August 1929, in particular. The provocations of the Jewish demonstrators of 15 August tended to lend credibility to the villagers fear of a Jewish attack on the *Buraq*.

On Friday 23 August great numbers of Muslim villagers came up to Jerusalem for the midday prayer armed with clubs and sticks. An order to disarm the incoming villagers, given by the British police officer in charge of one part of the city, was cancelled by his superior officer on the ground that the measure could not be carried through effectively without taking up the energies of more of his seventy British policemen than he could afford to spare.

The outbreak of 23 August, which began around noontime, was from the beginning an attack by Arabs, armed with sticks, revolvers and some with swords, on Jews. When the Arab crowds attacked the Jewish suburbs in the early afternoon, the police opened fire, and shortly afterwards aeroplanes flew over Jerusalem. By 4 pm armoured cars from Ramleh had arrived and seventy special constables had been enrolled. Half an hour later the Old City of Jerusalem was quiet but firing directed on to outlying Jewish suburbs continued and so did Arab attacks on Jewish villagers within a few miles of Jerusalem.[51]

When news of the outbreak of Jerusalem reached Nablus and Hebron there were angry demonstrations by excited crowds, and in the course of an attack on a Jewish school in Hebron one Jew was killed. On the following day Arabs in Hebron made a bloody attack on the Jewish quarter and on isolated Jewish houses lying outside the crowded quarters of the town. More than sixty Jews were killed and more than fifty were wounded.

Jewish Counter-attack

On the same day a determined Arab crowd who wished to obtain arms, attacked the police barracks in Nablus, where serious trouble was averted by the action of the police firing on the crowd. In Beisan an attack was made on the Jews. There was a minor disturbance at Jaffa, and several Jewish colonies were attacked. On 25 August attacks by Arabs were made on the outlying Jewish districts. Isolated attacks on Jewish colonies continued and burning. In Haifa there was an outbreak in the old quarter, and several attacks were made on Hadar Hacarmel, a Jewish suburb of Haifa. In Jaffa a police officer who opened fire on an Arab crowd succeeded in beating off an attack on the quarter which lay between Jaffa and Tel Aviv:

> In this quarter there occurred the worst instance of a Jewish attack on Arabs, in the course of which the Imam of a mosque and six other people were killed. On the 26th August, there also occurred a Jewish attack on the Mosque of Okasha in Jerusalem, a sacred shrine of great antiquity held in much veneration by the Muslims. The mosque was badly damaged and the tombs of the prophets which it contains were desecrated.[52]

On 29 August, Arab mobs attacked the Jewish quarter in Safad where some forty-five Jews were killed or wounded and several Jewish houses and shops were set on fire.

Apart from isolated incidents and attacks the hostilities soon subsided and the situation began to improve from day to day. During the disturbances 133 Jews were killed and 339 were wounded, of whom 198 were treated in hospital; 116 Arabs were killed or died in hospital, while the number of Arabs who received treatment in hospitals for injuries was 232.[53]

The Watershed

The events of the last week of August 1929 proved to be the watershed in Arab-British relations in Palestine. The rising began as an anti-Jewish outburst, since the Mufti had no desire to fight the British, and his men were believed to have nourished the impression that the Government was in sympathy with the Arabs (*Doleh Ma'-ana*). Although the events of 23 August in Jerusalem did not entail any hostile actions against the Government, both the Government and the Muslim Supreme Council (see to have) lost control of the situation less than 48 hours after the initial Arab attacks on the Jewish Quarter. In the course of their defence of Jewish lives and property the British troops fired at the Arab mobs inflicting many casualties. The immediate effect was reflected in the attitude of the purely Arab towns — Nablus, Acre, Jenin, Tulkarem and Gaza — where the demonstrations assumed a pure anti-British character. In the meetings of the Arab Youth (*Shabab*) which took place in various places in order to decide on the form of solidarity towards the Jerusalem Arabs two tendencies emerged. The stronger tendency, advocated by the clerical class and the Muslim notables, called for attacks on Jews and revenge on Zionists. The second tendency supported by the 'left' national element led by Hamdi Husseini in Jaffa and the active members of the young Muslim Society in Haifa, called for directing activity 'against the English and not against the Jews'.[54]

With the arrival of British troops on 25 and 26 August the situation took a sharp turn. Zionist leaders who were critical of the Government suddenly returned to advocating the necessity of maintaining the Jewish goodwill towards Britain and the Palestine Administration. Correspondingly, Muslim notables — Hajj Amin, Ragheb Nashashibi and Musa Kazem — signed a Proclamation, in which they dissassociated themselves from mob actions leaving the unarmed and unorganised fellahin and bedouins to face aeroplanes, armoured cars and British troops. The British military machine inflicted devastation on the Arab villages of Lifta, Deir Yassin, and Colonia. Over one thousand persons — more than 90 per cent of these being Arabs — were tried on charges relating to the disturbances of August 1929. In the final instance the courts confirmed twenty-six death sentences, twenty-five of these being upon Arabs, and one upon a Jew.[55]

Moreover, the Collective Punishments Ordinance was applied to the towns and villages whose inhabitants were guilty of participation in the concerted attacks on Jews at Hebron, Safad, Motza, Artuf, Beer Tuvia, and heavy fines were inflicted.

For the villagers and the masses of the Palestinians two important facts were made clearer and sharper by the events of 1929. The first was that Zionism and the JNH depended, ultimately and inevitably, on

British bayonets, and it was therefore necessary to fight Britain if the struggle against Zionism was to achieve its goals.[56] The second concerned the cowardice of the Palestinian notables and their inadequacy to lead the Arabs in the struggle against Zionism and British policy in Palestine.

A further blow in this direction was meted out by J. Chancellor (the H.C.) who issued on his return to Palestine an angry proclamation in which he accused the Arabs of committing atrocious acts and announced that in view of recent events he was going to suspend those discussions with His Majesty's Government on the subject of constitutional changes in Palestine.

No Arab Atrocities

On top of Chancellor's general accusations there were Zionist allegations of Arab atrocities at Hebron on 24 August. When the Arabs denied that any acts of mutilations had taken place, a formal request by the Palestine Zionist Executive was made to the High Commissioner to authorise the exhumation of bodies of Jews who had been killed at Hebron.[57] Thereupon, Chancellor instructed the Director of Health to appoint a special committee, composed of British doctors, to examine the exhumed bodies with a view to ascertaining whether they had been mutilated or not, in the presence of Jewish and Arab representatives.

The special committee submitted a report on 13 September in which it stated that the charges of 'mutilation' were not substantiated in the cases of the twenty bodies which were exhumed, four of which were referred to them by the Jewish representatives.[58] The report of the medical committee was looked upon as a political and moral victory for the Palestinian Arabs who, in their turn, had insisted that the exhumation should be carried out.

In their turn the Arabs complained that the Attorney-General Norman Bentwich was pro-Zionist and demanded his dismissal.[59]

There were other complaints as well: 'the severity of the Police which had reached a limit that they thought was unheard of in a civilised country', in addition to the rigorous supression of the Arabic papers 'for trivial reasons'.[60]

The High Commissioner was anxious that the Executive should use their influence to prevent incitement by boycott:

There was a serious danger at the present time when public opinion was inflamed that some small incident connected with boycotting might develop into a disturbance on a large scale. They must bear in mind that there was a large number of troops in the country now, and any disturbance might lead to bloodshed.[61]

Chancellor's insinuation that any disturbance would soon develop into a clash between the Arabs and British troops was hardly necessary, as the Arab Executive were already advising moderation and were only looking for Government help that would strengthen their hands.[62] Far from offering the Arab Executive any concessions, Chancellor affirmed the extension of the application of the much hated Collective Punishment Ordinance over the whole country.

The Mufti's Attitude

While a growing anti-Government militant mood was making itself felt all over the country, Hajj Amin was assuring Chancellor, in a private interview on 1 October, that 'there could be no doubt that the mass of the Arab population were amicably disposed towards Great Britain'.[63] The Mufti's statement implied that he still believed it possible to confine Palestinian opposition to Britain's Zionist policies and to the Zionists themselves and thus avoid a direct clash between Britain and the Arabs. During the latter part of September, Police sources stated that:

> Shekib Wahab, Syrian revolutionary leader, in conversation with the Grand Mufti, offered to organise bands for a guerrilla campaign to last not less than a year. The Grand Mufti reported to have considered this unnecessary at present.[64]

Hajj Amin sought to impress Chancellor of his loyalty when he told the High Commissioner that he considered himself 'as one who was, in a sense, an officer of the State'.[65] A week later:

> The Mufti said he promised to help in the maintenance of order and to cooperate with the Government. He had always held this attitude and he held it still and should continue to hold it even if Government did not listen to his representations. He regarded this as his duty not only to the Government but to God and the people and also to his own conscience.[66]

The Mufti pointed out to the High Commissioner the difficulties involved in his pro-Government position which was particularly unpopular in view of the Government's refusal to abolish the Collective Punishment Ordinance: 'during the last few days he had been charged himself with being in league with the Government in this matter'. On

19 October, Hajj Amin despatched Jamal Husseini, Secretary of the Supreme Muslim Council, to London to conduct political discussions at the Colonial Office.

The Government and the Colonial Office proved that they were alive to the importance of maintaining Hajj Amin's friendly attitude because of his opposition to a direct Arab-British confrontation in Palestine. In deference to the Mufti, the Colonial Secretary eliminated any mention of whether the 1929 outbreak 'may be regarded as having been pre-concerted or due to organised action'[67] in the final terms of reference of the Shaw Commission of Enquiry.

By 12 October Chancellor felt compelled to convey to Passfield his alarm at the evolution of Arab political attitudes following the disturbances of 1929:

> The feeling of the Arabs against the Jews is still bitter. Boycott is being enforced and instigators are working clandestinely and avoiding detection. There is amongst the Arabs a growing feeling of hostility to the Government which is being fermented by skilful propaganda conducted by Arab leaders. I am informed that this feeling is not as previously confined to political circles, but also now extended to lower classes of the population and to the villagers.[68]

This process of radicalisation posed a threat to the Arab Executive and the traditional leadership:

> A full meeting of the Arab Executive had been summoned for 12th October to consider the question of calling a general strike as a protest against the Regulations and other alleged acts of partiality and injustice. Younger Moslems declare that the strike will be held whether the Executive approve it or not.[69]

Though successful in calling the strike off, 'Awni' Abdul Hadi told Chancellor in the course of an interview on 14 October, that 'the Executive Committee in their actions are not always their own masters, but have to yield to the pressure of their followers'.[70] The Committee 'were following a policy to do all they could to win over public opinion and to avoid estrangement'. Nevertheless, the Executive Committee assured Chancellor that 'The principle that guided them was that there should be no difference between them and the British Government',[71] as they believed they could not attain their rights otherwise.

A State of Desperation

Though speaking on behalf of the majority of the notables and the propertied classes, the views expressed by the Executive Committee were not universally embraced by all the members of these classes. According to a Police Report some participants in a meeting of leading Muslim and Christian merchants at the offices of the Arab Executive, spoke openly in favour of revolution:

> That a general rising is the only means to save the country is common talk among all classes of the population; also that the people have become desperate and unmindful of the risks; further villagers are stated to have become affected by political propaganda and by the economic depression, influence by purchase of lands by Jews and resultant ejection of Arab farmers.[72]

Nor was this militancy presumed to be of a transient character, as Chancellor was of the opinion that it would not be possible to reduce British troops below two battalions even after the crisis was over.

A week later Chancellor reiterated that 'the Moslem population appear to be approaching a state of desperation on account of Government's failure to meet their wishes in any way. This feeling is not confined to the leadership only but has spread to the lower classes and to the rural population'.[73]

Among other factors, the spread of agitation against Zionism and British policy in Palestine to the neighbouring countries, the smuggling of arms to Palestine and the possibility that volunteers from Syria, Transjordan and Lebanon might join the Palestinians in any future uprisings added to the anxieties of British Authorities in Palestine.

During the third week of October police sources reported that money was being collected, and 400 Arabs selected to form an armed force. A week later Police Intelligence reported that 'gangs of Criminals to attack Jews and British officials have been formed and will first function in areas at Haifa and Nablus.[74] Intelligence summary of the 19th October from Trans-Jordan Frontier Force reported that

> experienced bandits are being consulted as to the best means of carrying out guerrilla warfare which may commence after the Commission from London arrives and completes its report. Committees are being formed in many parts of Palestine for the purpose of helping these bands.[75]

The new level of political activism was conducive to the emergence of students[76] as a political element, and to the birth of the Palestine Arab Women's Congress which was held on 26 October 1929. The latter was attended by over 200 delegates, both Muslim and Christian from various parts of Palestine. The participants were members of the leading Palestinian families, the most prominent of whom were wives of Palestinian political leaders. The wife of Musa Kazem was elected to the Chair and

> many speakers considered the Mandatory Power, as represented by the Palestine Administration, to be solely responsible for all that took place, and a national movement for consolidated action on the part of all women's organizations was earnestly urged.[77]

The resolutions of the Congress rejected the Balfour Declaration and Zionist immigration, called for the establishment of a National Government responsible before a Representative Council, and urged the development of National Industries.

A day later a 'General Assembly of Arab Congress' called by the Arab Executive was held at Jerusalem, Delegates to the Assembly included Beduin Sheikhs from all parts of Palestine and some representatives from Transjordan. According to Police reports,

> Great enthusiasm and determination to 'save the country' even at the cost of their lives was manifested. Judging from the attitude of the Assembly it was apparent that the people were in a state of extreme excitement and approximated to a revolutionary disposition. It is said that the Arabs now await the 'decision' of the commission, and if these are unsatisfactory the only course open to them is a general uprising.[78]

A General strike was called and observed on the Balfour anniversary.

The participation of Trans-Jordanians in the Assembly indicated the state of feeling in the adjacent Arab countries. According to a report by the British Resident in 'Amman,

> Transjordan was kept out of the riots in August because. . .a plan of action had not been prepared. Should a further outburst against the Jews be arranged, I fear the country might not behave so well.[79]

An intelligence report dated 13 November stated that a secret

Committee called the Boycott Committee has been formed for terrorist purposes with a view to the assassination of persons considered to be acting against Arab nationalist interests.

These threats were reported to have led to the drying up of the Arab sources of Police Intelligence. The Committee was reported to have been formed 'with knowledge and consent of Supreme Moslem Council and Arab Executive who have subscribed to expense'.[80] One Arab working for the Zionist Intelligence was assassinated, and a warning was sent to a British Judge. A later report tended to shed some doubt on the links between the Executive Committee and the Boycott Committee as eleven of the twenty-four persons of the latter were reported to be members of the Palestinian Communist Party.[81]

The period between 1923 and 1929 which began with a whimper ended with a bang as Arab opposition to the Anglo-Zionist partnership struck deeper popular roots with a disposition towards waging an armed struggle as a means of forcing a change in British pro-Zionist policies in Palestine. From now onwards the Arab struggle against Zionism involved a direct confrontation between the Palestinian Arabs and the Mandatory Government.

Mention should be made of Zionist attitudes towards the prospect of bringing about an Arab-Jewish understanding in 1929. One month after the August outbreak Weizmann told one of the members of the Middle East Department that

> The Government should try and get a conference between the Zionists and the Arabs, the latter not necessarily Palestinian Arabs, with the idea of getting both sides to come to a concordat.[82]

A month later H. St. John Philby, one of the major British officials in the East in the early twenties, paid a visit to Jerusalem and Damascus with the intention of drawing up the 'Basis of an Arab-Jewish understanding in Palestine' and found the Arab leaders moderate and reasonable.[83]

When Dr Judah Magnes, head of the Hebrew University, said in a speech at the reopening of the University that it was necessary for Jews and Arabs to find ways of living and working together he was heckled by the students, and the Jewish press attacked both him and the Brith Shalom Organisation. The Administrative Committee of the American Jewish Committee expressed its 'feeling of outrage over Dr Magnes's utterances and his irresponsibility in breaking the united Jewish front.[84]

Notes

1. See Monthly Political Report, October 1923, Samuel to Devonshire 16 November 1923, CO 733/51, p.1.
2. Ibid.
3. Ibid.
4. Monthly Political Report, November 1923, Samuel to Devonshire, 14 December 1923, CO 733/52, p.1.
5. Monthly Political Report, December 1923, Samuel to Devonshire, 10 January 1924, CO 733/63.
6. Monthly Political Report, January 1924, Samuel to Devonshire, 21 February 1924, CO 733/65, p.3.
7. Ibid., p.2.
8. Ibid., p.4.
9. Monthly Political Report, February 1924, Samuel to Thomas, 21 March 1924, CO 733/66.
10. Monthly Political Report, April 1924, Samuel to Thomas, 23 May 1924, CO 733/68, p.2.
11. Monthly Political Report, May 1924, Samuel to Thomas, 6 June 1924, CO 733/69, p.1.
12. Monthly Political Report, June 1924, Clayton to Thomas, 17 July 1924, CO 733/71, p.1.
13. Monthly Political Report, July 1924, Clayton to Thomas, 13 August 1924, CO 733/72, p.1.
14. Monthly Political Report, August 1924, Samuel to Thomas, 11 September 1924, CO 733/73.
15. Monthly Political Report, September 1924, Clayton to Thomas, 24 October 1924, CO 733/74, p.2.
16. See 'Report on Palestine Administration', Jerusalem, 5 October 1924, CO 733/74, p.13.
17. See Monthly Political Report, December 1924, Samuel to Colonial Secretary, 21 April 1925, CO 733/92, p.1.
18. Another topic of interest was the French Consul General's show of 'considerable sympathy with Zionist enterprise throughout Palestine'. See Monthly Political Report, February 1925, Samuel to Colonial Secretary, 18 March 1925, CO 733/90, p.1.
19. Monthly Political Report, March 1925, Samuel to Colonial Secretary, 21 April 1925, CO 733/92, p.1.
20. Ibid., p.2.
21. Ibid., p.2. Solidarity with the Palestinian Arab national movement was lavishly displayed during Balfour's visit to Damascus where his life was in danger and the French Authorities had to speed his departure from the Arab city.
22. 'Minutes of the meeting between the Right Hon. L.S. Amery, Secretary of State for the Colonies, and the Arab Deputation composed of members of the Executive Committee, the National Party and the Peasant's Party held at Government House on 21 April 1925', CO 733/92, p.1.
23. Ibid. Also see a memorandum submitted to the President of the League's Council by the Executive Committee, 12 April 1925, CO 733/93, p.8.
24. Monthly Political Report, July 1925, Symes to Colonial Secretary, 26 August 1925, CO 733/96, p.1.
25. The Supreme Muslim Council with its budgets, courts, schools, levies, jobs and elections had the illusion of being a government and in a limited sense it was an *Imperium in imperio.*
26. For the correspondence between the Palestinian politicians and Mr Mills, see

Darwaza op.cit., pp.271-280.

27. See Minute by Shuckburgh, 10 July 1928, CO 733/158.
28. See Shuckburgh to Eder, 4 January 1927, CO 733/118, p.2. Also see Plumer to Amery, 7 October 1927, CO 733/133.
29. Same to Same, 22 December 1927, CO 733/145.
30. Same to Same, 26 April 1928, CO 733/155, p.2.
30. See Departmental Comments between March and December 1928, CO 733/155, *passim.*
31. See *The New Palestine,* (New york), 26 October 1928.
32. Chief Secretary to Plumer, 1 April 1928, CO 733/155. Another factor was the constitutional progress of the neighbouring Arab states towards self-government and independence.
33. See 'Report of the Commission on the Palestine Disturbances of August 1929' (British Parliamentary Paper Cmd. 3530 of 1930), hereafter referred to as the Shaw Commission Report, p.150.
34. The Muslims call the Wall the Holy *Buraq.* For details of its religious importance see a Memorandum by President of the Supreme Muslim Council on 'The Moslem Buraq', 4 October 1928, CO 733/160.
35. Peel Commission Report, op.cit., p.67.
36. Weizmann to Shuckburgh, 31 October 1928, CO 733/160.
37. Peel Commission Report, op.cit., p.66.
38. The General Muslim Conference for the defence of the *Buraq* comprised delegates representing Muslim bodies in Palestine, Syria Lebanon and Trans-Jordan and submitted protests to the High Commissioner and Secretary, 7 November 1928, CO 733/160.
39. See 'Summary of a meeting held in the High Commissioner's Office on 30 October, 1928', CO 733/160.
40. Shaw Commission Report, p.34.
41. 'Note of Interview of High Commissioner with Grand Mufti', 6 April 1929, CO 733/163, p.2.
42. 'Minute of a meeting held in the office of HE the HE the E.Cr. on 6 May 1909', CO 733/163.
43. Chancellor to Shuckburgh, 15 May 1929, CO 733/173.
44. A memorandum by the Secretaries of the Executive to the Palestinian Arab Congress 17 June 1929, CO 733/167.
45. Telegram from Sheikh Said al-Khatib to the National League, 4 August 1929, CO 733/163.
46. Acting H.Cr. to Colonial Secretary, 16 August, CO 733/160.
47. See Shaw Commission Report, op.cit., p.53.
48. Muslims claimed that the demonstration openly cursed Islam and caused terror to the women and children in Jerusalem, see Petition to the High Commissioner by Mohammad il-Mahdi and others 15 August 1929, CO 733/175.
49. OAG to Colonial Secretary, 17 August 1929, CO 733/163.
50. Shaw Commission Report, op.cit. p.57.
51. THE OAG Telegraphed for naval assistance and wired to the Colonial Office for British troops to be sent without delay. By 27 August five British warships, three battalions and one company of infantry, a company of armoured cars, a squadron of the RAF and a detachment of auxiliary troops were on their way to Palestine. see Ibid.
52. Ibid.
53. Ibid., p.65.
54. See a Manifesto by the Central Council of the Palestine Communist Party, 'The Boody War in Palestine and the Working Class', September 1929, CO 733/175. Hamdi Husseini and his group were jailed by the British.

55. See 'Report on the Administration of Palestine and Trans-Jordan for the year 1929' (Colonial No.47 of 1930), p.7. All the death sentences were commuted with the exception of three sentences on Arabs who were hanged on 17 June 1930.

56. The Communist manifesto referred to earlier, quoted one of the Jewish dailies as saying 'The Jewish Yishuv is a part of the British Empire. The Jewish Community is a British position in the country, and must be protected as such. The spilt (Jewish) blood is the price which is paid to England for her assistance in building the JNH'.

57. See Chancellor to Passfield, 21 September 1929, CO 733/175, p.3.

58. See ibid., Enclosure IV to XII.

59. See Memorandum by the Executive Committee to the H.Cr.1 October 1929, CO 733/175.

60. Chancellor to Passfield, 5 October 1929, CO 733/175.

61. Ibid.

62. Ibid. Two weeks later the Executive requested that Jewish immigration be suspended until the Commission of Enquiry had submitted their recommendations. See 'Meeting of interview of the Arab Executive with the High Commissioner', 17 October 1929, CO 733/163, p.10.

63. Ibid., Enclosure II, p.1.

64. Cabinet, 'Situation in Palestine', 28 November 1929, CO 733/17 p.4.

65. Ibid., p.3.

66. Chancellor to Passfield, 12 October 1929, CO 733/163, Enclosure II, p.3.

67. Passfield to Shaw, 19 September 1929, CO 733/176

68. H.Cr. to Colonial Secretary, 12 October 1929, CO 733/175.

69. Ibid.

70. Chancellor to Passfield, 19 October 1929, CO 733/163, Enclosure I, p.4.

71. Ibid., p.5.

72. 'Situation in Palestine', 28 November 1929, op.cit.

73. H.Cr. to Colonial Secretary, 19 October, CO 733/163.

74. Ibid., p.5.

75. ibid., p.6.

76. Same to Same, 23 October 1929, CO 733/163.

77. Mogannam, *The Arab Woman*, op.cit., p.70.

78. 'Situation in Palestine', 28 November 1929, op.cit., p.6.

79. Ibid.

80. Ibid., p.7.

81. Ibid., p.8.

82. Departmental Note, 23 September 1929, CO 733/175, p.2.

83. See Letters from Philby to Passfield, 1 November 1929, CO 733/175.

84. See Extract from *The Jewish Guardian*, 29 November 1929, CO 733/175, p.1.

6 PRELUDE TO REVOLUTION: 1930-1935

In January 1930, Chancellor reported to Lord Passfield, the Colonial Secretary, that as a consequence of the recent outbreaks 'a wave of Pan Arab nationalist sentiment has swept over Palestine and the neighbouring Arab countries, and it is certain that the political situation will never again be as it was, or appeared to be, before last August'.[1]

The reference to Pan Arab nationalist sentiment was indicative of Chancellor's awareness of the impending radical change in the Palestinians' political outlook. The Palestinians' political strategy would no longer be confined to resisting Jewish colonisation but would also aim at attaining national independence and getting rid of British rule.

Prior to the 1929 disturbances the Palestinians were alarmed at the revival of the Zionist threat in the wake of the World Jewish Congress of July 1929, when the agreement between Zionist and non-Zionist Jews committed the latter to contribute funds to promote the establishment of a JNH in Palestine. Far from protecting the Arabs from the renewed Zionist threat the Government were committed to help Zionist immigration and land settlement. The attitude of the Palestine Administration and the Arab clashes with the Police during the summer of 1929 strengthened the hand of the Palestinian Arab radicals who advocated violent opposition to the British Mandate, as an effective means of preventing Zionist hegemony in Palestine.

Indicative of the New Palestinian mood and the profound effect of the events of 1929, was the growth of an armed band of guerrillas operating in the Safad-Acre-Samakh region. The idea of organising armed bands to fight against Zionism and the Mandate was entertained during the hot summer of 1929. The band itself was composed, initially, of twenty-seven persons who participated conspicuously in the August outbreaks and had, as a result, to take refuge in the hills near the Syrian frontier.

The existence of an armed band waging guerrilla operations against British troops and police as well as Zionist settlers was both novel and significant. Although largely ignored and overlooked by most of the published books on the modern history of Palestine, including those of Darwaza and Sifri, a good account of that movement was provided by Chancellor.[2] In his 'Survey' Professor Arnold Toynbee maintained that these armed bands were 'quickly broken up with the assistance of the

155

French authorities in the territory mandated to France'.[3] In fact, this was not the case.

The 'Green Hand Gang'

The 'Green Hand Gang' was organised in October 1929 under the leadership of Ahmed Tafish and mounted an operation during the same month against the Jewish Quarter in cooperation with their supporters within the town of Safad. During the following month the band was reinforced by a number of seasoned Druze revolutionaries who fought the French in the famous Druze Rebellion of 1925 and who soon became the backbone of the enlarged band. A second attack on Safad in mid-November spurred the Administration to despatch Palestinian and British Police reinforcements to the area. Shortly after the arrival of the reinforcements in Safad, the guerrillas appeared in the Acre Sub-District where they started ambushing police patrols. Towards the end of December the arrival of large troop reinforcements made driving operations against the guerrillas possible. The French 'afforded valuable assistance by patrolling the Syrian frontier with a large force of French troops'.[4]

The guerrillas proved to be elusive as they were 'working in an area where many of the villagers were sympathetic to them'.[5] However, lack of coordination and cooperation between the band and the Palestinian political leadership dimmed the prospect of the spread of armed resistance to other areas, notably, the Nablus District. Combined military operations conducted against the band in the first two months of 1930 caused a temporary break-up of the band and the apprehension of sixteen of their original number. As late as 22 February Chancellor reported that the band was reassembling and that further operations were being undertaken against the remaining fighters.

The coming of the dry season, the arrest of the band leader in Trans-Jordan, the combined efforts of the Police and the Army and the failure to organise armed bands in other parts of the country provide possible clues to the failure of the 'Green Hand Gang'.

The Foremost Arab Grievance

The Shaw Commission were convinced that Zionist land acquisition and Jewish colonisation were the foremost Arab grievance, 'the fears of the Arabs that the success of the Zionist land policy meant their expropriation from the land were repeatedly emphasised'.[6] When the Jewish National Fund acquired Wadi Hawarth lands at an auction ordered by a court in satisfaction of a debt, Chancellor was certain that trouble was inevitable as

> further purchases of agricultural land by the Jews can be made only
> by dispossessing Arab cultivators of the land they are occupying and
> so create a class of landless peasantry.[7]

The Shaw Commission reiterated the opinion expressed by the Haycraft
Commission that 'The Arab fellaheen and villagers are therefore
probably more politically minded than many of the people of Europe'.[8]

The villagers, however, were not the only victims of pressure created
by Zionist immigration. The Arabs, the Shaw Commission reported,
were convinced that Zionist land settlement and immigration schemes
would inevitably result in the complete subordination of the Arabs as a
race, the expropriation of their people from the soil, the unemployment of a large number and their displacement by Jews.[9]

Despite the plight of the *fellahin,* the threat to urban Arab workers,
and the failure of the Mandate to establish self-governing institutions,
the political notables were determined to stick to their traditional
attitudes towards the British Government. Encouraged by the findings
of the Shaw Commission, the personal disposition of Chancellor and
the emergence of a new Labour Government under Ramsay MacDonald,
a new Arab Delegation elected by the Executive Committee proceeded
to negotiate with HM Government in London a change of policy that
would prevent disturbances and bloodshed in the future. The
Delegation was headed by Musa Kazem and included Hajj Amin,
Raghed Nashashibi, 'Awni 'Abdul Hadi, Jamal Husseini and Alfred
Rock.

Negotiations in London

The composition of the Delegation represented the desire of the
Palestinian political notability to reach an understanding with the
Government that would prevent Zionist domination in Palestine and
thus render their peaceful disposition towards the Government
acceptable to the discontented Palestinians.

The Delegations reached London on 30 March 1930, and were
received the following day by the Prime Minister and Lord Passfield,
the Colonial Secretary. In subsequent discussions the Palestinian leaders
demanded the prohibition of land sales from Arabs to non-Arabs,
stoppage of Jewish immigration, the re-establishment of the (Ottoman)
Agricultural Bank and the institution of a national parliamentary
government in accordance with Article 22 of the League's covenant.[10]

The British Government maintained that they were under the obligation to carry out the administration of Palestine in accordance with the Articles of the Mandate. MacDonald and Passfield, however, promised to act on land sales and Jewish immigration after Sir John Hope Simpson, the land expert, had investigated the situation and submitted his recommendations.

The British Government described the talks with the Delegation as inconclusive. The Palestinian leaders, though clearly convinced that their mission was a failure, refused to publicise their belief that it was not possible to effect a radical change of British policy by peaceful means. Instead they declared that they were hopeful that the British Government would eventually accept their demands for the sake of peace in Palestine.

The despatch of Sir John Hope Simpson to Palestine reflected the Government's serious view of the plight of the landless peasants and unemployed workers in Palestine. A number of surveys were conducted by various committees in that period. According to a report on the 'Arab farmers' economic condition' submitted by the Commissioner of Lands in Palestine, the two burdens which weighed most heavily on the Arab cultivators were excessive taxation and indebtedness to Government and to money lenders.[11] These two factors were closely interrelated, and their interplay forced the Arab farmers to sell their lands to the Zionists.

The Plight of the Fellah

A consistent campaign in the Arabic Press emphasising the same facts reported by the Commissioner of Lands was directed against the Government's policy and complicity, which facilitated the implementation of the Zionist plans for the gradual conquest of Palestine and the dispossession of the fellahin. An article by a farmer from Tulkarem, published in *Falastin* of 24 August 1930, explained the interplay of factors that forced the Palestinian peasant to sell his land to the Jews:

> I sell my land and property because the Government compels me to pay taxes and tithes at a time when I do not possess the necessary means of subsistence for myself and my family. In the circumstances I am forced to appeal to a rich person for a loan which I undertake to refund together with an interest of 50% after a month or two. . . I keep renewing the bill and doubling the debt. . .which eventually forces me to sell my land in order to refund my debt out of which I

took only a meagre sum.

During October 1930 the Press drew attention to the Administration's neglect of the unemployed Arabs,[12] while spending large sums of money to relieve the Jewish workers, and complained against the granting of concessions for the exploitation of the country's resources by Jewish and foreign concerns.

Before Simpson submitted his report and recommendations, Chancellor found it necessary to take action in respect of immigration and land sales which was calculated to have a tranquillising effect upon the Arabs. The action was prompted by investigations which revealed that the Jews had 'recently bought or acquired options over large areas of land and acquisition of land by them is now proceeding at such a rapid rate. . .'[13]

On receiving Chancellor's legislative proposals Shuckburgh anticipated that actions designed to protect Arab peasants were bound to detonate 'further Jewish agitation on what may well be a most embarrasing scale'. The interests of the local inhabitants in Palestine were not, according to Shuckburgh, the paramount consideration:

> We have there to consider (or are always being told that we ought to consider) not merely the existing population, but the 14 odd millions of Jews all over the world who regard themselves as potential Palestinians. The embarrassing results of this position are obvious. But they are inherent in the Zionist policy, and must be faced.[14]

The accuracy of Shuckburgh's assessment of the situation became apparent in October 1930 following the publication of the report of Sir John Hope Simpson,[15] and the Statement of Policy by His Majesty's Government on Palestine, later known as Passfield's White Paper, which was based on Simpson's findings and recommendations.[16]

According to the Simpson Report the amount of cultivable land available in Palestine — excluding the Beersheba Sub-District — was only 6,544,000 *dunums* considerably less than the figure given by some Zionists (16,000,000) and appreciably below the estimate of 10,952,000 given by the Commissioner of Lands.[17] From that basic calculation Simpson drew two far-reaching conclusions:

1. If all the cultivable land in Palestine were divided up among the Arab agricultural population, there would not be enough to provide every family with a decent livelihood.

2. Until further development of Jewish lands and of irrigation had taken place and the Arabs had adopted better methods of cultivation, 'there is no room for a single additional settler if the standard of life of the *fellaheen* is to remain at its present level.' On State lands, similarly, there was no room, pending development, for Jewish settlers.

Furthermore, Simpson expressed his conviction that Arab unemployment was serious and widespread and that it was wrong to admit Jewish immigrants to fill vacancies in Palestine when unemployed Arabs were capable of filling the vacancy.

Passfield's White Paper

While upholding the theory of 'Dual Obligation' under the Mandate, and the principle of 'Economic Absorptive Capacity' as a regulative guide to the number of Jewish immigrants allowed into the country, Passfield's White Paper adopted, by and large, Simpson's estimates and promised to implement his recommendations. Furthermore it declared that the time had come to establish a Legislative Council on the lines indicated in the Churchill White Paper.

The Zionist outcry against the Simpson Report and the 1930 White Paper was vehement and overpowering. Weizmann protested that the White Paper was inconsistent with the terms of the Mandate and informed Passfield that he had resigned his joint office of President of the World Zionist Organisation and the Jewish Agency. The Zionists staged demonstrations in many Western countries and their attitude was openly supported by leading British politicians. The ensuing 'public ventilation of the controversy was an impressive demonstration of the Political power the Zionists could mobilise in England'.[18]

Zionist agitation over this issue did not subside until it was announced in November that the Jewish Agency had been invited to confer with HMG on the White Paper, as a prelude to swinging back to a pro-Zionist British policy in Palestine.

While not completely satisfied with the White Paper, the Palestinian leaders were, nevertheless, encouraged by the implication of what seemed to be a fresh attitude on immigration and land settlement. They were hopeful that further favourable changes would be forthcoming.

Thus the Arab Executive announced on the eve of the Balfour Declaration's anniversary that for the first time there would be no strike proclaimed.[19] Significantly, the Students' Higher Committee called for a strike on that occasion.[20]

Another indication of the conciliatory outlook of the Palestinian notability was Jamal Hasseini's 'attitude of great reasonableness' during his conversations with the officials of the Colonial Office in December.[21] In the course of these conversations, Jamal Husseini, who was in London as a personal representative of the Mufti, agreed to a Round Table Conference provided the Jewish representation was confined to Palestine Jews to the exclusion of Weizmann and other non-Palestinian Zionists. Any negotiations with Weizmann, Husseini argued, would involve an 'acceptance of Zionism', which the Palestinians were not prepared to accept under any circumstances.

On receiving news of the official talks between the Government and the Zionists over the 'White Paper', the Arab Executive hastened to give public expression to their apprehensions and misgivings at the prospect of a revision of the White Paper in favour of the Zionists. Even before the news of the talks broke out, the Arabs were alarmed by the Government's grant of 1,500 immigration certificates. These ominous signs did not deter Jamal Husseini, on his return to Palestine, from 'going round the country speaking warmly of the courtesy and consideration with which he was treated by the Officials of the Colonial Office, who, he states, are sympathetic to the Arab case'.[22]

The 'Black Letter'

Early in January 1931, Passfield informed Chancellor that in view of the necessity of finding a 'Modus co-operandi' with the Jewish Organisation in the wake of the outcry against the White Paper, the Government

> seem to have no alternative to writing and publishing, or allowing to be published, a letter to Dr. Weizmann, defining our policy in Palestine in terms more precise and more acceptable to the Jews than those of the White Paper of which it is to be the authoritative interpretation on the matters with which it deals.[23]

Shortly before the publication of MacDonald's letter to Weizmann, Passfield anticipated that the intended letter may have the effect of increasing Chancellor's difficulties with the Arabs and that the result was unavoidable 'for political and international reasons'[24] arising from Zionist pressure.

In his letter to Weizmann, MacDonald asserted that HMG intended to stand by the Mandate, which they viewed as an obligation to World Jewry and not only to the Jews of Palestine, to uphold the JNH policy by further land settlement and immigration by Jews and to condone the Zionist policy of insisting on Jewish labour for work on Jewish enterprises. In Weizmann's considered opinion the MacDonald Letter was a decisive factor 'which enabled us to make the magnificent gains of the ensuing years'.[25]

Not unnaturally, the Arabs read MacDonald's 'Black Letter', as they called it, with distress and indignation. They took the Letter as proof of Zionism's decisive influence on Whitehall and Westminster and hence the futility of expecting any degree of justice from Britain.

The political notability were hard hit by the MacDonald Letter and did not hesitate to tell Chancellor, in their first interview with him after the publication of the 'Black Letter', that their position before the public had become 'precarious and anxious'.[26] At the end of the interview the Arab leaders handed Chancellor a memorandum of protest in which they professed their loss of confidence in HMG and their vehement objection to what they considered a sanctioning of Jewish boycott of Arab labour. In turn they were considering boycotting the Jews by virtue of the principle of reciprocation.

In their manifesto to the Palestinian public, the Arab Executive declared that they were turning to the Arab and the Muslim worlds for help as they had given up all hope and confidence in Britain. The Arab Executive called for 'lawful and active' struggle to restore the Palestinians' violated rights. On 3 March 1931, Reuters news agency reported that Arab indignation over MacDonald's Letter was rising to fever pitch. Under popular pressure the Arab Executive had decided the previous day to boycott Jewish products and to encourage national handicrafts and local goods.

Settling the Palestinians across the Jordan

At this point Weizmann decided to visit Palestine ostensibly to promote an Arab-Jewish rapprochement. When the Zionist leader arrived in Palestine, the Arab Executive boycotted him and vigilantly watched every move he made. They published a declaration in the Press denouncing anybody who dared to defy public opinion on a matter that involved recognition of Zionism, the Balfour Declaration and the Mandate. Furthermore, they accused him of contemplating bribing some Arabs with the intention of exploiting them for propaganda and fund-raising purposes.[27] The Arab Executive were not far off the mark as Weizmann had informed Chancellor that he believed that most of the Arab leaders could be bribed.[28]

Chancellor took a dim view of the possibility of achieving an Arab-Jewish entente through bribery and suggested instead a meeting in London attended by both parties and representatives of HMG. Weizmann

did not follow the matter through and directed his attention to a
question which really interested him, namely, 'developing land in
Trans-Jordan for the settlement of Palestinian Arabs'.[29]

MacDonald's Letter dealt a severe blow not only to the traditional
political leadership but also to the underlying assumptions of their
conciliatory policies of the 'Black Letter'. The Administrative Officer
of Nablus Area was reporting that the Arab extremists used the Letter
as a means of regaining their political prestige. The implications of the
Letter were unmistakable: the Palestinians were compelled to adopt a
new strategy of closer alliance and cooperation with the Arab and
Muslim[30] worlds to achieve 'Palestinian independence within the framework of Arab unity'. This set the stage for two political forces which
were already assuming greater importance and initiative, namely, Hajj
Amin and the Arab nationalist radicals.

An Islamic Revolutionary Scheme

In May 1931, the British authorities in Palestine began receiving secret
information regarding a certain revolutionary scheme throughout the
Arab and Islamic countries to deliver the Arab countries, particularly
Palestine and Syria from foreign suzerainty.[31] The preliminary reports
indicated that Amir Shakib Arslan, the prominent Lebanese Druze
personality, was the leader of the movement and that he was in touch
with all the major Arab Nationalists in Syria, Iraq, Lebanon, Egypt and
Palestine and with various potentates in the entire Arabian Peninsula
and the Islamic countries. According to these reports Hajj Amin and
Shaukat 'Ali, the Indian Muslim leader, were parties to this 'scheme'.
The 'scheme' itself consisted of organising gangs in Trans-Jordan, wadi
Sirhan and Sinai Province for guerrilla operations in Syria and Palestine,
perhaps simultaneously.

The neighbouring countries would extend material assistance, and
forces from various Arab countries would co-operation to renew the
Syrian Revolution, perhaps, gradually.

A month later it was reported that Arab dissensions in Palestine
and the incompatibility of various Muslim elements militated against
the 'scheme''s early materialisation. These reports also indicated that
Arslan was in very close touch with Moscow which regarded Palestine
as the principal base for Soviet activities in the area. This was significant
as the Comintern had succeeded, in the wake of the 1929 events, in
achieving a semblance of unity between the Arab and Jewish
Communists in Palestine.[33]

Two factors gave added weight and credence to the police reports on this elaborate 'revolutionary scheme'. The first factor was the fear 'that the anti-Italian agitation which has been sedulously fostered in connection with alleged atrocities in Tripolitania may be converted into an anti-European movement'.[33] The second factor was the belief of the Police, shared by the Officer Administrating the Government, that the murder of three Jews near Ahava Yajour on 11 April 1931, was 'committed by members of a gang acting under the direction of a political organisation'.[34]

The Ascent of the Activists

During the summer of 1931 Arab agitation was directed against the British and the Zionists. In the purely Arab sections, particularly Nablus, Arab discontent and hostility to British rule was most apparent. The initiative was being seized by the younger Arab Nationalist activists. A top Colonial Official described the position in the following terms:

> The relations of the moderates, who so far have controlled the Arab Executive, with the extremists have long been obscure and equivocal; but there are now definite signs that the moderate element has been compelled to make some concessions to the extremists in order to maintain a perhaps precarious leadership.[35]

These concessions included the Arab Executive's refusal to accept the Government's development scheme as it was based on the Mandate and the MacDonald Letter which was unanimously rejected by the Arabs.[36] A Press campaign led to a strike against the arming of the Jewish Colonies by the Government.

The Palestine Administration retaliated by suspending Arabic newspapers accused of incitement, by suppressing a strike in Nablus with troops assisting the Police and by breaking a taxi drivers' strike in August. A number of activists were also arrested.

On 18 September two conferences were held in Palestine. The first comprised the Arab journalists who had assembled in Jaffa to denounce the oppressive British policy in Palestine, which was 'inspired by the principles of imperialism and Zionism and applied since British occupation'.[37] They were particularly resentful of the administrative suspension of Arab newspapers and the various restrictions on the freedom of the Press.

The second conference which was held on the same day was of greater significance and of more far-reaching effect. The Nablus activists had summoned the Conference to protest against the arming of the Jewish Colonies, the supression of their August demonstration and a general review of the Palestine situation. The Conference was attended by young activists from various Palestinian towns who denounced the underlying assumptions of the policy adopted by the political notability and the Arab Executive towards the Government. It was resolved that the demands of the national movement should concentrate on 'independence within Arab unity'.[38] Propaganda should be directed at the Arab and Muslim worlds. Moreover, the Palestinians were advised to encourage national industries and boycott all imports as the customs on these constituted a considerable proportion of the Government's income which was being spent on oppressing the Palestinians. A Palestinian Youth Conference was called for to endorse these principles and work for their implementation.

The General Islamic Congress

But the biggest Conference of all was the General Islamic Congress that was convened at Jerusalem in December 1931.[39] It was hoped that the Islamic Congress would focus international Muslim opinion on the Palestinian problem which had arisen after the *Buraq* incidents of 1929. Hajj Amin, assisted by Shawkat 'Ali and others, was the moving spirit of the movement. To the Mufti's own thinking the Congress would tend to strengthen the hands of the Palestinians *vis-à-vis* Zionism and the Mandate as well as consolidate his political overlordship in Palestine and his prestige in the Islamic world. A preliminary committee under his chairmanship sent invitations to Muslim religious and political leaders all over the world. The date of the Congress was fixed to coincide with a significant religious event.

The prospect of a world-wide Islamic Congress in Jerusalem specifically convened to demonstrate solidarity with the Palestinian Arabs irritated the Zionists. The fact that Hajj Amin would derive added prestige and power from it piqued his Palestinian political adversaries. As the enthusiasm for the Congress gathered momentum, the Nashashibi-led politicians who had organised themselves in the Palestine Arab Liberal Party exerted considerable political effort to thwart it and convened a rival 'Islamic Nation' Conference.

Against a background of festive preparations, the Islamic Congress was solemnly inaugurated by Hajj Amin in the presence of leading political personalities in the Arab and Muslim worlds. His speech stressed the importance of Palestine to Islam and the Muslims. After two weeks of deliberations the conferees resolved to elect an Executive Committee and establish branches all over the Muslim world. They declared the sanctity of the *al-Aqsa* Mosque and its surroundings the *Buraq,* and the central importance of Palestine to the Muslim world and denounced Zionism and British policies in Palestine. Furthermore, they proposed to build an Islamic University — The Aqsa Mosque University — and an Islamic Land Company to save Arab Lands from falling into Zionist hands. During their last session the conferees denounced Western (including British) imperialism in all Muslim lands, whereupon, British indifference to the Congress gave way to resentment.

The euphoria created by the Congress was somewhat deceptive as no great material advantage was reaped by the Palestinians later on. The Executive Committee relapsed, through the negligence and self-ishness of its members, into an honorary inactive body. A trip by Hajj Amin to collect money for the University and the Land Company was a failure owing, according to Darwaza, to British influence on the rich Muslims.[40]

The Arab National Charter

The Islamic Congress comprised a large number of the leading members of *al-Fatat* and *al-'Ahd* (1908-1918), the pillars of Faisal's regime in Damascus, known as the *Istiqla*lists (Independents). They held Arab nationalist rather than Islamic political views and availed themselves of the opportunity to discuss the affairs of the Arab world and to devise a plan for concerted action. A day or two before the Islamic Congress came to an end around fifty members met at 'Awni 'Abdul Hadi's house and drew up an 'Arab national charter'.[41]

In this remarkable document, the Arab nationalist leaders pointed out the evil political effects of the division and fragmentation of the Arab world and resolved to fight imperialism and to struggle for independence and unity for all the Arab countries. An Executive Committee, most of whose members were Palestinians, was elected mainly to propagate the 'national charter' and prepare the ground for a general conference comprising delegates from all Arab countries to devise the means and lay the plans for the implementation of the 'national charter' on a popular Pan-Arab level.

The Executive Committee lost no time in conducting the necessary contacts. In particular they were eager to obtain Faisal's backing for their conference as he was their old associate and friend, and as a monarch of an 'independent' neighbouring Arab state. At first Faisal welcomed the idea of an Arab nationalist conference in Baghdad and promised non-governmental interference. Later, however, Faisal reneged, after the British High Commissioner had advised him not to involve Iraq with Arab problems.[42] The idea collapsed to the chagrin of its sponsors and the Palestinians among them in particular.

The Islamic Congress dealt a *coupe de grace* to the Arab Executive as it led to public mutual recriminations and denunciations between the Nashashibi and Husseini factions. The formation of the Arab Liberal Party constituted another step towards the disintegration of a largely ineffective political front.

The Arab National Conference and the 'national charter' of 13 December 1931, boosted the Palestinian *Istiqlal*ists and a new level of activity became evident. The new attitude towards the British was demonstrated in the country-wide celebrations on the anniversary of Saladin's victory over the Crusaders at Hattin and in the anti-British speeches delivered on that occasion. Concurrently, the director of the Arab Executive office Subhi al-Khadra wrote a fiery article in *al-Jami'a al-'Arabiyya* attributing the calamities of Palestine and the Arabs to British policies. Other articles by Darwaza in the same paper exhorted the Arabs to fight British policies, to unite in the face of growing dangers and to renew their drive to attain freedom and independence.

The Arab Independence Party

This anti-British agitation was prelude to the emergence of the Arab Independence (*Istiqlal*) Party, of which Darwaza and al-Khadra were founding members. Before they announced the establishment of their party in August 1932, the *Istiqlal*ists held several talks with the Mufti urging the necessity of opposing British policy and the Mandate head-on. For reasons closely connected with his official positions and personal interests Hajj Amin declined to commit himself to an openly anti-British political platform. The Palestinian *Istiqlal* Party leaders were prominent members of the old *Istiqlal* movement of 1919-1925.

In their first manifesto the *Istiqlal*ists attributed the lamentable disarray in the ranks of the national movement to the egocentric and self-interested political notables who were subservient to the imperialist rulers.[43] The party founders vowed to struggle against imperialism face-to-face and fight against Jewish immigration and land sales and to endeavour to achieve a parliamentary Arab government and work for the attainment of complete Arab unity.[44] Their attacks against the political notability were followed by a call to abolish the feudal Ottoman titles of *Pasha, Bey* and *Effendi*. Their public meetings and conventions sought to propagate the principles and slogans of the Party as well as to invite wider Palestinian participation in the political process.

In 1932, a Palestinian Youth Congress was held in Jaffa to discuss ways and means of mobilising Arab youth in the service of the Arab national movement in Palestine. The Congress resolved to adopt the principles of the 'national charter', to establish branches in towns and villages, encourage national industries and organise a national Scout movement comprising a great number of able-bodied Arab youth.

Palestinian women were also spurred into action. In a long memorandum to the Permanent Mandate Commission, the Executive Committee of the First Arab Women's Congress of Palestine put forward the grievances of the Palestinians, particularly, the predicament of the *fellahin* and the failure of the Mandate to protect them against eviction,[45] and called for the abrogation of the Balfour Declaration, the abolition of the Mandate and 'the establishment of a National Government responsible to an elected representative Council with a view to attaining complete independence within an Arab Federation'.[46]

Special conferences on taxes were convened in the spring of 1932, which submitted memoranda of protest against the Government's tax policies. The (Arab) National Fund formed an Arab Redemption of Lands Corporation to save Arab lands that were likely to fall into Zionist ownership.[47]

The Zionists' uncompromising attitudes and the failure of the Government to implement promises over the introduction of self-governing institutions, i.e. the Legislative Council, tended to strengthen the hand of the *Istiqlal*ists.

In September 1932, they induced the Arab Executive to pass a resolution declaring that no Arab should serve on any Government Board or in any way cooperate with the Government. Nevertheless, Wauchope reported that 'the Mufti and a number of Nashashibi party who support me will probably arrange that this resolution shall not be acted on'.[48]

Despite the agitation of the *Istiqlal*ists against Britain Hajj Amin was remarkably cooperative with the Government:

The Mufti has definitely responded to the measure of confidence placed in him, and it is doubly satisfactory to Government that he and some of the more moderate men of the Nashashibi party are now working together with Government.[49]

Two weeks later, Wauchope reported that 'Awni 'Abdul Hadi, the prominent *Istiqlal*ist, had resigned from the Road Board to the embarrassment of other Palestinian members on Government Boards. Thereafter, Wauchope advised the Colonial Secretary, that unless the Government proceeded with the establishment of the Legislative Council, Arab 'extremists would obtain complete ascendency and that Arab cooperation would become increasingly difficult and ultimately impossible'.[50]

The *Istiqlal*ists' fresh approach was eloquently expressed in their reply to a speech delivered by the High Commissioner before the Mandates Commission in Geneva. In it they reiterated their rejection of the Balfour Declaration and the Mandate and exposed the basic aspects of the alliance between Zionism and British Imperialism. They alleged that one-third of the budget had to be allocated to defence and security expenses because of the Mandate's attempt to build an alien national home against the will of the Palestinians. As a result of this policy the Palestinians were overburdened with all kinds of taxes, and the *fellah* in particular was in a desperate position. Furthermore, the Mandatory Government had deliberately failed to live up to its duty towards the Arabs, 'the legitimate owners of the country', in the crucial fields of education, land legislation and immigration.[51]

The Prospect of Civil Disobedience

The initiative of the *Istiqlal*ists and the increase of Jewish immigration compelled the Arab Executive to invite a number of political leaders including those of the *Istiqlal* and the Youth Congress to an Assembly on 24 February 1933, under the presidency of Musa Kazem. In the course of the discussions several attacks were launched by the militants against the 'lethargic leaders', and land commission agents were denounced as traitors. Suggestions were made to the effect that civil disobedience and the boycott of British goods constituted the only effective method of forcing the Government to listen to their grievances.[52] Musa Kazem induced the Assembly, against the better judgement of the majority of those present, to elect a deputation to meet the High Commissioner on the same day. The deputation put to the High Commissioner the necessity of protecting the Arab population from dispossession and eviction[53] by prohibiting land sales and Jewish immigration, to no avail. Discouraged by Wauchope's reply, the Arab leaders finally decided to call a general assembly on 26 March in Jaffa to lay down the basis of non-cooperation with the Government.

The Jaffa meeting was attended by five to six hundred persons, townsmen and villagers of all classes and parties, including the Arab Executive, Hajj Amin and most of the mayors of the principal towns of Palestine. The policy of non-co-operation was discussed and the *Istiqlal*ists suggested social and political boycott of Government, the non-payment of direct taxes such as tithes, *werko* (a rural tax), urban property tax and the boycott of British and Jewish goods as well. However,

> Party conflict between the pro and anti-Mufti factions reigned. . . It was clear that the anti-Mufti faction was mainly concerned in placing Haj Amin in a critical position in insisting on his resignation.[54]

from the Muslim Supreme Council as a first act in the policy of non-cooperation. The Husseini-Nashahibi antagonism was not the only snag to the adoption of the policy of non-co-operation. The propertied participants were apprehensive of the consequence of non-payment of taxes. The assembly adopted the principle of non-co-operation and restricted its application to the boycott of Government receptions and Boards on the political-social level and the boycott of British and Zionist goods on the economic level. On the more crucial aspects of the non-co-operation policy, namely, the non-payment of taxes, the wiser counsels of the propertied classes prevailed.[55] The issue was referred to a committee of the members of the Arab Executive including a member representing each of the parties in the country, to study the various implications, and methods that would lead to the execution of the idea of non-co-operation. A similar decision taken ten years earlier led to the suppression of the idea altogether. The assembly was dominated by pro-Mufti elements. Ragheb Nashashibi did not attend and his supporters withdrew before the meeting came to an end, and the watering down of the policy on non-co-operation reflected Hajj Amin's friendly relations with the High Commissioner, as well as the vested interests of some of his political associates.

The lukewarm attitude of the leadership notwithstanding, the general Palestinian mood was becoming increasingly militant. When the Colonial Secretary toured Palestine in April 1933, the Arab Executive called for his boycott and alleged that he had come to 'strengthen the pillars of British and Zionist colonization'[56] and to pave the way for evicting Arabs to bring more Jews into the country.[57]

The proposed committee on non-co-operation did not materialise and the High Commissioner reported that the leaders were afraid of legal liabilities, that the pro-Nashashibi Party were definitely not disposed to participate in the proposed Committee, and that even the

Istiqlalists were not enthusiastic.[58] The eviction of the Arabs of Wadi Hawareth by the Jews, with the aid of Government forces, was the subject of Arab agitation against Jewish immigration and Government policy throughout the summer of 1933. On 10 August, the CID reported that political leaders were 'interesting themselves in finding a means to redeem lands' and that delegations were visiting villagers in Wadi Kabbani to warn against sale of lands to Jews.

The Pressure of Jewish Immigration

The flow of legal and illegal Zionist immigration assumed alarming proportions[59] and the resolutions of the Zionist Congress in Prague, which dwelt on opening the gates of Palestine to unrestricted Jewish immigration in view of the Nazi persecution, added oil to the Palestinian's fire.[60] Even the lethargic Arab Executive were induced to take a more radical stand and decided during a meeting in early September to stage a general demonstration in Jerusalem on 13 September without applying for Government permission. Other towns were to observe a strike on the same day.

At first the Government endeavoured to talk the leaders out of this challenge to its authority,[61] but later requested that the demonstration should not transcend the limits of the Old City. The well advertised demonstration was led by leaders from all political groups which inspired an unprecedented feeling of national unity and determination. Eventually, the demonstrators clashed with the police, and the authorities took legal action against a number of Arab leaders. Following the demonstration the members of the Arab Executive met at Musa Mazem's house and resolved to stage another demonstration in Jaffa four weeks later. In a memorandum to the High Commissioner, dated 30 September 1933, a number of Arab Nationalists from Nablus accused the Government of Palestine of working for the destruction of the Palestinian Arabs and their replacement by Jews and threatened to adopt self-defensive measures against the flood of Jewish Immigrants.

On 8 October, the Arab Executive decided to hold another demonstration on 13 October in Jerusalem, in defiance of the orders of the High Commissioner. Before the Friday prayers were over, the shops were closed and scores of Christians and about 50 women were waiting outside the *Haram* to join the demonstration at its starting point. The demonstration of several thousand strong revealed the depth of hostility towards the Police, and baton charges by the latter against the demonstrators reinforced that feeling. Five members of the Police and six members of the public were injured.

The prevalent sentiments and the new strategy were expressed in an article which appeared in *al-Jami'a al-'Arabiyya* on 17 October:

> Kick this Zionism with your feet and stand face to face with Great Britain. . .Zionism is nothing but a criminal enterprise encouraged by Britain and protected by its bayonets, aimed at oppressing the Arabs and bringing them under its control.

The Cause of the Poor

Although the bulk of the *Istiqlal*ists, the advocates of the new strategy, did not have pronounced leftist tendencies, their agitation against the 'lethargic leadership' swayed some of them towards the adoption of a leftist interpretation of patriotism. In a remarkable article published by *al-'Arab* on 21 June 1933, Darwaza launched a vehement attack against the Palestinian vested interests. The national cause, he argued, was in fact the cause of the poor, the majority of the people who had to bear the brunt of imperialist and Zionist oppression. The propertied and notable classes were in touch with, and subservient to, the imperialists and the Zionists. He reported that rich people were ready to leave Palestine to live in Egypt or Switzerland if the going got rough, while the poor had to stick it out and die in their battle against oppression.

As the *Istiqlal*ists' radical drive gathered strength, the position of the traditional leadership became more precarious. Two days before the Jaffa demonstration, the notables explained their 'predicament' to Wauchope in the following terms:

> We have never in the past resorted even to peaceful demonstrations; now we have been pushed to it by the people themselves. Being so pushed, we hoped that Government would help us and not force us to lead people to more serious trouble.[62]

Three days later the Arab leaders informed Wauchope that 'In the past, the leaders were able to appease the people, but now they have lost their influence'.[63]

The 1933 Revolt

Anti-Government agitation tended to point out that an outburst of feeling was imminent. The arduous preparations undertaken by Palestinian youth organisations for the Jaffa demonstration indicated the time and place of the expected clash with the Authorities. Political activists from Palestinian towns, a delegation of women from

Jerusalem[64] and special delegations from Syria and Trans-Jordan converged on the Arab port.

On the appointed day, over seven thousand angry demonstrators armed with sticks, took to the Jaffa streets. During the ensuing clashes with the Police one policeman was killed and twenty-five wounded. Twelve demonstrators were shot dead and seventy-eight wounded. Scores of arrests including the more prominent militant leaders were made.

On hearing the news of what the Arabs subsequently referred to as the Jaffa massacre, Palestinian public opinion was inflamed, and a general strike in the country was declared. Spontaneous riots and demonstrations came into conflict with the Police at Haifa and Nublus in the evening of the same day. On the following day, the streets of Haifa were barricaded and the Railway Station attacked. Scores of casualties were inflicted by police fire. A curfew was imposed, and the Harbour in Haifa was closed for three days. The District Commissioner of the Northern District was satisfied that the notables of Haifa 'did do their utmost to assist in preventing the thing getting wider'.[65]

Safad, Nazareth and Tulkarem were occupied by British troops in the early hours of 28 October, but this did not prevent the demonstrators from throwing stones at the troops. At Acre, Sheikh As'ad Shuqairi used his influence to prevent a proposed demonstration. At Nablus tension prevailed, but no clashes took place owing to the good offices of the Mayor who received the personal thanks of the District Commissioner. At Wadi Hawareth trouble was prevented by 'the timely arrival of the Royal Airforce planes'[66]

Jerusalem awaited the news of the Jaffa riot with considerable concern and nervousness. Parties of excited youths arrived from Nablus by car and visited the leaders who had returned from Jaffa. On the following morning shops began to close and crowds of demonstrators attacked the Police with stones and during the night sniping took place in the neighbourhood of Mount Scopus 'directed either at the British Police camp or at the Mayor's house'.[67]

On 29 October, Arab crowds hurled missiles, including home-made bombs, at the police and at one place the Police opened fire and inflicted considerable casualties. Tension increased as successive victims died, and sniping at the troops and Government Offices was resumed during the night. Arab shops remained closed, and it was common belief that the strike was maintained by Husseini influence strongly supported from the Supreme Moslem Council, in protest at the continued detention of Jamal Effendi Husseini. Press censorship was reimposed, and the Arabic press in protest declined to publish. The general strike was maintained until 2 November, when the Arab Executive called off the strike.

A Genuine National Feeling

Wauchope did not hesitate to inform Cunliffe-Lister that the disturbances of October 1933 were 'anti-British and anti-Government in character...No Jews were molested'.[68] The High Commissioner attributed the immediate cause of the rooting to an overpowering desire to protest against Jewish immigration:

> It would be a mistake however to imagine that sole cause of riot was Jewish National Home Immigration. A genuine national feeling is growing constantly more powerful in Palestine and more bitter against British Government and moreover reflected in other parts of Arab world.[69]

The reaction of the neighbouring Arab countries to the 1933 demonstrations was strikingly strong. Palestine was increasingly becoming the focal point of Arab nationalist agitation and concern.[70]

Following the disturbances, persistent Palestinian Arab allegations of police brutality compelled Wauchope to appoint a Commission of Enquiry. The Murison-Trusted Commission of Enquiry confined themselves to the narration of the facts and the developments that took place during the week of disturbances in the major towns of Palestine. According to their report one policeman and twenty-six Arab citizens were killed while 56 policemen and 187 Arabs were injured.[71]

The events of 1933 demonstrated a growing purposefulness among the Arabs of Palestine. An unprecedented week of strikes and clashes with Government forces throughout Palestine revealed the depth of Arab feelings against the JNH policy. Furthermore, the disturbances revealed that the Arabs were disposed towards the use of violence[72] to deflect the Mandatory from its policy, and that the real aim of the Palestinians was national independence.

Britain's Imperial Interests

The British Government, too, viewed the deteriorating situation with concern. British Imperial interests in Palestine were no longer confined to the defence of the Suez Canal. The Mosul-Haifa pipeline, the Haifa harbour and the Imperial Airways air route to India via Gaza, rendered Palestine an essential link in the Imperial strategy and the Empire's system of communication.[73]

However, rebelliousness of the Arabs tended to strengthen the bonds of alliance and cooperation between the Zionists and the British. The Government were inclined to react favourably to the Zionists' demands 'to postpone the question of a Legislative Council indefinitely'.[74] In return Ben Gurion, the influential Zionist leader, assured Wauchope that

> ...the Jews wanted Palestine to become a fraction of the British Empire; there alone safety lay.[75]

Explosive as the situation was, Wauchope was not as alarmed as might have been expected for three main reasons:

> First, because their character was purely political; second because the fellaheen did not join in the riots; and third, because the leaders showed no powers of organization.[76]

Wauchope rightly assessed that Hajj Amin was the only Palestinian force capable of altering the situation. This safety valve was under control owing

> To the agreement government made last year with the Supreme Moslem Council and to my own (at present) most happy relations with the Mufti and other members of the Supreme Moslem Council.[77]

The agreement in question was a provisional one, whereby the Government conceded to the Supreme Muslim Council complete control over *waqf* funds, as a reward for the Mufti in exercising 'his great authority over the *fellahin* to stop them heeding the extremists'.[78] When Hajj Amin succeeded in restraining Arab demonstrations against British policies in mid-January 1934, the grateful Colonial Secretary approved a permanent agreement with the Mufti over the control of *waqf* finances.[79]

It was a remarkable feat on Hajj Amin's part to achieve ascendency within the national movement in Palestine while maintaining friendly relations with the High Commissioner and a conciliatory attitude towards the British at a time when the contradiction between the two forces was becoming increasingly sharp. This could only be explained in the light of the situation obtaining inside the Arab camp at that period.

Hajj Amin's main opponents were the Nashashibis who were more pro-British than he was and their accusations against him that he was acting under Wauchope's instructions were ineffective. On the other hand there was no real challenge from the more militant Arab nationalist groups as the *Istiqlal* Party had ceased to be an effective organised force in the latter part of 1933, partly owing to Hajj Amin's efforts to sabotage their reputation and position within the national movement.[80] According to Emile Ghoury, one of Hajj Amin's more eloquent and educated assistants, the Mufti had worked out an understanding of cooperation and alliance with many of the leading *Istiqlal*ists following the decline of the Party in 1933.[81]

In the wake of the 1933 riots, the Mufti persevered in his conciliatory attitude towards the British without attaching great hopes to any significant change in British policy. Wauchope was convinced that Hajj Amin was moderate and willing to help the Government maintain order:

> I am confident that the Mufti likes me, respects me and is anxious to help me...He realizes the folly of unlawful demonstration and clashes with the authority but he fears that the criticisms of his many opponents that he is too British may weaken his influence in the country. The fact, however, that his influence is on the side of moderation is of definite value were it contrawise I consider widespread disturbances would be inevitable.[82]

Hajj Amin's reverence for authority, and 'the folly of unlawful demonstration' reflected his fear of British military prowess and his realization that the Arabs could not possibly win in a head-on collision with Britain. On the other hand as a leader of the national movement in Palestine he could not remain quiescent while Zionist immigration was assuming threatening proportions.

Self-Organisation

The Arab Bank, established in 1930, was strengthened in 1934 to become a major financial and political Arab national institution. An Arab agricultural Bank was started with a capital of £60,000 for development of Arab land. The (Arab) National Fund campaigned for public subscriptions and started buying lands that would otherwise have been sold to the Jews. An active propaganda campaign against sales of land to Jews was waged by the Supreme Muslim Council in the mosques and in the Arab Press. Small landowners were encouraged to register their lands as family *Waqfs* to prevent subsequent alienation.

A more difficult task to cope with was the prevention of illicit Jewish immigration which was on the increase owing to greater Nazi pressures on German Jewry. This task was entrusted to the Arab Youth Conference which organised Arab Scout units to patrol the coasts and intercept boats smuggling Jewish immigrants during the night.[83]

Another measure of self-defence and self-organisation was brought about by the Histadrut's attempt to prevent the employment of Arab labour by Jewish entrepreneurs through 'intimidation of employer and employed'.[84] Arab Labour Garrisons to prevent intimidation and attacks by Jewish labour were formed in Jerusalem, Jaffa and Haifa. These were followed by the formation of Arab Labour Committees which made their political debut on the occasion of the Balfour anniversary when the transport workers observed a national strike.

The third Arab nationalist demand, that of self-governing institutions could not be achieved without the cooperation of the British. Hajj Amin told Wauchope that the Arabs 'looked forward towards a Parliament with full powers and not to a Legislative Council with limited powers'.[85] The Arabs, in fact, were willing to accept a Legislative Council where the demographic composition of the population would be reflected.[86] Zionist opposition to the Legislative Council proved insurmountable and no substantial progress on this issue was made before the latter part of 1935.[87]

Instead of establishing a national self-governing institution which would focus the Palestinians' attention on the basic issues at stake and promote a sense of purposefulness to the Arabs' political efforts against the JNH policy, Wauchope introduced an electoral side-show on the local municipal level. This innocuous dose of participatory democracy sharpened family dissensions and rivalries as might have been expected. However, the defeat of Ragheb Nashashibi in the Jerusalem Municipal elections of 1934 upset the Husseini-Nashashibi balance, which had been maintained since 1920, and concentrated more power in the hands of Hajj Amin. The bitterness engendered by the elections and the death of Musa Kazem dealt a final flow to the moribund Arab Executive, and each political faction proceeded to form a party of its own.

The Palestinian Arab Parties

The first party to emerge in December 1934 was the National Defence Party headed by Ragheb Nashashibi. Four months later the Palestine Arab Party emerged led by Jamal Husseini, the Mufti's political protagonist. The National Defence Party comprised a number of rich powerful notables and mayors who vowed

> To endeavour to achieve independence for Palestine with full Arab sovereignty, and not to recognize any international obligation which is calculated to culminate in any foreign predominance or influence.[88]

The Palestine Arab Party, which was a popular party with numerous branches throughout Palestine was more unequivocal in its determination to fight Zionism and the Mandate at one and the same time.[89] Unlike the Nashashibi-led rival, the Arab Party was in favour of Arab unity and engaged themselves in practical efforts to prevent sales of Arab lands to Jews.

A month later the second meeting of the Arab Youth Congress was convened. The discussions were devoted to social and economic self-improvement and the mobilisation of the younger Arab generation in sports clubs and youth organisations dedicated to fighting Zionism in a down-to-earth practical manner.[90] Though not politically antagonistic to either party the upshot of their second conference was to establish the Youth Congress as another political body in Palestine. Two other political parties were founded before the end of 1933, the Khalidi-led *Islah* (Reform) Party and the National Bloc led by Abdul Latif Salah, a well-known lawyer from Nablus, both of whose declared aims were close to those of the Palestine Arab Party.

The personal and selfish motives behind the proliferation of Arab parties were apparent to all Palestinians, and the ceaseless bickering between these parties exposed them to public derision.[91]

Eviction of Arab Peasants

While the politicians and notables were promoting their respective personal and family interests and adding to internal dissensions, the bulk of the Palestinian Arabs were growing increasingly bitter and desperate. The spectacular increase in Jewish immigration exerted additional pressures on the Zionist organs to acquire new lands for Jewish settlement. Out of 673 land transactions effected in 1933, most of which were from Arabs to Jews, 606 were in respect of areas each less than 100 *dunums* in extent. In the following year the number of sales increased to 1,178 including no fewer than 1,116 for areas each less than 100 *dunums* in extent.[92] The vendors were either rendered landless or left with lands not adequate to provide subsistence level income for the peasant landlords. The landless Arabs were becoming a major political issue because of the rapid increase in their numbers and the fears this engendered among the Palestinian rural population. The implementation of eviction orders (by the Courts) could no longer be effected without the efforts of large numbers of Police. The Arab peasants were showing greater determination in resisting the execution of eviction orders. During January 1935, the Hartieh Lands eviction was resisted by the tenants, *'Arab el-Zubeidat,* and the battle between them and forty-three British and Palestinian Police ended with seven British Police and five Palestinian Police injured by the stone-slinging villagers.

Facing an increasingly delicate and precarious situation, Hajj Amin had to adopt a stronger public stand against Zionism. While endeavouring to avoid direct personal involvement in the mutual recriminations of the newly formed parties, he involved himself in public efforts to mobilise the Islamic religious machine in the fight against Zionism. On 25 January, Hajj Amin, as President of the Supreme Muslim Council, convened a meeting of some five hundred religious functionaries, mostly *qadis,* Sheikhs and *'ulamas* at Jerusalem to discuss, principally, the sale of land to Jews, brokerage and Jewish immigration. The Mufti, however, confined himself to threatening with religious penalties Muslims who sell their lands or act as land brokers, without advocating more violent methods to fight Zionism.[93]

In his relations with the British the Mufti continued to display a friendly disposition. In the course of denying allegations levelled against Hajj Amin by the Nashashibi faction that the Mufti was intriguing with the Italians, Wauchope reported:

> I have noticed no change in Hajj Amin's attitude towards this Government — his attitude for the last two years and now is definitely friendly, and especially so towards me, as you already know. The Mufti is always troubled by the thought he may lose influence on this account, but I see no signs of his power waning or of his adopting a hostile attitude towards this Government.[94]

The Mufti, as a matter of fact, had asked the CID chief for police protection and obtained a bullet-proof jacket as he feared hired assassin.

The bullet-proof jackets were not the only hedge Hajj Amin had against extremists. According to Emile Ghoury, a secret youth organisation in Jerusalem formed after the October-November events of 1933, was turned into *Munazzamat al-Jihad al-Muqaddas* (The Organisation for

Waging Holy War) under the leadership of a young revolutionary, 'Abdul-Qader Husseini, son of Musa Kazem and an associate of the Mufti.[95] Furthermore, Hajj Amin was in touch with Sheikh 'Izzeddin al-Qassam.

Qassam's Revolt

The Syrian-born Qassam immigrated to Haifa in 1921, after the failure of the Syrian revolt against French occupation in which he was a prominent leader. As a man of immense religious learning and as an eloquent orator, he had no difficulty in joining the staff of the Islamic School at Haifa. He later joined the Muslim Young Men's Association[96] and became its President in 1926. As an ardent Muslim and a patriot, he stood against Zionism and British rule, and in 1929 he started roaming the villages of the North as an employee of the Shari'a Court of Haifa. His contacts with the *fellahin* in the villages and the prayers in the *Istiqlal* mosque in Haifa enabled him to recruit some revolutionary elements which he organised in secret groups not exceeding five members.[97] He preached to them the necessity of revolt against subservience to the alien infidels – Jews and Britons alike. In 1932, he joined Haifa's *Istiqlal* Party branch. After the events of 1933, he started collecting contributions to buy small quantities of arms in preparation for a revolt against the Government, the real sponsor of Zionism in Palestine. His preparations were managed with the utmost degree of secrecy.

Qassam's stronghold was the shanty-town of Haifa where 270 poor peasants who had moved to the bustling harbour-town were compelled to live as they were unemployed or poorly paid. He showed genuine concern for their welfare and started a night school to fight illiteracy among these worker-peasants. His frequent visits to the villages and his personal decency endeared him to the peasants of Northern Palestine.

By 1935, Qassam had organised five committees: propaganda, military training, supply, intelligence and foreign relations. It was not unlikely that Qassam was in touch with the Italians, whose interests in Palestinian affairs was enhanced by their Ethiopian campaign and the ensuing tension with Britain over the matter.[98] This secret contact with the Italians was solely motivated by a practical need to cooperate with the enemies of Britain.

Although Qassam had recruited two hundred members and organised 800 sympathisers, he had no real contact with the peasants and workers – on which he depended – in Southern or Central Palestine. According to Subhi Yasin, a Qassamite, the Sheikh had actually sent one of his followers, Mahmud Salem, to the Mufti asking him to declare a revolt in the South simultaneous to Qassam's declaration of revolt in the North. Hajj Amin reportedly answered that he was working for political solution rather than an armed revolt.[99]

A number of events that took place during 1935 forced the hand of Qassam and his fellow *Mujahidin* to initiate an armed revolt against the British and the Zionists in November of that year.

Before the end of 1935 Wauchope reported to the Colonial Secretary that one-fith of the Arab villagers were already landless, the number of Arab unemployed workers in the towns was rising, and resentment against the Government was growing day by day.[100]

Furthermore, no hopeful developments were anywhere in sight as the immigration figure for 1935 approximated a record number of 60,000 and the rise in unemployment compelled Wauchope to conclude that this figure was 'beyond the absorptive capacity of the country'.[101]

Zionist provocations, such as open military drilling and assaults on Arab villagers by the Revisionists, enraged Arab public opinion. The discovery of a considerable consignment of arms to the Zionists confirmed the Palestinians' worst fears. As there was no hope that the Government would respond to Arab demands over immigration, land sales and Parliamentary Government, armed uprising was the only alternative left to the Arabs to prevent Zionist hegemony in Palestine.

While the Palestinian politicians were exposing their compromising and faint-hearted attitudes towards the Government, Qassam and twenty-five of his armed associates left Haifa on the night of 12 November and headed towards the vicinity of Jenin to call on the peasants to take up arms against the British and the Zionists. Before they could propagate their message and capture Haifa by surprise, an accidental clash with the Police alerted the Authorities to the presence of an armed band, and Police and troops were quick to cordon off the area.

Inspired by the Islamic duty of *Jihad* (Holy War), Qassam refused to surrender and urged his followers to fight and die as martyrs for the sake of God and the Homeland. On 19 November, Qassam and two of his comrades were killed, five others were captured and the rest disappeared in the mountains.

The news of Qassam's heroic death had a tremendous impact throughout Palestine. He soon become the symbol of self-sacrifice and martyrdom, and his funeral at Haifa was a great national demonstration against the Government and the JNH during which the Police were stoned. The political leaders declined to attend his funeral and their goodwill messages on that occasion were lukewarm. They could not help feeling that Qassam's revolt was an indictment of their futile methods and that his selflessness contrasted with their selfish motives and pursuits.

Subsequently, however, the Palestinian leaders felt compelled to adopt a less conciliatory policy towards the British. In an interview with Wauchope six days after Qassam's death, representatives of the five Arab parties submitted a memorandum and told the High Commissioner that

Unless they received a reply to their memorandum which could be generally regarded as giving satisfaction to their requests, they would lose all influence with their followers; extreme and irresponsible counsels would prevail and the political situation would rapidly deteriorate.[102]

In his covering letter Wauchope informed J.H. Thomas, the new Colonial Secretary, that the Arab leaders were

right in saying that otherwise they will lose such influence as they possess and that the possibility of alleviating the present situation by means of moderate measures suggested by me will disappear.[103]

Qassam's revolt cast a long shadow on the Palestinian political scene, and any attempt to effect a detente in the situation was doomed to failure. Less than a month after the troops' encounter with Qassam, the CID was expressing its concern at the turn of events. Hostility against the Government, they reported, had spread to the villages of Palestine. Qassam and his followers were held in high esteem as heroes and martyrs. There were popular discussions over the fact that the Egyptian nationalists had obtained concessions from the British only after they resorted to more violent means than hitherto. A more serious development was the emergence of radical youth groups under revolutionary leadership to replace the discredited older political leadership.

The new formations popped up in the major towns and were led or inspired by the young radical with whose name the group was associated. Akram Zu'ayter was associated with the Nablus group and Hamdi Husseini led the Jaffa radicals in collaboration with Michel Mitri, leader of the Arab Labour Society of Jaffa. At Qalqilya a new Revolutionary Youth Committee was formed; in Tulkarem, Salim 'Abdul Rahman and the Arab Scout leaders led another youth group;

and at Haifa 'Aref Nuralla led a similar movement. These groups were supported by Darwaza and 'Ajaj Nweihed, both of them founding members of the *Istiqlal* Party. Hamdi Husseini and Akram Zu'ayter contributed regular articles to Jamal Husseini's newspaper *al-Liwa* (The Standard).

According to CID reports these combined groups intended:

(a) To direct political agitation against the British authorities, and not against Zionism. This is clear from their writings and speeches.

(b) To force the Party leaders to adopt some firm decision at the Nablus meeting on the 15th January, such as non-cooperation, non-payment of taxes, demonstrations, etc.

(c) To stimulate agitation and public feeling until the meeting on the 15th January.

(d) Subsequently to create disorders.[104]

The shape of things to come had already been determined, and the showdown between the British and the Palestinian Arabs became only a matter of time.

Notes

1. Chancellor to Passfield, 17 January 1930, CO 733/182, p.2.
2. Chancellor to Passfield, 22 February 1930, CO 733/190.
3. Toynbee, Arnold *Survey of International Affairs, 1930.* London, 1931, p.282.
4. Chancellor to Passfield, 22 February 1930, op.cit., p.8.
5. Ibid., p.9.
6. Shaw Commission Report, op.cit., p.113.
7. In the years 1921-1925 the Jews acquired 236,000 *dunums* almost exclusively from individual absentee landlords. Between 1921 and 1930 the Jews gradually acquired undivided shares in the village lands, which they sought to partition and dispossess the villagers of the lands. Ibid., pp.51-2.
8. Ibid., p.129.
9. Ibid., p.98.
10. For a report submitted by the Delegation on the London negotiation to the Executive Committee on 27 July 1930, see Documents, op.cit., pp.181-8.
11. See Chancellor to Passfield, 17 April 1930, Enclosure, CO 733/185.
12. According to a report by Hyamson, Chief Immigration Officer, the number of unemployed was in excess of 12,000 in December 1930, see Chancellor to Passfield, 18 July 1931, Enclosure A, CO 733/202.
13. See Departmental Note by Shuckburgh, 18 June 1930, June 733/185.
14. Ibid.
15. 'Palestine: Report on Immigration, Land Settlement and Development by Sir John Hope-Simpson', Cmd. 3686, 1930.
16. 'Palestine: Statement of Policy by His Majesty's Government in the United Kingdom', Cmd. 3692, 1930.
17. These estimates were quoted in the Peel Commission Report, op.cit., p.71.

18. Ibid., p.74.
19. See Chancellor to Passfield, 4 November 1930, CO 733/182.
20. Documents, op.cit., pp.189-90.
21. Note by Shuckburgh to S. Wilson, 15 December 1930, CO 733/178.
22. Chancellor to Shuckburgh, 16 January 1931, CO 733/178. Also see same to same, 13 February 1931, CO 733/197.
23. Passfield to Chancellor, 9 January 1931, CO 733/197.
24. Passfield to Chancellor, 6 February 1931, CO 733/197.
25. Weizmann, op.cit., pp.415. In July 1931, the Zionists put forward their claim for 'parity' with the Arabs in Palestine when they constituted one-fifth of the population, and then advanced their official claim to be treated as 'partners' of the British in Palestine. See Note by Shuckburgh to Colonial Secretary, 24 July 1931, CO 733/197. According to the Palestine census of 1931, there were 759,952 Muslims, 90,607 Christians and 175,000 Jews in Palestine. See 10 December 1931, CO 733/206.
26. See Chancellor to Passfield, 17 February 1931, CO 733/197, p.7.
27. Documents, op.cit., p.232.
28. See 'Note on Interview given to Dr Weizmann by the High Commissioner on 20 March, 1931', CO 733/203, p.2.
29. Ibid., p.5.
30. In 1930 the Muslims of India, Ceylon and Burma demonstrated their solidarity with the Palestinian Arabs by declaring 16 May of every year a 'Palestine Day'. See Documents, op.cit., pp.171-2.
31. See report on 'The Pan Islamic Arab Revolutionary Movement', by Criminal Investigation Department, Palestine Police, 20 May 1931, CO 733/204.
32. For the Communists' roles and attitudes in the early thirties, see Laqueur, op.cit., pp.86-95.
33. Officer Administrating the Government (OAG) to Passfield, 30 May 1931, CO 733/204.
34. Ibid.
35. O.G.R. Williams, 'Arab Incitement', 3 September 1931, CO 733/204.
36. See Documents, op.cit., pp.236-7.
37. Ibid., p.245.
38. Ibid., pp.243-4.
39. See H.A.R. Gibb, 'The Islamic Congress at Jerusalem in December 1931', in *Survey of International Affairs, 1934*, edited by A.J. Toynbee, London, 1935, pp.99-108.
40. See Darwaza, op.cit., p.86.
41. Professor Brodetsky, the Zionist leader and liaison officer with the Colonial Office, expressed Zionist anxiety regarding Pan-Arabism in Palestine. 'He regarded the pan-Islamic Congress movement as a failure, but pan-Arabism, he thought, was a much more serious thing'. 'Note on conversation with Professor Brodetsky', 9 September 1932, CO 733/215, p.5. For the text of the document.
42. See Darwaza, op.cit., pp.88-9.
43. The *Istiqlal*ists' newspaper *al-'Arab* alleged that some members of the Arab Executive were land agents for the Jews. See *al'Arab*, 17 September 1932.
44. See Documents, op.cit., pp.261-5.
45. During the winter of 1932 Wauchope informed Phillip Cunliffe-Lister that the poorer fellahin were obliged to purchase flour, and many others lost half their flocks through starvation and that a feeling of general hopelessness prevailed. 5 March 1932, CO 733/215.
46. 28 January 1932, CO 733/221.
47. See Documents, op.cit., pp.257-69, passim.

48. Wauchope to Cunliffe-Lister, 16 September 1932, CO 733/219.
49. Ibid.
50. Cabinet. 'Palestine: Legislative Council', Memorandum by the Secretary of State for the Colonies, 3 November 1932, CO 733/219.
51. See Documents, op.cit., pp.284-298, passim.
52. Daily Intelligence Summary, No. 39/33, 25 February 1933, CO 733/234.
53. Two days before the assembly convened, an attempt to evict Arabs from lands bought by Jews in Tulkarem's vicinity led to clashes between the evicted Arabs and a Jewish *Chaffir* (village guard) which resulted in the death of the latter.
54. See Wauchope to Cunliffe-Lister, Enclosure III, 1 April 1933, CO 733/234.
55. *Falastin* stated that those who advocated non-payment of taxes were not tax-payers and those who advocated non-attendance of Government functions were those who were not invited.
56. Quoted in *Falastin,* 24 April 1933.
57. For measures taken to facilitate entry of German Jews see Wauchope to Cunliffe-Lister, 12 April 1933, CO 733/236.
58. see Extract from Periodical Appreciation Summary No. 17/33, 20 June 1933, CO 733/239.
59. In a despatch to the Colonial Secretary, Wauchope admitted that 'during the past twelve months the control of immigration into Palestine has broken down, and the principle of allowing settlers to enter in accordance with the absorptive capacity of the country has not been observed'. 3 August 1933, CO 733/236.
60. See Memorandum by the Supreme Muslim Council to the H.Cr. 3 September 1933, CO 733/239.
61. Ragheb Nashshibi opposed the idea of holding demonstrations and used his influence to persuade some villagers to keep away from Jerusalem that Friday. See Wauchope to Cunliffe-Lister, 23 October 1933, CO 733/239.
62. Interview between Wauchope and the Arab Executive on the 25th October, CO 733/239.
63. Interview between Wauchope and a group of Arab leaders, 28 October 1933, CO 733/239.
64. In their interview with Wauchope on 30th October, the Arab ladies displayed more courage and determination than their notable menfolk. See Wauchope to Cunliffe-Lister, 2 November 1933, Enclosure A, CO 733/239.
65. See Keith-Roach to Chief Secretary, 7 November 1933. Enclosure to Wauchope to Cunliffe-Lister, 24 November 1933, CO 733/239, p.6.
66. Ibid:, p.13.
67. Campbell to Chief Secretary, 'Summary of Events in Jerusalem Districts 27th October, 4th November, 1933', 6 November 1933, CO 733/239, p.2.
68. Wauchope to Cunliffe-Lister, 6 November 1933, CO 733/239.
69. Ibid.
70. See Consul MacKereth (Damascus) to Sir John Simon, 1 November 1933, CO 733/239.
71. 4 January 1934, CO 733/239, p.36.
72. See Wauchope to Cunliffe-Lister, 10 November 1933, CO 733/239.
73. See Royal Institute of International Affairs, *Political Strategic Interests of the United Kingdom,* London, 1939, 1940, pp.142-4.
74. Wauchope to Cunliffe Lister, 16 August 1934, CO 733/265.
75. Ibid.
76. Cabinet, 'The Situation in Palestine', 18 December 1933, Annex dated, 18 December 1933, Annex dated.
77. Ibid., p.2.

78. See Wauchope to Cunliffe-Lister, 5 February 1934, CO 733/254.
79. Cabinet. Palestine, 28 March 1934, CO 733/258, p.2.
80. See Darwaza, op.cit., pp.109-10.
81. Interview with Emile Ghoury, Beirut, August, 1967.
82. Wauchope to Cunliffe-Lister, 5 January 1934, CO 733/258, pp.3-4.
83. The Government resented this unsolicited help from Arab volunteers to apply the law against illegal Jewish immigration and subsequently prohibited the formation of these patrols.
84. OAG to Cunliffe-Lister, 12 September 1934, CO 733/257.
85. Wauchope to Cunliffe-Lister, 25 August 1934, Enclosure A, CO 733/265.
86. Hajj Amin insisted on the representatives being directly elected by the people while Ragheb Nashashibi preferred an appointed Legislative Council owing to his weak position with the electorate.
87. Cabinet. 'Palestine Legislative Council', 14 November 1934, CO 733/265. The Prime Minister was of the opinion that the Zionist demand for 'parity' with the Arabs in the Legislative Council 'was a good thing'. Also see Departmental note by Downie, 'Palestine Legislative Council', 4 October 1934, CO 733/265.
88. Mogannam, op.cit., p.237.
89. See Documents, op.cit., pp.359-68.
90. see Sifri, op.cit., pp.196-201.
91. See *Falestin*, 3 July 1935.
92. Wauchope to Cunliffe-Lister, 6 March 1935, CO 733/272.
93. For a report on the Conference of the 'Ulama, see Wauchope to Cunliffe-Lister, 4 March 1935, CO 733/278.
94. Wauchope to Cunliffe-Lister, April 1935, CO 733/278.
95. Ghoury related the gist of a conversation between 'Abdul Qader and a few young revolutionaries with Hajj Amin in 1934 to the effect that the Mufti thought their enthusiasm to fight the British face-to-face was premature.
96. For the Constitution of the Association, see Documents, pp.97-101.
    Not to be confused with the Egyptian association bearing the same name.
97. Some of Qassam's followers reported that the revolutionaries of the early thirties were impatient members of Qassam's secret organisations who opposed their leader's call for further preparations before declaring the Revolution. See SubhiYasin, *Harb al Isabat fi-Falastin* (Guerrilla Warfare in Palestine), Cairo, 1967, pp.68-70.
98. See Naji Allush, *Al-Muqawama al-'Arabiyaa fi Falastin, 1917-1948* (The Arab Resistance in Palestine), Beirut, 1967, p.102. The Italians were much assailed in Palestine for their oppression of the Muslim Arab population of Libya, in addition to a violent anti-Italian campaign waged by *Falastin* in the wake of the Ethiopian invasion.
99. Subhi Yasin, *al-Thawra al-'Arabiyya al-Kubra fi Falastin, 1936-1939.* (The Great Arab Revolt in Palestine), Damascus, 1959, p.23.
100. 7 December 1935, CO 733/294.
101. Ibid.
102. Wauchope to J.H. Thomas, 7 December 1935, CO 733/294.
103. Ibid.
104. See Rice to Chief Secretary, 14 December 1935, CO 733/297.

7 THE GREAT PALESTINE REVOLT: 1936-1939

The gathering clouds of autumn 1935, presaged the impending storm of 1936. The number of landless Arab peasants and the number of unemployed Arabs in the big cities was on the increase. The Arabs were becoming increasingly convinced that if no restrictions on Jewish immigration were imposed they would soon become a minority in their own country, and that if no limitations were imposed on land sales, the Arab peasants would be uprooted and evicted from their homeland. The economic crisis of 1935 further aggravated the situation. Qassam's revolt, though abortive, pointed out the only way left to the Palestinians to resist a Zionist take-over of their country, and many of Qassam's associates and disciples were still at large ready to take up arms against the JNH and the British at the earliest opportunity. Rising tides of nationalist struggle in Egypt and Syria against foreign rule encouraged radical Muslim and Arab nationalist elements to adopt similar methods to attain the same ends in Palestine. The Mediterranean crisis precipitated by Italy's Ethiopian campaign gave rise to hopes that a European War, which was believed to be imminent, would provide an opportunity for the Arabs to realise their long-sought political and national aims. The smuggling of arms on a relatively large scale by the Jews attracted attention to the prospect of armed conflict between the Arabs on the one hand and the Jews and the British on the other.

Alive to the dangerous state of Arab opinion in Palestine the High Commissioner was authorised, one month after Qassam's revolt, to make an announcement regarding the setting up of a legislative council, which was followed shortly by a proposal in connection with the limitation of land sales. The Jewish leaders categorically rejected the scheme while emphasising 'their desire and determination to maintain cooperation with Government in all matters save only that of the Legislative Council'.[1]

The proposals were critically received by the Arabs, but even Jamal Husseini, who was very critical of the scheme, thought it well to give Wauchope a private assurance 'that nothing that he said should be regarded as rejection of the proposals'.[2] Arab objections to the composition and powers of the Legislative Council notwithstanding, the scheme itself and the Land Transfer Legislation proposals had a tranquillising effect on the Arabs. The agitation against the Government continued, albeit in less violent forms, and sums of money were being collected in Egypt and elsewhere to subsidise the pro-Mufti elements and the *Istiqlal* groups.

Zionist efforts to fight the Government's Legislative Council proposals were instrumental in bringing about a change of policy. In February a debate in the House of Lords took place, followed by a debate in the Commons in March which revealed the existence of 'serious doubt in all parts of the House as to the desirability of proceeding with the proposals'.[3]

The impact of the Commons debate on the Arabs was predictable. It reminded them of the Zionist efforts that preceded the publication of the 'Black Letter'[4] and justified the radicals' call for a total boycott of all negotiations with the Government.

Despite the setback represented by the Commons debate and the hostile public mood, the National Defence Party displayed a singular eagerness to accept the proposals of the Legislative Council. On 29 March the National Defence Party officially declared their acceptance of the proposals and two days later Ragheb Nashashibi urged the leaders of the other parties to do likewise. Jamal Husseini refused to comply as it was the responsibility of the Arab Party's Executive Committee to determine the attitude of the Party on major issues.

On 2 April 1936, the High Commissioner summoned the leaders of the Arab parties and told them that the Colonial Secretary had extended an invitation to representatives of the five Arab parties to send a deputation to London to lay their views before him. After a short discussion the Arab leaders agreed that it was their unanimous wish to accept the Secretary of State's invitation. Twelve days later, however, the Arab Party issued a manifesto in which it declared its rejection of the Legislative Council proposals as these were not in consonance with the aspirations of the country for complete independence and Arab unity.[5] The decision was a shrewd move calculated to enhance the popular standing of the Arab Party and embarrass all the other parties which had already accepted the proposals. The objection to the Legislative Council scheme was not accompanied by a withdrawal from the membership of the delegation.[6] The disputes over the membership of the delegation delayed the departure of the Arab leaders and, before they could reach agreement, events had overtaken them yet again.

Tension between Arabs and Jews had been steadily rising since the beginning of autumn 1935, as a result of Zionist opposition to self-governing institutions. Continued Jewish immigration on a large scale and further land acquisition did not relax the prevailing tensions. In February 1936, the Government awarded a contract to build three Arab schools in Jaffa to a Jewish contractor who refused to employ a single Arab labourer. An Arab Labour Garrison was formed to picket the site of the school and racial animosity ticked like a time-bomb ready to explode at any moment.

The incident which triggered the violent events was trivial yet enough to throw the country into turmoil and revolution. On 13 April, one Jew was killed and two Jews were seriously wounded in the course of a general hold-up by Arab bandits on the main roads between Nablus and Tulkarem. The following night two Arabs on the main road north of Petah Tikvah were murdered in their huts, as an act, so the Arabs believed, of Jewish reprisal. The funeral of the Jew killed in the hold-up on 17 April led to angry Jewish demonstrations where the demonstrators attempted to penetrate into Jaffa but were turned away by the Police whom they stoned.[7] A series of assaults on Arab vegetable merchants began in Tel Aviv and on 19 April following the circulation of rumours that more Arabs had been killed by Jews, clashes occurred between Arabs and Jews on the border between Jaffa and Tel Aviv, and a number of casualties on both sides were inflicted.

A curfew was imposed on Tel Aviv and Jaffa and the Palestine (Defence) Order in Council and the emergency regulations thereunder were brought into force throughout Palestine.

Spontaneous Reactions

During the clashes of 19 April, scores of Arabs were injured and many Arab houses were burnt. Arab reaction to the news in all parts of Palestine was spontaneous and violent.[8] On 20 April an Arab National Committee was formed at Nablus, where it was resolved that a general strike should be declared throughout the country and maintained until such time as the Government had conceded the demands put forward in the previous November.

On the following day National Committees led by *Istiqlal*ists, young students and activists were formed in Haifa, Jaffa and Gaza which declared themselves in sympathy with the national demands and the national strike declared by the Nablus Committee. Wauchope admitted to the Colonial Secretary that 'the strike was begun independently and spontaneously in various places by various committees and groups'.[9]

The Arab parties were quick to react. The National Block and the Youth Congress associated themselves, without hesitation, with the

Nablus and Jaffa National Committees respectively. The Arab Party, anxious not to repeat its loss of initiative (of November 1935), declared its support for a general strike as from 21 April.

> The moderates of the National Defence Party under the leadership of Ragheb Bey Nashshibi and the commercial element who stood to lose most heavily, while recognising the necessity for some strong national manifestation were inclined to limit the strike for a definite period.[10]

On 21 April Wauchope interviewed the party leaders and asked them to use their influence to check all forms of disorder and to name their delegates to London to meet the Colonial Secretary on 4 May in London.

Anti-British Feelings

The Arab leaders told Wauchope that they were quite willing to help him in restoring order 'but their task would be facilitated if immigration was stopped at once'[11] as a temporary measure pending further negotiations. Jamal Husseini complained that 'The attitude of the Police had given the impression to the Arabs that their real enemies were the British'.[12] In view of the situation, the leader of the Arab Party added that the deputation would not proceed to London until peace was re-established in the country.

Anti-British feeling was the outstanding feature of the National Committee's call for a general strike. In its manifesto, the Haifa National Committee attributed the root of evil to the oppressive policy of the British Government.[13]

Anxious to associate themselves with the sweeping popular sentiments the leaders of the five Arab parties issued a manifesto on 22 April where they declared the postponement of the departure of the deputation to London and requested 'the honourable nation to continue its present strike exhibiting patience, quietness and determination until further notice. Flour mills, bakeries, clinics, dispensaries, means of transport and cafes are temporarily and until further notice excluded from this strike'.[14]

Two days later, the National Committee of Jerusalem met and formed special organs to supervise the general strike. Committees for relief,[15] fund-raising, promotion of national industries and products, transport, legal and medical services were formed to help the people maintain the general strike and sustain hardship thereof. On the same day Arab owners and drivers of public and private motor cars and trucks in Palestine joined the Arab shopkeepers, students, workers and the Jaffa Port labourers in their general strike.

On 25 April a meeting of all Arab parties took place and a supreme committee later known as the Arab Higher Committee was established. Hajj Amin reluctantly accepted the presidency of the Committee. He attributed his hesitation to his fear that the other political leaders would not cooperate with him. It was more than likely that the real reason for his reluctance was connected with his unwillingness to come into direct clash with the British. The other members of the Committee were 'Awni 'Abdul Hadi (Secretary), Ahmed Hilmi Pasha (Treasurer), Ragheb Nashashibi, Jamal Husseini, 'Abdul Latif Salah, Dr Hussein Khalidi, Ya'quob al-Ghussein, Ya'quob Farraj and Alfred Rock. In an atmosphere of enthusiasm the Higher Committee announced that the leaders were now committed 'to continue the General Strike until the British Government changes its present policy in a fundamental manner, the beginning of which is the stoppage of Jewish immigration.'[16] They also reiterated their adherence to the three national demands of the 'national charter', stoppage of immigration, prohibition of land sales and a national government responsible to a representative council.

The Higher Committee delegated the task of co-ordinating the activities of the various National Committees to 'Awni 'Abdul Hadi who maintained daily contact by telephone. He immediately embarked on a course of involving the Arab Kings and soliciting their assistance. A memorandum to the H.Cr. dwelt on Jewish plans to make Arab Palestine the land of Israel — a national state for all the Jews of the world and maintained that the continuation of the British policy would lead to the immediate annihilation of the Arabs of Palestine.[17] Arab bitterness against the Jews was accentuated by a speech delivered by Weizmann in Tel Aviv on 23 April, in which he said that the Arab-Zionist struggle was one between the forces of the desert and destruction on one side and the forces of civilisation and building on the other.[18]

Before the end of April Arab work and trade were virtually at a standstill and violent clashes between Arab demonstrators and the police had already led to sabotage and terrorist acts in Jerusalem.

The Aim of the Palestinian Struggle

On the eve of the general convention of the National Committees, a meeting of the Arab Women in Jerusalem urged the Higher Committee and the National Committees to boycott the Government and refrain from entering any negotiations until the Arab demands were conceded. A similar manifesto in Jenin declared that no party or Committee had the right to negotiate with the Government or take any decisive step without prior consultation with a national convention. On 8 May the Convention of the National Committees was held in Jerusalem. The Arab radicals carried the day, and the convention resolved not only to continue the Strike but also to press for 'no taxation without representation'. The aim of the Palestinian struggle was declared to be 'complete Palestinian independence within the framework of Arab Unity'.[19] The Arab Transport Committee urged that government officials (Arab) should be asked to join the strike but no resolution to that effect was adopted.

It soon became evident that women and students were playing a major role in maintaining morale and providing personnel for the organisation of relief, demonstrations and medical aid.[20]

Two days after the Convention the student committees held a convention in Jaffa and resolved to support the national demands, to boycott British and Zionist goods and to withdraw from the British Baden-Powell Scout Movement. On the same day several bombs exploded near government offices and on the following day outside the Central Police Station. Already there were signs that disorders were spreading to the rural areas of Palestine. A conference of the rural National Committee was held at Nablus where it was resolved to advocate the non-payment of taxes, to denounce the installation of Police stations in some villages at the expense of the villagers, and to establish National Committees in all the Arab villages of Palestine. On the same day Wauchope reported to the Colonial Secretary that 'The whole population of village and towns is united'. In the same telegram Wauchope predicted that henceforth each week would see the manifestation of resistance to authority. 'In spite of more than 600 arrests', Wauchope stated, 'arson, shooting, bomb throwing and destruction of railways continue and will grow in intensity'.[21]

At that point Wauchope was authorised to play the only card left in his hands; namely, the appointment of a Royal Commission of Enquiry to investigate the causes of the unrest after civil order had been re-established. He soon found out, however, that the politicians, the Mayors and the non-political leaders were powerless 'in view of the strength of public opinion all over the country, to call off the strike'.[22]

Wauchope's predictions proved to be accurate; demonstrations in the big towns, shouting of slogans against Britain and Zionism increased, clashes with the Police strengthened Arab bitterness against the Government and the Arab youth organised the National Guard in an effort to maintain morale and defend the shops and the population in a prolonged strike.

A Full-Fledged Revolt

More threatening still were the developments that were taking place in the countryside where discontent expressed itself in two forms: non-payment of taxes and violence. Air Vice-Marshall Peirse reported that:

> At village meetings in the Northern districts the people identified themselves with the strike movement. On the 18th May a large meeting took place at Abu Ghosh, between Jerusalem and Jaffa, which was attended by several thousands of people from neighbouring villages. The general feeling abroad was that the time had come when the Jewish question had to be settled once and for all and that it was necessary to sustain the struggle against the Government until the national political aims had been realised.[23]

On 18 May the Government announced a new Jewish Labour Schedule of 4,500 immigrants for the next six months which influenced Arab public opinion and committed the Palestinians to further defiance of the British. On the same day it was announced in the House of Commons that it had been decided to appoint a Royal Commission to investigate the causes of unrest in Palestine but that the Commission would not proceed to Palestine until the strike was called off and order restored. The announcement did not produce the desired effect as the Arabs were committed to continue the strike until the Government announced the stoppage of Jewish immigration.

Military reinforcements began arriving from Egypt and Malta. On 23 May sixty-one Arab activists and strike organisers were arrested. No sooner had the news spread than demonstrators took to the streets of Nablus where Police killed four of them and wounded seven. Armed villagers also headed for Tulkarem, and a battle took place at Bal'a where four of them were wounded including a woman who was carrying water to the fighters. These incidents turned the peaceful strike in Samaria to a full-fledged revolt.

The stepping up of the armed resistance exerted greater pressures on the Arab bodies that had refrained from joining the general strike: the municipalities, government employees and workers in Haifa's harbour.

The workers were threatened by the complete loss of their jobs if they joined the strikers as the labour force in the harbour was mixed and the Jews would have replaced them immediately and permanently. As for the municipal workers the matter was in the hands of the Mayors who were not as resolute in the defiance of the Government as other Arab sectors were. Under considerable pressure, the Mayors agreed to meet to discuss the situation and take concerted action, but the Government cancelled the meeting. On 31 May they met in secret and subsequently half of them decided to go on strike.[24]

Despite popular demands Government employees were not asked by the Higher Arab Committee to join the strike. Instead the senior officials and judges submitted a strong-worded memorandum to the Government in which they recommended the stoppage of immigration and advised that 'the trouble cannot be removed by force, but only by removing the causes of it'.[25]

Responsibility for the failure of the Government employees to join the strike, which would have crippled the Administration, must necessarily be attributed to the lack of militancy on the part of the Arab Higher Committee. Out of the ten members on this Committee only one, 'Awni 'Abdul Hadi was interned in June in a 'concentration camp' at Sarafand because of what Wauchope described as his organising capabilities.[26] Despite Hajj Amin's position as the President of the Higher Committee which was nominally leading the Arabs in their anti-Government strike and non-payment policies, Wauchope showed appreciation and gratitude for the Mufti's moderation. On 7 June, Wauchope reported these feelings to W. Ormsby-Gore, the new Colonial Secretary:

> It is a remarkable fact that the religious cry has not been raised during the last six weeks, that the Friday sermons have been far more moderate that I could have hoped during a period when feelings of the people are so deeply stirred, and for this the Mufti is mainly responsible.[27]

Five days later Jamal Husseini, Shibil Jamal, Dr 'Izzat Tannus and 'Abdul Latif Salah were granted visas to England, and the first three were given a letter of introduction by Wauchope to Sir John Maffey of the Colonial Office. These leaders were willing to negotiate a way out of the impasse in Palestine which would be acceptable to the British Government and the Palestinian Arabs at the same time. During one of their interviews at the Colonial Office 'they admitted that the leaders were largely now in the hands of the people, and they mentioned threats which had been made against Jamal Husseini himself and Awni Bey in the event of any weakening on their part'.[28]

Punitive Measures

The British authorities were convinced that the Strike had the 'full sympathy of the Arabs', that they could see 'no weakening in the will and spirit of the Arab people'.[29] and that the armed bands were backed by the villagers. Peirse and the military concluded that:

> It was quickly evident that the only way to regain the initiative from the rebels was by initiating measures against the villages from which the rebels and saboteurs came... I therefore initiated, in co-operation with the Inspector-General of Police, village searches. Ostensibly these searches were undertaken to find arms and wanted persons; actually the measures adopted by the Police on the lines of similar Turkish methods, were punitive and effective.[30]

These punitive measures were not only distasteful to the Palestinian Police but were also instrumental in bringing about a greater degree of cohesion and identification between the villagers and the rebels. The pro-Government Mayor of Nablus informed Wauchope that 'During the last searches effected in villages, properties were destroyed, jewels stolen, and the Holy Qoran torn, and this had increased the excitement of the *fellahin*'.[31]

Two days later the *'Ulama* interviewed Wauchope and made vigorous representations on the same subject. They further informed the High Commissioner that the Arabs were aware 'that by attacking His Majesty's troops they commit suicide, but, as Your Excellency is aware, a desperate man often commits suicide'.[32] The object of Arab disorders was simply 'letting their voice reach England and induce the British people to help them in considering their desperate position', for they would rather commit suicide or be shot down by British troops rather than suffer Jews to become dominant in Palestine.

Although largely a peasant movement armed resistance was not restricted to the rural areas. Before the British troops entered Nablus in late May, barricades were erected across the main roads and in the narrow alleyways of that ancient Arab town. The camp of the troops and the Fort were heavily sniped from the steep slopes of the surrounding mountains which directly overlooked them. A similar situation arose at Tulkarem and the village of 'Aqraba. Around

Jerusalem Jewish buses and armoured car patrols were attacked. In Gaza barricades were placed across the streets and rioting took place after clashes with the Police on 25 May and armoured cars and tanks had to be despatched to clear the barricades. In almost all other towns and villages there was sniping at the Police and the troops.

The most serious situation, however, arose in the old city of Jaffa which, according to Wauchope, 'formed a hostile stronghold into which the Government forces dare not penetrate'.[33] The old city of Jaffa afforded refuge for the rebels by the impenetrable labyrinth of narrow alleys and the maze of closely packed old houses. British troops and military installations were subjected to continuous sniping from that strategic quarter which dominated the town while being unaccessible to wheeled traffic. The military demanded the driving of a wide road over the crest of the hill through the old city in order to bring it under their control. This involved the demolition of a large number of houses and wiping out a good deal of the town. After some opposition from the Civil Administration, a circular, emanating from the Government Press, was distributed to the inhabitants of the old town announcing that for sanitary and town-planning reasons it had been decided to demolish a number of houses in their quarter.

A great deal of hardship and bitterness was caused by these extensive demolitions and many of the tenants were forced to live in hovels built from old petrol tins on the outskirts of Jaffa.

The punitive measures of the military and the amendment of the emergency regulations to enable the death penalty to be passed in cases of discharging firearms and malicious damage, and the wholesale arrests of Arab nationalist activists served to add determination and perseverance to the general strike and to spread armed resistance in the countryside. Jamal Husseini's negotiations in London did not lead to an acceptable formula for ending the strike, and Amir 'Abdullah's efforts with the Higher Committee in that direction were also futile. Memoranda of protest against the Government and the brutality of the military were becoming even more violent. The *'Ulama* were offended by the destruction of certain segments of various mosques and their mild attitude gave way to a more defiant one in July.

Impressive as the general strike certainly was, it began to look like a side-show or a smoke-screen as the sporadic activities of the armed bands began to assume revolutionary dimensions. In his report for the month of June, Peirse stated:

Armed bands which a fortnight previously consisted of 15-20 men were now encountered in large parties of 50-70. The bands were not out for loot. They were fighting what they believed to be a patriotic war in defence of their country against injustice and the threat of Jewish domination.[34]

The military endeavoured to counter the upsurge of sabotage and rebel activists by blowing up houses of people suspected of harbouring rebels and imposing collective fines on villages known to be actively backing the rebellion. Nevertheless, the military authorities were fully expecting greater armed resistance because of enhanced efforts to smuggle arms into Palestine, and because of 'the fact that the fellaheen were hastening on with the harvests so that the men would be free'.[35]

The Rebel's Military Formations

Inside the villages and the towns the rebels depended on the National Committee to provide food, recruits, shelter and information. Their military formations which operated on a regional-local rather than a national basis were divided into three categories. The first category comprised the full-time guerrillas (*mujahidin*) who took to the mountains, engaged the troops, sabotaged the oil pipeline etc. and formed the military backbone of the rebellion. The second category consisted of the town commandos who carried on their ordinary civilian life but performed specific terrorist acts on the request of their command. These were particularly instrumental in the liquidation of Arabs suspected of collaborating with the British as well as the assassination of British officers accused of committing excesses against the villagers and prisoners. The third category, by far the largest in number, was the partisans or auxiliary formations which were in the majority ordinary peasants and practising farmers who took up arms to relieve the guerrillas in case of a battle taking place in their vicinity.

During July the British military intelligence reported that the rebel bands were being reorganised by ex-officers from Syria and Trans-Jordan evidenced by the considerable improvement in their tactical handling during recent engagements. The rebel formations were divided into four fronts headed by a District Commander who had armed formations varying between 150-200 *mujahidin*, led by a platoon leader.

While hoping that the military repressive measures would succeed in crushing the rebellion, Wauchope and Ormsby-Gore were thinking of breaking the general strike and weakening the armed bands by means of political action. To appease the Arabs, without yielding to terrorism,

Wauchope accepted Ormsby-Gore's suggestion that should the Arabs stop acts of disorders unconditionally the British Government would of their own volition suspend all immigration while the Royal Commission were conducting their Enquiry. On the other hand Wauchope dropped his opposition to the cantonisation of Palestine,[36] which was supported and promoted by Weizmann.[37] While cantonisation was being discussed at length at the Colonial Office, Ormsby-Gore assured Jamal Husseini and his associates on 14 July that Britain meant to remain in Palestine and to govern it justly in the interest of all the inhabitants.[38]

The Role of the Arab Rulers

At the same time the British Government decided to use the influence of the neighbouring Arab rulers to talk the Palestinian Arabs out of their rebellions, general strike and armed resistance.[39] Communications with Sa'udi Arabia and the Foreign Minister of Iraq, Nuri el-Said, took place for that purpose. About the middle of July, 'Abdullah of Jordan 'was encouraged by the Government to attempt to mediate with the Arab High Committee in the cause of peace'.[40]

On 7 August, 'Abdullah invited the Higher Arab Committee to Amman whose members hastened to inform him that they were powerless to stop the strike unless Government decided to suspend Jewish immigration. Two weeks later Nuri Pasha arrived in Palestine as the Government's guest and offered his services as an unofficial mediator between the Government and the Higher Committee. As the Iraqi Foreign Minister could make no promises on the Government's behalf the negotiations broke down. In a manifesto published on 30 August, the Higher Committee declare that while they were willing to trust to the mediation of the Government of Iraq and their Majesties and Highness the Arab Kings and Prince the Nation, nevertheless, 'will continue its general strike with the same steadfastness and conviction it has shown'.[41]

The failure of Nuri's mission was not the only setback to British hopes for an early termination of the general strike and the rebellion. During August Wauchope reported to Ormsby-Gore that communications were still constantly being seriously damaged and trade hampered in every direction.

Simultaneous with the arrival of Nuri the Syrian revolutionary leader, Fawzi (ed-Din) al-Kawukji, entered Palestine at the head of an armed band and declared himself the Commander-in-Chief of the Arab Revolution in Southern Syria (Palestine).[42] Soon after Kawukji's assumption of control, Peirse reported:

Rebel tactics improved and the bands showed signs of effective leadership and organization. They were well supplied with arms and ammunition and the extension of their sphere of operations to districts outside the habitually active areas showed that their numbers had increased considerably.[43]

Other Syrian rebel leaders like Said el-'As (who was killed in October 1936) and Sheikh Muhammad al-Ashmar arrived during the first week of September probably as a result of the Mufti's efforts.[44]

Despite the growing strength of the rebels and the perseverance of town-dwellers in their general strike, the Palestine political leaders were anxious to hammer out a compromise with the Government. During the second part of August, 'Awni wrote to Wauchope 'saying in effect, that the Arab leaders might be prepared to call off the strike and disorders if they could be assured that the restoration of order would be followed by the complete stoppage of immigration',[45] which was largely in line with the solution Wauchope and Ormsby Gore had advocated a few weeks earlier, which was supported by many British officials, in view of 'the growth of the Arab national spirit'.[46] Time and again Wauchope warned that the alternative, advocated by the military, was the 'adoption of most drastic means to end disorder which will become more violent than now, a large increase of present garrison and an end to all hope of securing a settlement, that will also leave as embittered, sullen, and in their hearts, rebellious Arab population ready to rebel in any future year'.[47]

Convinced though he was that Wauchope's recommendations constituted the best course of action, Ormsby-Gore found himself unable to act in accordance with his convictions. On 19 June 1936, the House of Commons discussed the situation in Palestine. In the speeches of the members the immense strategic value of Palestine in war and peace was emphatically stressed. The speakers tended to equate the security of British interests with the success of Zionism in Palestine. The Zionist campaign against the proposed temporary suspension of Jewish immigration was highly effective in forcing the Government to change its attitude. In an interview with Ormsby-Gore, Weizmann and Ben Gurion intimated that if Britain appeased the Arabs the Zionists might change alliances and assist in dislodging Britain from the area 'but they had steadily rejected any overtures of this kind'.[48]

Britain's Course of Action

In a meeting of the Cabinet devoted to the discussion of the latest developments in the Palestine situation:

> The Secretary of State for the Colonies observed that the Govern-
> ment were faced with a most serious situation both in Palestine and
> in the Near East and at home. As a result of the events of the last
> few days, the whole Jewish world was in a turmoil. Mr Lloyd George
> and others were showing increased anxiety, and Mr Attlee wished
> Parliament to be specially summoned.[49]

At the end of their meeting the Cabinet resolved that 'intensive
measures, designed to crush Arab resistance, should be taken, and that
for this purpose the troops in Palestine should be reinforced by a
complete division sent from home, and that at an appropriate moment
martial law should be applied either to the whole of Palestine or to
selected parts thereof'.

Five days after the Cabinet's decision to crush the rebellion the
Colonial Office issued a rigorous statement regarding the 'direct
challenge to the authority of the British government in Palestine'.
The British Government, the Colonial Office asserted, had made several
attempts at reasonable conciliation to no avail. Their patience was now
exhausted and the state of disorder must be brought to an end without
delay. An additional division of troops was being sent to Palestine
and Lieutenant-General J.G. Dill would assume the supreme military
command.

Three days after this uncompromising announcement Wauchope
saw Hajj Amin, Ragheb Nashashibi and 'Awni 'Abdul Hadi individually,
before the Higher Committee met to discuss the latest British move.
According to Wauchope the Arab leaders were ready ,to urge
cessation of acts of disorder and to call off without any precedent
condition if so requested by Arab Kings'.[50]

On the following day, the Higher Committee published a manifesto
which referred to the Arabs' loss of confidence in the usefulness of
commissions of enquiry and refuted the Government's claim that the
Arab Kings and statesmen had offered their mediation as a result of
a request to do so by the Palestinian leaders. Significantly, the manifesto
added that the Arabs' reverence for their Kings was well known and it
was unthinkable for the Palestinians not to act in harmony with this
particular tradition. The mediation of the Arab Kings, the manifesto
asserted, was the best solution to the problem.[51] Kawukji issued a
manifesto the same effect, despite the fact that 'large numbers of the
population are perfectly ready to continue the fighting, more especially

as they receive assistance in men and arms from over the border'.[52]

These conciliatory declarations notwithstanding, the British reinforcements began to arrive in Palestine on 22 September, boosting the number of British troops in the country to over 20,000 and extensive operations were immediately undertaken to crush the rebels. The last week of September and the first ten days of October witnessed the sharpest battles, in the 1936 rebellion, between the British troops and the Arab rebels.

Towards the end of September a delegation from the Higher Committee set off to confer with Ibn Sa'ud and on 29 September 'Awni 'Abdul Hadi went to Trans-Jordan to interview 'Abdullah. As a result of these contacts and in accordance with prior consultations with the British Government Ibn Sa'ud, King Ghazi of Iraq and 'Abdullah despatched, on 10 October, an identically worded appeal to call off the strike and discontinue the rebellion and 'rely on the good intentions of our friend Great Britain, who has declared that she will do justice'.[53]

The End of the First Phase

On the following day the Higher Committee published the appeals of the Arab rulers and announced that after obtaining the approval of the National Committees they had decided to call upon the noble Arab nation in Palestine to resort to quietness and to put an end to the Strike and 'disorders'.

The strike and the rebellion were effectively and immediately called off, and the bands were permitted to disband and the rebels from the neighbouring Arab states were eventually allowed to cross the border. The general atmosphere began to cool down.

As a result of the rebellion sixteen Police and twenty-two military had been killed and 104 Police and 148 military wounded,[54] 80 Jews had been killed and about 308 wounded. According to official reports there were 145 Arabs killed and 804 wounded, but these figures were based on verified deaths and treatment in hospitals. The Peel Commission was inclined to believe that 1,000 Arabs were killed mostly in fighting.[55] The Jewish Agency reported 80,000 citrus trees, 62,000 other fruit trees, 64,000 forest trees and 16,500 *dunums* of crops belonging to Jews or Jewish bodies had been destroyed by the Arabs.

Britain's inability or unwillingess to suspend immigration reinforced the Arabs' belief that Britain was irrevocably committed to a pro-Zionist policy in Palestine which could not be changed unless and until independence was achieved.

The military punitive measures, village searches, wholesale arrests, collective fines, demolition of houses and what was euphemistically termed 'excesses'[56] added to Arab resentment against the Government. According to O.G.R. Williams of the Colonial Office, these measures 'provoked a very considerable amount of ill feeling not unmixed, I think, with contempt for His Majesty's Government'.[57]

The Peel Commission

The reasons that induced the Higher Committee to call off the strike and the rebellion were connected with their assessment of the seriousness of the military situation after the arrival of the new British division. In view of the destitution caused by the rebellion and the arrival of the citrus season, which touched on the interests of many members of the political notability, any decision to extend the Strike was bound to be controversial as was borne out by the opposition to boycott the Peel Commission shortly afterwards.

Simultaneous with the departure of the Royal Commission of Enquiry to Palestine on 5 November, the Colonial Secretary announced in the House of Commons the Government's decision that there would be no suspension on immigration during the course of the Royal Commission's investigation.

On the following day the Higher Committee denounced in vigorous terms the Colonial Secretary's statement which they viewed as a breach of faith and as contrary to what they had been expecting. As a result of this affront the Committee declared its resolve not to co-operate with the Royal Commission and asked all the Arabs of Palestine to abide by its decision.

The decision to boycott the Peel Commission exposed the inherent weaknesses of the Palestinian national movement. Although the National Committees were strongly in favour of a firm stand, the Nashashibi faction resented the tough lines represented by the boycott decision. 'Abdullah went out of his way to have the decision rescinded and Ibn Sa'ud threatened that he would sever all relations with the Higher Committee if the latter did not appear before the Royal Commission.[58]

Encouraged by the attitude of 'Abdullah and Ibn Sa'ud, the Nashashibi opposition to the boycott of the Peel Commission began to make itself felt. On 24 December *Falastin,* the organ of the Nashashibi Party, criticised the Higher Committee's decision to boycott the Commission and a few days later Hasan Sudki Dajani, a prominent member of the Nashashibi faction, announced his intention of giving evidence before the Royal Commission. Behind the increasingly bold dissident stand of the Defence Party lay the apprehensions of the propertied classes which were largely identified with it, that the new radicalism of the Mufti and the growing power of the extremists would inevitably lead to a total armed confrontation with the British aimed at achieving national independence. The expected upheaval would inflict severe losses to their interests and properties and should the impending rebellion achieve its aims Hajj Amin would, no doubt, reign supreme.

Faced with a lack of consensus inside their own shaky ranks and with strong pressures from the Sa'udi monarch, the Higher Committee had to succumb once more to the good offices of the Arab rulers. The decision to boycott the Peel Commission was abandoned on 6 January 1937, and the Arab case was largely presented by members of the Arab Higher Committee. Unlike Jewish and British evidence before the Royal Commission, Arab evidence was presented in the course of a few days in a manner not altogether appealing to a Western political tribunal.

The Arab Demands

In their statements before the Commission the Arab leaders asserted the inclusion of Palestine in the McMahon pledge to King Hussein, denied the validity of the Balfour Declaration and held that they never admitted the right of the powers to entrust a Mandate to Britain, which was inconsistent with the principle of self-determination embodied in the League of Nations.

The Higher Committee demanded the removal of the Mandate and the establishment of a national independent government. In their conclusions about the 'underlying causes of the disturbances' of 1936, the Royal Commission stated that the desire of the Arabs for national independence and their hatred and fear of the establishment of the JNH were the basic causes of all the Palestine disturbances. Additional causes were provided by the fact that the neighbouring Arab countries had attained national independence while the no less deserving Palestine had not. 'The intensive character of Jewish nationalism'[59] accentuated Arab fears of Jewish domination in Palestine.

Unlike the Arabs, the Zionist were opposed to Palestinian independence 'since a free Palestine in present circumstances means an Arab State'.[60] Jewish nationalism, the Commission Report stated, could not refuse 'allegiance to the British Government, which alone protects it from the enmity of the Arab world'.[61]

On 29 December Wauchope reported that the situation in Palestine was one of political tension and that

It is common belief among Arabs and Jews that if the report of the Royal Commission and His Majesty's Government's decision thereon are unfavourable to the Arabs, disturbances will break out again.[62]

An article published on 21 December in *al-Difa* 'reflected the prevalent Arab resentment of Britain when it declared that 'The Arabs of Palestine are looking at the Government with an eye of hate'. The responsibility for all the trouble fell 'first on the Government and then on the Jews' and hinted that more sacrifices might be needed to save Palestine from 'the madness of imperialism'.

These feelings of resentment and hostility were reflected, slowly but surely, in Hajj Amin's relations with the Government. By the end of the summer the British were anxious that the Mufti was firmly backing the strike and providing 'relief' funds, which were collected in Palestine and the neighbouring countries towards the upkeep of the armed bands and the purchases of arms.[63] Both the High Commissioner and the Colonial Secretary were determined to remove the Mufti from the political scene. Wauchope, however, warmed Ormsby-Gore against an exaggerated impression of the role of Hajj Amin.

> . . .it would be the height of folly to imagine that by the removal of the Mufti or this Committee the danger of a fresh Arab rising will be ended or even greatly reduced. Compare the tenacity of villagers who have opposed us for six months with little pay and no loot, with the feebleness and a lack of any great qualities of leadership among the Committee of Ten. Remember Arab genuine fear and deep hatred of Zionism.[64]

The High Commissioner rightly pointed out that the fear of imminent Jewish domination was felt by all from the highest to the lowest and was the mainspring of the disturbances and that the bodies which organised the strike and the rebellion 'sprang up locally and spontaneously'.[65] In view of the fact that the bands were not disarmed and the National Committees were still in close touch with the population and with the rebels, the British expected a renewal of serious disturbances after the Royal Commission submitted their report and recommendations.

Aware of the opportunities provided by the explosive situation, the Jews pressed for further concessions from the British. During the first week of January 1937 Dr Brodetsky informed the Colonial Office that the Arabs were collecting funds in preparation for future disorders and suggested a tougher policy with the Mufti and his associates. He added that although the Jews 'appreciated the action of the High Commissioner in authorising the formation of the Jewish Constabulary', they wanted a large Jewish force that would enable them to hold their own in any future disturbances.[66]

Although Wauchope fully expected the renewal of disturbances following the publication of the Peel Commission Report, he availed himself of the opportunity provided by the 'interlude' to use the influence of the Higher Committee in the interest of moderation. In particular, he was anxious to restore respect for law and order and stop the continuing campaign of political assassinations, which was renewed after the Royal Commission's departure.

For their part the Higher Committee were willing to show a more friendly attitude towards Wauchope, although for reasons connected with the state of public opinion they could not agree to the presence of a Palestinian at the coronation of the King. In the course of an interview with Wauchope, Hajj Amin (and 'Awni 'Abdul Hadi) stated that the sooner friendly relations with the British were re-established the better for the Arabs.[67]

Wauchope attributed the Mufti's more conciliatory attitude to the influence of Ibn Sa'ud and the influence of moderate Arabs outside Palestine:

> But I fear under certain circumstances that the influence of local Shabab and the Istiqlal Party may later on bring pressure to bear against satisfactory co-operation with Government and counsels of moderation which the Mufti now preaches and, as regards his Sheikhs and Qadis at present practices.[68]

Factors Against Moderation

The influence of the Shabab and the *Istiqlal*ists was not the only factor militating against moderation. In addition to the landless Arabs, which according to Government estimates constituted one quarter of the Arab rural population,[69] there was the question of Arab unemployment, which Wauchope described in the report as 'most serious problem and is neither temporary nor local'. This problem was raised 'in every town and village' he visited and threatened to loom larger both in the political as well as in the economic field. The Government's discrimination against Arab labourers in favour of the Jews added fuel to Arab resentment: 'On many roads the Arab receives little more than half the wage for equal output'.[70]

The granting of a new labour schedule and rumours of proposed partition of the country by the Peel Commission were subjects of Arab protests.[71] In view of the growth of nationalist feelings on both sides Wauchope saw little hope of maintaining security without a large and permanent garrison.[72] Tension was accentuated by a hunger strike declared by 180 political internees in Galilee which threatened to snowball after the declaration of a sympathy strike in Acre and Haifa.

While urging the Government to release all political internees and protesting against the issuing of immigration schedules, Hajj Amin was able to do so 'in a friendly way', and to offer co-operation on settling the dwellers of the tin shacks in Haifa on *waqf* lands.

As the rumours regarding the recommendations of the Peel Commission became more persistent Hajj Amin's moderation gave way to a more militant and defiant attitude. On 22 June, the Mufti, accompanied by four of his closest lieutenants, arrived in Damascus where he received all the prominent nationalist leaders, journalists and politicians of Syria and Lebanon in addition to a few Iraqi Arab nationalists and the Sa'udi Arabian Consul. According to a report by the usually well-informed British Consul in Damascus, Hajj Amin's discussion centred around two inter-related subjects. These were a 'general review of the pan-Arab political position' involving the 'immediate merging of the Palestine Istiqlal party in the Syrian National bloc...in all its aspects',[73] and the impending scheme for the partition of Palestine. Hajj Amin raised objections to partition, and a majority of the politicians was against the acceptance of 'Abdullah as sovereign of the proposed Arab State of Palestine. A Pan-Arab Congress was to be convened to discuss the future of Palestine at a later stage. Apart from the Syrian politicians and journalists, Hajj Amin had more than one lengthy private meeting with Syrian and Palestinian rebel leaders such as Mohammad al-Ashmar and Sheikh 'Attiyeh and other persons known for their gun-running activities. Moreover, the Mufti was reported to have stated on several occasions that he would 'declare war on the British on the 8th July',[74] following the publication of the Royal Commission's report. Days before the report was due to be published Ragheb Nashashibi and Ya'qoub Farraj resigned from the Higher Committee ostensibly on the ground that the Mufti was acting without reference to the rest of the members of the Committee. They also deplored recent acts of terrorism and hinted that the Mufti was responsible for these acts. The fact was that their continued membership on the Higher Committee would have restricted their freedom of action when the Government announced the Partition Scheme. In league with 'Abdullah, the National Defence Party intended to accept the proposed partition[75] and annex the new Arab state to Trans-Jordan with 'Abdullah as sovereign. With the aid of the British Government the Defence Party expected to assume political leadership after Hajj Amin had been removed from the scene by Government order. On hearing of the resignation of Nashashibi and Farraj, the Mufti returned to Jerusalem and British military authorities immediately predicted that he would soon attempt to terrorise the opposition by political assassinations.[76]

Peel's Partition Plan

On 7 July, the Royal Commission Report was published together with an official announcement that the British Government had accepted in principle its recommendations.

The Report recommended that the Mandate should be abandoned and that the country should be divided into three parts: an Arab state comprising those parts of Palestine predominantly Arab; a Jewish state comprising the predominantly Jewish parts; and certain areas comprising those parts that were of particularly strategic or religious importance were to remain under British Mandate. In view of the fact that the proposed Jewish state would include the best land in Palestine, the Report recommended that the Arab state be assisted by an annual subvention from the Jewish state.[77]

The Zionists protested that the Partition boundaries were not to their liking, but Weizmann was in favour of the scheme. In an interview with Ormsby-Gore, he promised 'to do his best to get the Zionist Congress to accept partition'[78] and help the British in getting Arabs out of Galilee into Trans-Jordan. The French were also reported by Weizmann to be in favour of 'the idea of partition and of the establishment of a Jewish State as assuring a bulwark for Western democracy at the eastern end of the Mediterranean.[79]

The Report was received with indignation by the majority of the Palestinian Arabs who were adamantly opposed to the creation of a Jewish state on what they regarded as Arab land.[80] In view of the vehement Arab reactions to partition, the Nashashibi faction refrained from making any public declaration in favour of the scheme.

On 8 July the Higher Committee rejected the partition scheme and appealed to the Arab rulers as well as to the Arab and Muslim worlds, to whom Palestine belonged, for solidarity. They communicated their rejection of partition to the League of Nations and submitted that the Royal Commission had asserted what they repeatedly claimed, namely, that the Mandate was unworkable. The Higher Committee demanded that the British Mandate be replaced by a *Palestinian* independent state, treaty-bound with Britain, guaranteeing reasonable British interests and minority rights of the Jews.[81]

Petitions of protest were submitted from all parts of Palestine but the strongest reactions were those voiced in Galilee, which was included in the Jewish State, where the Report was received 'with shock and incredulity'. According to an official report:

> Christians, Moslems, Fellahin and landowners are probably more united in their rejection of the proposal than they have ever been before. Their common feeling in this district is that they have been betrayed and that they will be forced to leave their lands and perish in some unknown desert.[82]

As a result new local National Committees of a large size were formed in which the rural population was represented by a majority of two-thirds.

Aware of the logical implications of Arab opposition to the partition scheme, the British unsuccessfully attempted on 17 July to arrest the elusive Hajj Amin, in order 'to prevent his making further appeals and preventing his giving any support to those who may wish for disturbances'.[83]

The Bludan Pan-Arab Congress

Having narrowly escaped arrest Hajj Amin kept within the sanctuary of the *Haram* from where he managed to keep in touch with the rebel leaders and political activists. Unable to arrest him in the *Haram* area, Wauchope initiated measures for Government control of the administration of the *Shari'a* Courts and the *waqf* funds to curtail the power of the Mufti. Emulating the example of Zionist Congresses, the Higher Committee applied for permission to convene a Pan-Arab congress in Palestine to study the situation and take the necessary measures to protest the rights of the Palestinian Arabs but the Administration refused to grant permission on the grounds that the proposed congress would lead to excitement. Thereafter, the 'Committee for the Defence of Palestine' in Damascus undertook to convene the congress in Bludan, a Syrian summer resort. On 8 September, over four hundred delegates[84] from Egypt, Iraq, Syria, Lebanon and Palestine elected Naji Sweidi, an ex-Prime Minister of Iraq, for the Presidency of the Congress, 'Alluba Pasha, Shakib Arslan and Bishop Krayke for the Vice-Presidency and

Darwaza for the Secretariat. The Congress asserted that Palestine was part of the Arab homeland and that the Arabs had the right and were duty-bound to defend Palestine. The proposed Jewish state was viewed as a grave threat and a foreign base against the Arab world.[85]

The Congress proposed that the Balfour Declaration should be abrogated, the Mandate annulled, and an Anglo-Palestinian treaty concluded whereby independence was recognised and a stop put to Jewish immigration.[86] In the event of British insistence on the partition of Palestine, British and Jewish goods should be boycotted by the Arab States.

In his report on the Congress the British Consul in Damascus cabled that 'contrary to expectation general tone was not anti-British-although vehemently anti-Zionist'.[87] This moderation was imposed by politicians eager 'to stand well' with the British Government led by Sweidi, the President of the Congress. Thoroughly dissatisfied with what they described as the insipid resolutions of the Congress about a hundred Palestinian and Syrian nationalists held a secret meeting on 12 September for the purpose of discussing more effective measures that could and should be taken to fight British proposals for partition.

The method most favoured was the continuance of attacks on the persons of Arabs friendly to the British authorities and on Jews, with the idea of preparing the ground for more direct action later against the Mandatory should this dangerous course be necessary.[88]

Simultaneous with these secret meetings Palestinian activists were in touch with the Syrian rebels who had taken a leading part in the revolt of 1936 and arrangements were made for the immediate departure of thirty rebels and a rallying point somewhere between Beisan, Jenin and Nablus was fixed.[89] Considerable accumulation of arms and ammunition were stated to have been made around Nablus under the direction of the Mufti.

The Rebellion's Second Phase

Anticipating an outburst of violence in Palestine the British took two parallel measures to contain and suppress Arab reactions. In September 1937 the League Council met to approve a recommendation submitted by the Permanent Mandates Committee to accept the principle of partition in Palestine. But instead of asking for approval to proceed with partition, the British Foreign Secretary, Mr Anthony Eden, requested approval for sending a commission to Palestine to work out the details of partition, which implied a certain lack of resolution to carry out the proposed partition scheme.[90]

At the same time new military measures designed to crush the renewal of rebellion were carried out and on 12 September Lieutenant-General Wavell replaced Dill as General Officer Commanding (GOC).

The opportunity to carry out measures against the political leadership of the new phase of the Rebellion presented itself when L.Y. Andrews, District Commissioner of Galilee, and his police escort were assassinated at Nazareth. Despite their public condemnation of the act the Arab Higher Committee and all National Committees were declared illegal and the Mufti was deprived of his offices as President of the Supreme Muslim Council and as Chairman of the *Waqf* Committee. Several members of the Higher Committees were deported to Seychelles. Hundreds of political activists and suspected rebels were arrested. The Mufti remained secure in the sanctuary of the *Haram* and Jamal Husseini avoided arrest and left Palestine. A prohibition was laid on the local press to mention or comment on the events of 1 October.[91]

On 2 October, a strike of protest against the arrests was observed in Jerusalem and on the following two days it spread to many other parts of Palestine. Two days later, Hajj Amin issued a manifesto calling on the Arabs to return to work, thus bringing the strike to an end. A period of calm followed and on 14 October the Mufti, in spite of police precautions, managed to escape to Lebanon.

On the night of 14-15 October the lull was suddenly and violently broke. Two attacks were made on Jewish buses in the vicinity of Jerusalem, Jewish settlements were subjected to sporadic shooting, the Iraq Petroleum Company (IPC) pipeline was damaged just west of the Jordan River and the escaping oil ignited, telephone lines were cut, a passenger train was derailed and a troop train was heavily fired upon in the mountains south west of Jerusalem and a police patrol was heavily ambushed near Hebron.[92] Curfew was immediately imposed on Jerusalem. On the following night a large party of Arab rebels penetrated the premises of the Lydda airport and completely burned out the wooden buildings housing the customs and passport offices and the wireless installation. A twenty-three hour curfew was imposed on Lydda for four days, two houses were demolished and a collective fine of £P 5,000 was imposed. The second phase of the rebellion was already under way. Emergency regulations were soon declared, and police posts were established in various villages at the cost of the inhabitants. As early as November 1937, troops entering villages 'were fired on and some of the villagers attempted to resist and threw stones whereupon the troops returned the fire'.[93]

The renewal of the rebellion dealt a severe blow to Partition and to 'Abdullah and his moderate Palestinian friends 'whose influence in Palestine is now negligible'.[94] On 8 December the Cabinet after prolonged discussions resolved 'to inform the (Partition) Commission that it was open to them to represent that no scheme of partition that they could devise was likely to prove workable'.[95] Arab opposition to partition induced the Jews to stand even more firmly with the Government in a common front against the renewed Arab Rebellion. In an interview with Parkinson Dr Brodetsky informed him that 'the Arabs had approached the Jews with proposals for some kind of agreement between the Arabs and Jews on the basis that the connection with Great Britain would be completely severed. This the Jews rejected out of hand as they regarded the connection with Great Britain as essential'.[96] As soon as the rebellion was renewed the Jews demanded the formation of Jewish armed units to fight along side of British forces against the Arab rebels. The previous policy of self-restraint was abandoned, and scores of Arabs were killed and injured by Jews, as a result of Jewish reprisals.[97]

The strong punitive mesures taken in the wake of the resurgence of violence in mid-October induced some village chieftains to deny aid to the nascent rebel bands and thus cut them off from the essential link between them and their supporters in the villages, who were their basic source of supplies, information and cover. The rebels who were growing in numbers saw in the tendency of some village notables to co-operate with the Government a serious threat and soon regained the initiative by intimidating the collaborators.

Despite the Government's repressive measures, the rebels were attracting and training more recruits,[98] and the organisation of the renewed rebellion showed some improvement over that of 1936. To begin with Rebel Headquarters called *al-Lujnah al-Markaziyya lil-Jihad* were instituted at Damascus under the active administration of Darwaza and the guidance of the Mufti from Lebanon. Rebel Headquarters were responsible for effecting co-ordination and co-operation between the largely independent rebel formations headed by a local military leader and assisted by platoon leaders. These formations were led by Palestinians and maintained the closest contact with the peasants and the villages in their respective areas of operation. The most prominent leaders of the second phase of the rebellion were 'Abdul Rahim al-Hajj Mukammad (Tulkasen), 'Aref 'Abdul Razeq (Nablus), 'Abdul Qader Husseini (Jerusalem), and later Yusuf Abu Durra (Galilee).

Many of the new formations were named after the early leaders of Islam. Contact between Headquarters and the various formations was conducted through messengers and occasional visits by rebel leaders to Damascus. The precarious authority of Headquarters was maintained through financial and medical aid and the supply of arms to rebel bands.[99] Al-Maktab al-'Arabi al-Qawmi (The Arab National Bureau) in Damascus acted as the propaganda organ of the rebellion.

The Rebels Gain the Upper Hand

The rebels were not totally or even mainly dependent on assistance from Damascus, which collected contributions from various Arab and Muslim countries, as they were able to exercise authority in a large number of villages. In their headquarters in the hills the rebels established rebel courts, administrative offices and intelligence centres. In view of the breakdown of civil government the villagers frequently and often freely resorted to these courts, and the rebels were able to levy taxes and quotas of volunteers on the villages.

The rebel leaders in the hills were also able to maintain contact with activists and terrorists in the towns and cities. The activists collected contributions in the cities and provided information for the rebels while the terrorists attacked British and Jewish targets inside their cities. The terrorists also intimidated the Arab collaborators through threats and assassinations. A number of educated Palestinians acted as consultants and advisors to the rebel leaders and were particularly useful in the Courts established by the rebels.

In addition to the Palestinian peasants and town activists the rebellion attracted parties of young men 'with vague pan-Arab enthusiasms'[100] who formed themselves into small bands and acted as guerrillas on the frontiers of Palestine. 'They affected a kind of uniform resembling that adopted by the late King Faisal's followers in 1918. They received no payment, but obtained ample supplies of arms when they got into Palestine'.[101]

The dramatic growth of the rebels' strength and activities brought about a change in the British military leadership. Sir Harold MacMichael, the New High Commissioner, and Lieutenant-General Haining, the new GOC, took a number of drastic measures to wrest the initiative from rebels. A wire fence along the northern and north-eastern frontier was erected with police posts and fortifications in the Jordan Valley to isolate the rebels and cut their supply routes across the Jordan. In view of an expected 'enhancement of triumphant lawlessness amounting to insurrection', the High Commissioner contemplated the arming of Jews by Government 'for active operations and not merely for static as at present'.[102]

Following his arrival, General Haining launched a number of offensives, in which the RAF and armour units took an active part. These operations proved to be 'disappointing' and as the armed bands were no longer offering battle voluntarily Haining and his assistant adopted a plan 'for a prolonged occupation of a large number of villages in Galilee and Samaria, with the object of denying basis to the bands'.[103] The result was a decrease of incidents in the occupied areas, and an increase in sabotage on the roads, railways, telephone lines, IPC pipeline and increased attacks on military patrols and half-hearted attacks — to use Haining's description — on isolated Jewish colonies.

The intensification of the military effort against the rebels was accompanied by heavy-handed actions against the civil population. Wholesale arrests, long curfews, extensive demolitions and collective fines did not enhance the popularity of British rule. In the cities the situation was getting out of hand as strikes, demonstrations, Arab-Jewish reprisals and curfews became almost daily occurrences.[104] Haining took the success of the rebel courts and their system of tax collection as a symptom of rural hostility to government which 'produced a more united front'.

Alternative to Partition

It was at this point, when the rebellion was gathering momentum that Jamal Husseini attempted to articulate the Palestinian Arab national demands in a manner calculated to appeal to the hard-pressed British Government. In a private letter to Malcolm MacDonald, Husseini offered an alternative to partition:

> We are prepared to take in the present Jewish population in Palestine and give them full and equal rights and proportionate seats in all Government institutions with Municipal and communal autonomy in strictly Jewish settlements.[105]

Nothing came out of this initiative as the Zionists were determined to have a Jewish State and, as the British were equally determined to crush the rebellion before entering into any negotiations with the Arabs.

The initiative, however, remained in the hands of the rebels in the country and with the activists in the cities. The increase in sabotage and bombing incidents led to streets fighting in Jerusalem, Jaffa and Haifa. On 6 July, a bomb planted by extremists Jews[106] exploded in the vegetable market in Haifa killing 23 people and wounding 79 most of whom were Arabs. A general strike was declared in all the major cities and Arab centres and in Haifa the strike lasted more than one week.[107] Other bomb explosions in Jerusalem and Haifa exacerbated Arab-Jewish relations and triggered off a series of attacks on Jewish colonies. The organisation of night squads supplemented by Jewish super-numeraries under Captain O.C. Wingate to take the offensive against the rebels by night and to protect the IPC pipeline[108] represented the highest stage of British-Zionist convergence in the period under study.

On 7 July, MacMichael reported 'some extension and intensification of gang activities in northern and central areas. Number of rebels appears to be increasing and their organisation appears to be improving'.[109] Haining submitted that his troops were facing a people in rebellion for even where the bands were small it was difficult to control rural areas since the villagers took

every opportunity to indulge in sniping, minor sabotage and the laying of road mines. . .This form of resistance is difficult to deal with as it is extremely hard to find a target to hit. In addition, the sympathy of the inhabitants are with the gangs and not with the British Government.[110]

During the summer of 1938 the rebellion reached its climax. A Higher Council comprising the major rebel leaders was convened at the request of the Central Committee for *Jihad* to strengthen co-operation and co-ordination between the rebels. The Higher Council resolved to persevere in the struggle until Britain conceded Arab demands. At the height of their power the rebels constituted the supreme authority in most parts of rural Palestine with their own legal and administrative set-ups.[111] Reflecting their peasant origin and sympathies, the rebels issued a moratorium on all debts as of 1 September 1938, and warned that debt collectors and land-brokers should desist from visiting the villagers. Another warning was issued to contractors engaged in constructing police posts and roads.

The growing power of the rebels led to an exodus of thousands of rich Palestinians, land-brokers and pro-Government notables. During the summer of 1938 Arab city-dwellers had to adopt the villagers' head-dress, the *kuffiyya*, in order to protect the infiltrating village rebels from being detected by the Police and the troops.

The Rebels Occupy the Cities

By the end of August and despite harsh punitive measures against those harbouring the rebels,[112] Civil Government had almost completely broken down in the major cities and towns owing to systematic attacks on Government offices by the rebels and to the suspected collusion of Arab Police. In Haining's opinion, the increasing number of attacks in the cities and the damage and dislocation caused to government property and communications was

> symptomatic of what is now a very deep seated rebellious spirit throughout the whole Arab population, spurred on by the call of a Holy War. The rebel gangs have now acquired, by terrorist methods, such a hold over the mass of the population that it is not untrue to say that every Arab in the country is a potential enemy of the Government however moderate his own personal feelings may be.[113]

In view of these developments, Haining and MacDonald urged that a second division be sent out in October in place of the proposed Brigade. before the arrival of the requested reinforcements 'Civil administration and control of the country was to all practical purposes non-existent.'[114] Armed rebels took many cities by storm and in other cases they infiltrated and took control of major cities with the objective of wholesale insurrection to effect complete reversal of British policy with particular reference to Partition and Jewish immigration. The opening of the citrus season did not divert the attention of the rebels as they and their leaders had no interest in the citrus trade.

Alarmed by the deteriorating situation in Europe brought about by German irredentism, the new Colonial Secretary, Malcolm MacDonald, and the Cabinet resolved to take measures designed to contain the rebellion and induce the Arabs to come to terms with Britain. He proposed to issue a public statement announcing the increase of military and police forces in Palestine and disclosing his intention of inviting representatives of the Arabs of Palestine and of the Jewish Agency to discuss with HMG the recommendations of the Palestine Partition Commission Report in October,[115] He intended to make it clear that there could be no question of the Mufti or any other exiles from Palestine representing the Palestinian Arabs in the proposed discussions.[116] MacMichael lost no time in advising the Colonial Secretary against such terms, for

> When one has excepted Mufti and his staff there are no Arab

representative leaders except rebel leaders in the hills. The very name of 'moderates' has become a term of abuse.[117]

As the Palestine Government were against negotiations with the Mufti, MacMichael suggested bringing the more obliging neighbouring Arab rulers into the picture. He later suggested negotiations with the Arab Mayors of Palestinian cities and towns.[118]

As the European crisis worsened, MacDonald warned MacMichael that the proposed reinforcements might have to be diverted and the 'rapid organisation of a Jewish volunteer Defence Force may be necessary despite all objects'.[119] In view of the fact that Egypt might become an important theatre of war, in addition to Iraq's particular importance, the British Government were eager to restore friendly relations with the Arabs.[120] At the same time in case of war friendship and support of the United States, where the Jews 'are considerable factor',[121] would also be a matter of vital concern.

Nevertheless, British strategic interests demanded the achievement of reconciliation with the Arabs of Palestine and the neighbouring countries and the termination of the rebellion. MacDonald proposed to suspend immigration should war break out.

Haining and MacMichael were of the opinion that the postponement of partition and the complete cessation of immigration offered the only hope of eventual peace in Palestine. Haining warned that this did not imply an immediate settling down of the Arabs. The second phase of the rebellion, he submitted, was less dependent on outside help than in 1936, and there was no one 'to influence the rebels who are nationally minded people'.[122]

Certain Arab statesmen shared Britain's anxieties regarding the continuance of hostilities in Palestine at a time when a European war seemed imminent. In October, Tawfiq Sweidi, the Iraqi Foreign Minister, was a frequent visitor to the Colonial Office, and there were reports that a temporary cessation of Jewish immigration was being considered. A feeling that considerable concessions to the Arab viewpoint were imminent prevailed both among Arabs and Jews.

Chamberlain's policy of appeasement towards Hitler succeeded in preventing — temporarily — the outbreak of a war between the European powers. Before MacMichael returned to Palestine on 14 October, a policy had been set in London designed to bring an early end to the rebellion and to keep the Arabs quiet during the expected war with Germany.

Reconquering the Country

During October, the rebels infiltrated Jerusalem and by 17 October the Police had been driven out and the rebels had gained complete control of the Old City. On the following day it was announced that the military authorities had taken over control of the Jerusalem district from the civil power. Four days later military control was extended to the rest of the country, and the campaign to re-establish British rule, which amounted to a 'virtual military reoccupation'[123] of Palestine, commenced.

With two divisions, squadrons of airplanes, British Police, Trans-Jordan frontier forces, as well as six thousand Jewish auxiliary forces under his command, Haining set out to re-establish control over the cities by a co-ordinated drive against the rebels which involved the occupation, cordon and search of virtually all the larger villages of Galilee and Samaria. These operations enabled Haining to start a general disarmament campaign and encouraged the anti-Mufti forces to make their presence felt by providing information and identifying captured rebels.

The mounting pressure on the rebels exposed their inner organisational weaknesses and the serious consequences of the absence of a political leadership able to mobilise the masses as well as the absence of an effective military leadership able to face the challenge of overwhelming modern British might. Confusion arising out of abuse in the collection of contributions and taxes harmed the prestige and the authority of the rebels. Excessive indulgence in some unnecessary political assassinations encouraged the pro-Government Arab elements to openly defy the rebels.

On 9 November 1938 the Report of the Palestine Partition Commission was published,[124] accompanied by a covering statement of Policy from the Government. The Report ruled out the Peel partition scheme as impractical and accordingly the statement of policy announced that the Government had decided to abandon partition and to continue with the Mandate as it was and make an endeavour to arrive at a solution between Arabs and Jews by holding a conference of Arab and Jewish leaders to which representatives from the independent Arab States would be invited. The purpose of the proposed conference was not an Arab-Jewish entente, but rather the imposition of a British solution, in which both parties would acquiesce, calculated to take the wind out of the sails of the Arab rebellion in the hills.[125]

The Palestinian Arabs welcomed the abandonment of Partition and derived comfort from the fact that representatives of the Arab States were invited to the London conference. On the other hand they were dismayed that immigration and land sales were to be excluded from the discussions. The Jews wanted the British to crush the rebellion first and foremost and then hoped that the disunity of the Arabs of Palestine would prevent them from sending a delegation to the conference. They were apprehensive that the proposed London conference would lead to concessions to the Arabs regarding immigration and land sales in return for an early end to the rebellion. The Zionist leadership regarded the participation of the Arab States as an undesirable precedent and 'they wished the United States of America to participate actively'.[126]

From the outset it was clear that Iraq and Ibn Sa'ud would be 'ready to use their influence (whatever it may be) with Palestine leaders to bring insurrection to an end and also to make the conference a success'.[127] When British objection to the participation of the Mufti in the Palestinian Arab delegation became known, MacMichael reported that the majority of the Palestinian Arabs were disappointed,[128] and that the anti-Mufti faction began to show signs of life. Less than a week after the British statement of Policy was published, Fakhri Nashashibi published an open letter to the H.Cr. in which he claimed to be writing on behalf of many moderates. In this letter he challenged the Mufti's leadership claiming that the moderate anti-Mufti leaders represented 75 per cent of the interests of the country and that their followers represented more than half of the Arabs of Palestine. In view of the strong hostile reaction to Fakri's letter Ragheb Nashashibi, then in self-exile in Egypt, issued an immediate *dementi* disavowing his cousin's views. MacMichael reported that the controversy was possibly a 'stage battle'. As for Fakhri's initiative MacMichael stated, 'I think it more than probable than Fakhri was induced by local Jewish politicians to write his letter'.[129]

It soon became evident that all efforts to discredit the Mufti had backfired. On 29 November, MacMichael reported to MacDonald that he had received more than 180 telegrams expressing confidence in the Mufti and the Higher Committee 'many of which bear a considerable number of signatures. They have come from all parts of Palestine and bear the names of persons in different walks of life ranging from Mayors, Municipal Councillors, Christian and Moslem religious dignitaries to shopkeepers'.[130]

The London Round Table Conference

The Nashashibi Party did not carry sufficient weight to replace the Mufti and on 23 November MacDonald announced in the House of

Commons that the Palestine Arab delegation would represent all the leading groups in the country. Early in December it was announced that the Seychelles deportees would be unconditionally released to give them an opportunity to being chosen to represent the Arabs at the proposed London conference. After their arrival in Cairo, the British announced that they had no objection to consultations between the deportees and the Mufti before deciding on the membership of the Palestine Arab delegation to London. Together with Jamal Husseini they proceeded to Beirut to confer with the Mufti and come to an agreement with him so that no settlement would be agreed to at the conference without his approval.

It was agreed that the Palestine Arab delegation would put forward the demands of the Palestine Arab 'national charter' including the demand for an independent Palestinian state with an Arab majority. The Arabs were not to sit with the Zionists, and later events indicated that the leaders agreed 'that it was essential to intensify terrorism rather than modify it, both before and during the discussions. . .to inform world opinion of what would happen if the Arab demands were not met'.[131] It was agreed that Jamal Husseini would lead the delegation as the Mufti's representative and that Hussein F. Khalidi, Alfred Rock, Musa Alami would be members of the delegation with George Antonius and Fuad Saba as secretaries.

The Higher Committee had earlier approached Ragheb and had invited him to accompany the delegation to London. At that time Ragheb gave no reply. Later, however, the Palestine Administration encouraged Ragheb, as did Tawfiq Abu el-Huda, 'Abdullah's Chief Minister, and prodded him to name a rival delegation composed of Defence Party leaders, which he did.[132] The Mufti refused to compromise at the beginning but he was induced by Arab statesmen to accept Nashashibi and Farraj, both ex-members of the Higher Committee, as members of the delegation.

Before the London Round Table Conference opened on 7 February 1939, the situation in Palestine began to show signs of renewed rebel initiative.

Haining's campaign against the rebels bands in the hills and villages had the effect of shifting terrorism to the cities where sabotage, bomb-throwing and assaults increased sharply. By late December a number of prominent band leaders were in Damascus to discuss plans and obtain rest and supplies. These leaders returned in January and were able to intensify their attacks against British and Jewish personnel and property, as well as collect levies in the cities. Severe restrictions on

Arab traffic and travel were imposed and a strike was observed in Jerusalem as a protest against the establishment of a Police post in the *Haram* in January 1939. Arab protests against British troop brutality and ruthlessness abounded[133] and the Palestinian propaganda offices in Damascus and London (The Arab Centre) were busily engaged in distributing pamphlets and photographs in this connection.[134]

During February 1939, however, London became the centre of attraction as people followed the news of the Conference with interest and hope.

As the Arabs refused to confer with the Jews, Chamberlain opened negotiations with the Arab Delegations in the morning of 7 February 1939, and with the Jewish Delegations in the afternoon of the same day. On 9 February Jamal Husseini put forward the Arab demands which called for the recognition of the Arab right to independence, the abandonment of the JNH, the immediate cessation of Jewish immigration and land sales, the abrogation of the Mandate and its replacement by a treaty of alliance with an independent Arab Palestine.

Weizmann on the other hand called for the maintenance of the *status quo,* i.e. the continued implementation of the Mandate and the Balfour Declaration and the refusal of the Yishuv and the Zionists to accept a minority status in Palestine.

Spurred by a feeling that Britain was about to jettison the JNH policy 'largely because of the strategic necessity to Great Britain of Arab friendship and alliances in the Near East'[135] the Zionists directed a great deal of argument 'to showing the usefulness to Great Britain of a loyal, industrious and progressive ally, namely the Zionists, in this part of the world'.[136] The Zionists also began to look more and more towards the United States, and the Arabs began 'to regard America as their enemy'.[137]

In the course of the discussions the Government put forward proposals embodying the termination of the Mandate and the convening of a Round Table conference in the autumn which would lay down the constitution of an independent Palestine under British protection in which the Jewish minority would be safeguarded by guarantees.

The Arabs demanded the immediate implementation of the proposals, as they were apprehensive that the proposed delay would give the Jews an opportunity to pressure the Government into abandoning a scheme acceptable to the Arabs yet again. Not unexpectedly, the Jews angrily rejected the proposal and the Government withdrew the proposal on the ground that it had been 'misunderstood'.

Toward the end of February, Cairo's *al-Ahram* published a report that as a result of the London Conference, Palestine would become independent and that a treaty would be concluded with Great Britain on the lines of the Anglo-Iraq Treaty. Spontaneous demonstrations of jubilation took place; Chamberlain and Hajj Amin were cheered; in some villages bonfires were lit and in the Nazareth area the rebel leaders ordered 'a temporary cessation of terrorism'. The Arab *fellah* saw in Palestinian independence a guarantee against eviction and subservience to the Jews. 'What the fellah wants', wrote MacMichael, 'is a severe restriction of immigration and land sales and some safeguard to prevent the Jews from ever securing a political or economic mastery over him'.[138]

Arab election was matched by violent Jewish opposition: 'On the morning of 27 February a series of bomb outrages occurred almost simultaneously throughout the country. 38 Arabs were killed or fatally wounded and 44 were injured'.[139] The Zionist 'moderates' became as militant and as uncompromising as the Revisionist extremists.

As the Conference went on it became clear that no agreement would be reached as the Arabs wanted independence while they were in the majority (two-thirds of the population) and the Jews opposed Palestinian independence as long as they were in the minority. Attempts to 'save' the Conference by attempts to obtain concessions and compromises from the Mufti ended in failure.

The 1939 White Paper

The failure to arrived at an agreed solution paved the way for the British to announce their own solution. In their Palestine Statement of Policy of 1939 the British Government declared 'unequivocally' that it was not part of their policy that Palestine should become a Jewish State. Similarly, HM Government 'cannot agree that the MacMahon correspondence forms a just basis for the claim that Palestine should be converted into an Arab State'. What HMG desired to see established 'ultimately' was an independent Palestine state 'in which the two peoples in Palestine, Arabs and Jews, share authority in government in such a way that the essential interests of each are secured. . .The object of HMG is the establishment within ten years of an independent Palestine State in such treaty relations with U.K. as will provide satisfaction for all commercial and strategic interests of both countries'. The British Government further declared that the transitional period of mandatory rule would promote gradual self-government. Jewish immigration during the next five years was fixed at 75,000 after which period no further Jewish immigration would be permitted without Arab consent. In certain areas of Palestine no transfer of Arab lands would be permitted whilst in other areas transfers would be restricted.

The Zionists received the White Paper with hostility[140] and vowed to fight it to the finish. From 1939 onwards the Zionists could no longer depend on the British Government as protectors and sponsors of their plan to establish a Jewish State in Palestine; they had to turn to the United States of America for that role.

Resisted by the Zionists as it were, the 1939 White Paper left something to be desired where the Arabs were concerned. Only 'Abdullah and the Defence Party came out in favour of the new British policy'.[141] Rebel Headquarters viewed the White Paper in a different light. As there was no promise of amnesty for the rebels and no inclination towards a rapprochement with the Mufti, they immediately announced the rejection of the British proposals and promised that the Higher Committee would issue a reasoned and detailed statement shortly thereafter. Before the promised reasoned statement was published, British sources 'had good reason to believe that the members are not unanimous'[142] as some members were inclined to co-operate with the Government's policy as the best means of obtaining further concessions.

Internal squabbles notwithstanding the Higher Committee's statement welcomed Britain's recognition of Arab rights in principle but regretted Britain's failure to grant Palestinian independence 'the holiest of rights and the most precious aspiration of a nation'. Even the postponed independence was subject to a Jewish veto and made condition on Jewish co-operation. Furthermore, the Arabs, the Higher Committee hinted, had no faith in the British Government,

> And as long as authority is not in the hands of the inhabitants of the country, there is nothing to prevent the use of means commonly practiced by imperialism.[143]

The Higher Committee's statement concluded by rejecting the White Paper as it did not meet Arab demands which were summarised by their motto 'Palestine Will Get its Independence within the Arab Federation and Will Remain Arab Forever'.

The Last Hurrah!

Although 'tired of disorder and anxious for peace' the majority of the Palestinians mistrusted the Government's intentions. As a result of rebel propaganda 'a district hardening of opinion against the White Paper' was apparent during the latter part of May 1939. Strenuous efforts were made to continue the rebellion;

> Reports from all parts of Palestine are unanimous in confirming that gangs are being reformed under the newly returned leaders and are beginning to move freely about the country. Further evidence of this fact is the occurrence of several engagements in the past 10 days.[144]

In Zionist circles, the High Commissioner reported, the policy of violence was 'gaining ground particularly among youths'.[145] For a while it seemed that each side of the Palestinian triangle was invvolved in a fight against the other two sides.

Mistrust of the Government's· intentions, Jewish terrorism[146] and illegal immigration as well as season factors supplemented to rebel headquarters' efforts to reinvigorate the Rebellion. Yet even before the outbreak of the Second World War, it was quite evident that after years of rebellion, the Arabs' power and ability to resist Britain and Zionism by the force of arms had been weakened and exhausted.

One by one the rebel leaders began to disappear, to lose influence or get killed. On 25 March the most sincere and best respect of the rebel leaders, 'Abdul Rahim, was killed in an encounter with British troops and a general strike of sympathy was observed by the all over Palestine. On 13 April, 'Aref 'Abdul Razeq decamped from Palestine and surrendered with twelve of his men to the French over the Syrian border in a state of complete physical collapse owing to hunger,[147] and, on 24 July, Abu Durra was captured near Jordan River by the Arab Legion of Trans-Jordan.

War weariness, continued military pressure, hope that the favourable aspects of the White Paper would be realised in addition to a shortage of arms and ammunition[148] militated against the continuation of the Rebellion. The approach of war brought forth the complete suppression of the rebel headquarters in Damascus by the French. Soon after the declaration of war, the rebellion started to peter out, and MacMichael was able to report that 'as a whole the Arab community has declared its support for the Government in the war with Germany in no uncertain fashion'.[149]

The outbreak of the War eclipsed local politics and disorders; the great Palestine rebellion had ended 'not with a bang but with a whimper'.

Notes

1. Cabinet. Palestine. Legislative Council,10 January 1936, CO 733/293.
2. H.Cr. to Colonial Secretary, 22 February 1936, CO 733/293.
3. Thomas to Wauchope, 25 March 1936, CO 733/293.
4. A week after the Commons debate Wauchope reported, 'I am told on good authority that they (the Jews) have boasted to the Arabs in private that they can square matters in London'. 31 March 1936, CO 733/293.
5. *Falastin*, 15 April 1936.
6. These disputes were bitterly criticised in the Press and were taken as another indication of the leadership's inadequacy. See *Falasin*, 19-22 April 1936.
7. H.Cr. to Secretary of State for the Colonies, 19 April 1936, CO 733/310. Also see Peel Commission, op.cit., p.96.
8. 'Alloush related that at this point Farhan al-Sa'adi, one of Qassam's assistants, reappeared and killed three Jews as a signal for renewed guerrilla action against the Jews and the Government, ibid., p.109.
9. See 'Memorandum of Comments by the High Commissioner on General Dill's report on events in Palestine from the 15th September to 30th October, 1936', CO 733/317.
10. See Sir Vice Marshal Peirse to Air Ministry, 15 October, 1936, CO 733/317, p.15.
11. See Wauchope to Thomas, 23 April 1936, Enclosure, CO 733/310, p.3.
12. Ibid., p.5.
13. See Wauchope to Thomas, 24 April 1936, Enclosure B, CO 733/310.
14. See Documents, op.cit., pp.377-8.
15. Relief of distribution for the poor was organised according to zones of residence and through special cards issued for that purpose. See *Falastin*, 27 April 1936.
16. See Documents, op.cit., p.378-9.
17. See Wauchope to Thomas, 29 April 1936, Appendix C, CO 733/297.
18. Ibid., Appendix A.
19. *Falastin*, 9 May 1936.
20. See Documents, op.cit., pp.381-5.
21. CO 733/297.
22. 14 May 1936, CO 733/297.
23. Peirse to Air Ministry, op.cit., p.29.
24. Water, electricity and garbage collection workers were excluded from the strike.
25. See Wauchope to Ormsby-Gore, 8 July 1936, Enclosure ICO 733/313.
26. His successor 'Izzat Darwaza was also rounded-up for the same reason.
27. CO 733/297.
28. 'Note of Interview', 23 June 1936, CO 733/321.
29. H.Cr. to Colonial Secretary, 16 June 1936, CO 733/297.
30. Peirse to Air Ministry, op.cit., p.34.
31. Wauchope to Ormsby-Gore, 6 June 1936, Enclosure 601, CO 733/310.
32. Ibid. Enclosure 602, p.2.
33. 16 June 1936, The three thousand Jewish inhabitants of Jaffa had to be evacuated to Tel Aviv.
34. Peirse to Air Ministry, op.cit., p.58.
35. Ibid., p.59.
36. Wauchope to Ormsby-Gore, 24 June 1936, CO 733/297.
37. See 28 June 1936, CO 733/302.
38. 'Record of an interview with the Secretary of State', 14 July 1936, CO 733/321.
39. Colonial Secretary to H.Cr. 7 July 1936, CO 733/314.
40. Pierse to Air Ministry, op.cit., p.66.
41. Darwaza, op.cit., p.140.

42. For his first declaration see Documents, op.cit., pp.433-6. Kawukji was an officer in the Turkish Army in the war and with the French after the War where he obtained the Legion d'Honneur for his work as an intelligence officer. He joined the Druze rebellion in 1925 and was sentenced to death by the French but managed to escape to the Hejaz where he became military advisor to King Ibn Sa'ud. Thereafter he joined the Iraqi Army from which he resigned in 1936.
43. Peirse to air Ministry, op.cit., p.94.
44. Wauchope to Ormsby-Gore, 22 August 1936, op.cit.
45. Ibid., p.97.
46. Ibid.
47. Same to same, 26 August 1936, CO 733/314.
48. 'Record of Conversation with the Secretary of State', 31 August 1936, CO 733/297.
49. Cabinet. The Situation in Palestine, 2 September 1936, CO 733/297.
50. 10 September 1936, CO 733/314.
51. See Documents, op.cit., pp.439-41.
52. Wauchope to Ormsby-Gore, 12 September 1936, CO 733/311.
53. Peel Commission Report, op.cit., p.101.
54. See Wauchope to Ormsby-Gore, 20 November 1936, Enclosure I, CO 733/311.
55. Peel Commission Report, op.cit., p.105.
56. For the most important case of these escesses see Wauchope to Ormsby-Gore, 16 November, 1936. Enclosure 'The Quleh Calamity', CO 733/287.
57. 14 December 1936, CO 733/287.
58. Darwaza, op.cit., pp.152-3.
59. Peel Commission Report, op.cit., p.112.
60. Ibid., p.120.
61. Ibid.
62. Cabinet. Palestine Situation, 1 January 1937, CO 733/297.
63. Rice to Moody, October 1936, CO 733/311.
64. 17 October 1936, CO 733/317.
65. Ibid.
66. 'Note of talk with Dr Brodetsky, 6th January 1937', by Parkinson, CO 733/328.
67. Kauchope to Ormsby-Gore, 13 February 1937, Enclosure, CO 733/311.
68. Wauchope to Ormsby-Gore, 8 April 1937, CO 733/311.
69. Ibid., p.2.
70. Ibid., p.4.
71. Same to same, 15 May 1937, CO 733/332.
72. Same to same, 20 May 1937, CO 733/332.
73. MacKereth to Wauchope, 5 July 1937, CO 733/326.
74. Ibid.
75. See Cabinet, Palestine Royal Commission Report, 19 July 1937, CO 733/332.
76. CHQ Palestine and Trans-Jordan to War Office, 5 July 1937, CO 733/332.
77. For Partition Plan, see Peel Commission Report, op.cit., pp.380-96.
78. Note by W.O.G. (Ormsby-Gore) dated 19 July 1937, CO 733/328.
79. See 23 August 1937, CO 733/53.
80. On 21 December 1937, Wauchope wrote Parkinson that 'Dislike of Partition as the dread of Zionism needs no working up by anybody among the Arabs. It is universal'. CO 733/332.
81. 13 September 1937, CO 733/333.
82. 'Extracts from the Monthly Administrative Report for July 1937 Galilee District', CO 733/333.
83. Wauchope to Parkinson, 19 July 1937, CO 733/332.
84. No minister of state from any country attended. Of the 411 delegates there were

160 Syrians, 128 Palestinians, 65 Lebanese, 39 Trans-Jordanians, 12 Iraqis, 6 Egyptians and 1 Sa'udi Arabian.
85. See Darwaza, op.cit., pp.183-85.
86. Scott to Eden, 17 September 1937, CO 733/353.
87. 11 September 1937, CO 733/353.
88. MacKereth to Eden, 14 September 1937, CO 733/353.
89. Ibid.
90. In a memorandum to the Cabinet Eden stated that since the Report was published the situation had changed. The British were 'faced with solid and growing opposition from the majority of the native inhabitants of Palestine, and, what is much more serious, from the whole Arab world'. See Cabinet, Palestine, 19 November 1937, CO 733/354.
91. See Battershill (OAG) to Ormsby-Gore, 14 October 1937, CO 733/332.
92. Same to same, 23 October 1937, CO 733/332.
93. Same to same, 5 November 1937, CO 733/332.
94. Same to same, 21 November 1937, CO 733/354.
95. Cabinet. 46 (37), 9 December 1937, CO 733/354.
96. 18 December 1937, CO 733/328.
97. Wauchope to Ormsby-Gore, 23 November 1937, CO 733/332.
98. Cabinet, Palestine, 1 December 1937, CO 733/354.
99. There were accusations to the effect that the Rebellion was largely financed by Italian funds, but according to a Departmental memorandum prepared by the CO entitled 'Italy and Palestine'. 'There has been little or no direct evidence of subsidies to promote disaffection in Palestine'.(February 1938 CO 733/374.) As a result of the Anglo-Italian Conversation during March and April 1938, the Italian Government undertook to abstain from creating difficulties for HMG in Palestine. See Shuckburgh to MacMichael, 7 April 1938, CO 733/374.
100. MacKereth to Eden, 21 January 1938, Enclosure, CO 733/368.
101. Ibid.
102. H.Cr. to Colonial Secretary, 25 May 1938, CO 733/367.
103. Haining to War Secretary, 'Report on the Operations Carried out by the British Forces in Palestine and Trans-Jordan from 1st April to 18th May 1938', 4 July 1938, CO 733/379.
104. The prospect of Partition did not ameliorate the situation, see same to same 24 August 1938, CO 733/379.
105. 27 May 1938, CO 733/370. A similar suggestion was submitted by 'Abdul Latif Salah. See 26 September 1938, CO 733/372.
106. See H.Cr. to Colonial Secretary, 7 July 1938, CO 733/367.
107. The interference of the Royal Navy prevented a probable outbreak in Haifa.
108. Haining to War Secretary, op.cit., p.6.
109. H.Cr. to Colonial Secretary, 17 July 1938, op.cit.
110. Haining to War Secretary, op.cit., p.8.
111. See copy of a manifesto by Sa'ud ed-Din el-Bashir, Enclosure to a letter to Downie, 20 September 1938, CO 733/372.
112. Following the assassination of a British Government official W.S.S. Moffatt, 96 dwellings and 6 walls were demolished in Jenin. See MacMichael to MacDonald, 21 January 1939, CO 733/398.
113. Haining to War Secretary, 'Report on the Operations carried out by the British Forces in Palestine and Trans-Jordan 1st August to 31st October 1938', 30 November 1938, CO 733/379, p.2.
114. Ibid., p.3. Also See H.Cr. to Colonial Secretary, 26 August 1938, CO 733/367.
115. Also called Technical Commission and Woodhead Commission.
116. See Colonial Secretary to H.Cr., 1 September 1938, CO 733/386.
117. H.Cr. to Colonial Secretary, 2 September 1938, CO 733/367.

118. Same to same, 24 September, 1938, CO 733/372.
119. 22 September 1938, CO 733/367. Two days later MacMichael reported that there were about 6,500 Jews already paid and armed by the Government.
120. Colonial Secretary to H.Cr., 24 September 1938, op.cit.
121. Ibid. American pressure on the British Government brought forth a wave of anti-Americanism among the Arabs of Palestine, and *Falastin* urged the boycott of American Churches, Missions, schools and other institutions.
122. H.Cr. to Colonial Secretary, 25 September 1938, CO 733/367.
123. A phrase used by C.L. Mowat, *Britain Between the Wars 1918-1940*, London, 1968 (first published 1955), p.624.
124. Palestine Partition Commission Report, Cmd. 5854, October 1938.
125. See H.Cr. to Colonial Secretary, 2 November 1938, CO 733/386.
126. MacMichael to MacDonald, 29 December 1938, CO 733/398.
127. Peterson (Baghdad) to FO, 31 October 1938, CO 733/386. Also see Bullard (Jedda) to FO, 30 October 1938, CO 733/386.
128. 10 November 1938, CO 733/386.
129. MacMichael to MacDonald, 19 November 1938, Enclosure ICO 733/386.
130. CO 733/386.
131. MacMichael to MacDonald, 27 February 1939, CO 733/398, p.5.
132. Ibid., pp.6-7.
133. For British confidential reports of the troops excesses see George Francis (Bishop of Jerusalem) to Ormsby-Gore, 6 April 1938, CO 733/370. Also see a report by Inspector-General of the Palestine Police Force, 3 May 1938, CO 733/370. Also see Memoranda by the Arab Women's Committee of Jerusalem, MacMichael to MacDonald, 31 January 1939, CO 733/406.
134. See copy of photographic report of demolitions etc. 'Palestine the Martyr', same to same, 27 December 1938, Enclosure, CO 733/412.
135. MacMichael to MacDonald, 24 March 1939, CO 733/398, p.5.
136. Ibid.
137. Ibid., p.2.
138. Ibid., p.4.
139. Ibid., p.8.
140. Weizmann viewed the White paper as an act of betrayal and as a 'death-sentence'. See Weizmann, op.cit., pp.499-503 *seriatim*.
141. See MacMichael to MacDonald, 31 May 1939, Enclosure, CO 733/400.
142. See Wing Commander S.P. Ritchie's 'Appreciation of the Situation in Palestine', 31 May 1939, CO 733/406, p.1.
143. 30 May 1939, CO 733/408.
144. Ritchie, op.cit.,
145. H.Cr. to Colonial Secretary, 2 June 1939, CO 733/398.
146. MacMichael to MacDonald, 1 September 1939, CO 733/398. pp.9-10.
147. He was detained by the French but later escaped to Iraq where he received a warm welcome.
148. Darwaza accused some of the Arab rulers of reneging on their promises to supply the Rebellion with arms and ammunition, p.248.
149. H.Cr. to Colonial Secretary, 23 October 1939, CO 733/398.

CONCLUSION

The emergence of the Zionist movement in the late nineteenth century coincided with the rise of nationalism in the Arab provinces of the Ottoman Empire. From the outset the Arabs of Palestine viewed Zionism as a territorial colonialist movement which threatened their national existence. They fought it as a community by all peaceful means available to them under Ottoman rule. In this fight the educated classes played an important role in mobilising public opinion through newspapers, petitions and the formation of anti-Zionist societies, while the notables played an innocuous patriotic role as an intermediary between the populace and the Government.

After the revolution of the 'Young Turks' in 1908, the rulers of Constantinople pursued a more oppressive attitude towards the Arab elements of the Ottoman Empire in the Fertile Crescent lands thus giving rise to bolder Arab secret movements which called for Arab autonomy and independence. This feeling of rebelliousness was enhanced in Palestine itself by the leniency the Government displayed in checking Zionist immigration and land sales to Jews.

The outbreak of World War I carried the promise of independence for the Arabs of Syria, of which Palestine formed the southern part. A number of Palestinians were hanged for joining the ranks of the Allies and Sharif Hussein's Arab Revolt against the Turks. Instead of the desired independence, the defeat of Turkey brought British rule, committed, through the Balfour Declaration, to the establishment of a Jewish national home in Palestine.

On hearing of the Balfour Declaration, the Palestinians protested to their new rulers in every peaceful way possible. Without surrendering their intermediary role the political notability sought to deflect what in their view was the convergence of British and Zionist interests in Palestine by pointing out to the British the importance of maintaining Arab good-will and the futility of the Zionist dream.

As the nature of the British firm commitment to Zionism became clearer, the Palestinians were faced with two alternatives: revolution or acquiescence. The older notability opted for acquiescence to preserve their vested interests which depended on the good-will of the Government. The younger generation and the lower classes were both harder hit by the implementation of the Zionist schemes and were more determined to resist what they considered a foreign invasion that would culminate in their eviction or subservience. The young activists depended on the rural masse. for their plans or armed resistance against Zionism and the British Administration. They succeeded in staging two short-lived anti-Zionist uprisings in 1920 and 1921, that involved defiance of British authorities, but failed to persuade the British to withdraw from Palestine or to rescind their pro-Zionist policies. The collapse of Faisal's Arab Government in 1920 in Damascus and America's endorsement of the Balfour Declaration militated against effective external pressure in favour of Palestinian national demands.

Even before the final ratification of the Mandate in September 1923, most of the Palestinian notables including some of the younger generation had succumbed to a policy of co-operation with the Government in one form or another. Yet at no point did the Arab national movement in Palestine recognise the British Mandate as this implied the acceptance of the Balfour Declaration and the right of the Jews to a national home in Palestine. It was this factor that prevented their acceptance of Churchill's Legislative Council and later the Arab Agency offer. The notability, however, were exercising their intermediary role by using their influence to suppress insurrectionist tendencies among the 'lower strata' of the Palestinian Arabs.

The period of political relaxation and stagnation between 1924 and 1929 saw a decline in Jewish immigration and land settlement. During this period the struggle for power between the Husseinis and Nashashibis exposed the factiousness and the inadequacy of the notables to measure up to the grave Zionist challenge.

The British attitude during the clashes of 1929 between the Arabs and the Jews over the *Buraq,* or Wailing Wall, convinced the Palestinians that Britain was the real sponsor and defender of Zionism in Palestine. As a direct consequence, the first Arab guerrilla bands emerged in the vicinity of Acre and Safad to fight the British Mandate as well as the Jewish colonists. On the political plane the advocates of co-operation with the Government were discreditied and the younger generation among the educated classes, which formed the *Istiqlal* Party, challenged the traditional leadership of the notables. The *Istiqla*lists defined their aim as the attainment of Palestinian independence within the framework of Arab unity and boldly called for a policy of non-co-operation with the British Government which they viewed 'as the root of evil'.

Revolutionary as *Istiqlal*'s aims were, it nevertheless failed to create the vehicle of revolution, namely, a mass peasant organisation capable of waging armed resistance. Yet despite the fact that the *Istiqla*lists failed to wrest the political leadership from the notables, they played a prominent role in the process of revolutionary fermentation between 1930 and 1935. During this period immigration and land acquisition assumed threatening proportions which rendered one-fourth of the Palestinian rural population landless. Moreover, these landless peasants were not able to obtain work in the cities or in Jewish factories owing to the Histradrut's boycott of Arab labour on Jewish enterprise. In view of these facts it was not surprising that Qassam's call for armed resistance against the British and the Jews found its greates echo in the tin shacks of Haifa.

Although Qassam's insurgency was nipped in the bud in November 1935, it heralded a new active revolutionary stage which started out as a general strike (which is probably the longest political strike in history) in the spring of 1936 and quickly led to the great Palestine rebellion of 1936-39 which was a peasant uprising backed by urban population.

The Rebellion succeeded in attracting the attention of Arabs and Muslims in the neighbouring countries to the Palestine problem. In 1938, the rebels ruled considerable areas of rural Palestine and even succeeded in occupying some of the major cities for short intervals. To face the challenge of the Palestinian rebels, Britain had to employ two divisions and squadrons of aeroplanes.[1] During the 1938 European political crisis the Palestinian resistance represented a military embarrassment. The Rebellion culminated in the London Round Table Conference and the 1939 White Paper, which offered the Arabs some concessions over Jewish immigration and future independence. The concessions were neither immediate nor substantial and the prospect of independence was tied to Zionist co-operation which failed to satisfy the Arabs. These minor concessions were achieved after great sacrifices and at the expense of weakening Arab power to face the Zionist challenge in the ensuing period.

The major causes for the failure of the Palestinian Arab nationalists to prevent the establishment of the Jewish National Home centred around the lack of balance of power between themselves and their adversaries: the British-backed Zionists. The Palestinian Arabs formed an under-developed rural society with meagre resources and minimal effective organisation, while the Zionists constituted a highly organised, well-financed movement led by a highly intelligent and determined leadership.

Inability to change the balance of power owed much to the international situation and to the fact that the neighbouring Arab countries were under foreign rule or influence, in addition to the Palestinians own indigenous clashing interests and rivalries.

No less important was the failure of the Palestinian Arab national movement to produce the required leadership. By choosing, as their first political priority, the protection of their interests, the majority of notables maintained a counter-revolutionary attitude. Then, the economic and educational superiority of the Zionists prevented the emergence of a strong Arab bourgeoisie capable of assuming effective leadership in Palestine. The 'lower strata', too, failed to evolve a new radical leadership of its own for a number of reasons, not least of which was the hold of tradition on the peasants which, no doubt, enhanced Hajj Amin's position of leadership.

During the 1936-1939 rebellion, which represented the highest stage of the Palestinian Arab struggle against the Anglo-Zionist convergence, the weaknesses of the Palestinian nationalist movement were exposed. The political leadership displayed its compromising attitudes when it called off the general strike and the rebellion of 1936, without insisting on prior concessions from the Government. Throughout the rebellion the political leadership was willing to entrust a great part of their cause to the rulers of the Arab states, who, however, were eager to stand well with the British. The absence of a modern revolutionary organisation denied the rebels the valuable role of political revolutionary cadres, and the lack of a loyal commitment to a common purpose prevented the necessary co-ordination between the military and the political efforts.

In view of the absence of a capable revolutionary leadership, it was not surprising that the Palestinians failed to adopt an adequate strategy to prevent the establishment of the Jewish National Home in their country and against their will.

Note

1. Professor W. Khalidi put the number of Palestinian Arab casualties during the 1936-1939 Rebellion at 5,032 killed and 14,760 wounded and the number of detainees at 5,600 in 1939. See W. Khalidi (ed.), *From Haven to Conquest*, Beirut, 1971, Appendix IV, pp.848-9.

BIBLIOGRAPHY

A. Unpublished Materials

(i) Cabinet Papers. Discussion, reports and memoranda relating to Palestine during the period under study is scattered throughout the records of the British Cabinet between 1915 and 1939. The most important among the papers relating to Palestine are to be found under CAB 23/..., 24/..., 25/..., 27/..., 37/..., and 43/..., Public Record Office (PRO), London.

(ii) Colonial Office Archives. Correspondence between the Palestine Administration, Jerusalem and the Colonial Office, London between 1921 and 1939, classified under Palestine CO 733/1-415.

(iii) Foreign Office Archives:

1. Correspondence between the British Consul, Jerusalem and the Foreign Office, London, from 1839-1914, classified under Turkey F.O. 78/...
2. Correspondence between military authorities in Palestine (and Egyptian Expeditionary Force, Cairo) and the Foreign Office, London between 1917 and 1920, classified under Turkey, F.O. 371/...
3. Arab Bureau Papers. Covers British activities, treaties, etc. in the Middle East during World War I, classified under F.O. 882/...

(iv) Hagana Archives. Microfilms covering Zionist Intelligence reports between 1919 and 1921, which were made available to me in London.

(v) National Archives, Washington. Charles R. Crane and Henry C. King, *Report of the American Section of the Inter-Allied Commission of Mandates in Turkey, Section One, Report upon Syria, Paris.* 28 August 1919, Department of State 181.9102/9.

(vi) Zionist Archives, Jerusalem. Microfilms covering certain documents of the Executive of the Zionist Organisation in Palestine between 1917 and 1923, classified under Z 4/..., Central Zionist Archives (C.Z.A.), Jerusalem.

(vii) Private Papers:

1. *Balfour Papers,* at the Public Record Office, London, F.O. 800/199-217.
2. *Clayton Papers,* at the University of Durham, School of Oriental Studies.
3. *Lloyd George Papers,* Beaverbrook Library, London.
4. *King Papers,* Oberlin College Library, Oberlin Ohio, U.S.A.

5. *Samuel Papers*, at the Middle East Centre, St Antony's College, Oxford.
6. *Sykes Papers*, at the Public Record Office, F.O. 800/221.
7. *Yale Papers*, at the Middle East Centre, St Antony's College, Oxford.

(viii) Unpublished Works:

1. Ruhi al-Khalidi, *al-Mas'ala al-Sahyuniyya* (The Zionist Question), 1911, in the custody of Professor Walid Khalidi.
2. Neville Mandel, *Turks, Arabs and Jewish Immigration into Palestine*, 1882-1914. (unpublished D.Phil. Dissertion, St Antony's College, Oxford), 1965.

B. Reports and Command Papers

(i) *Report of the Court of Inquiry convened by order of H.E. The High Commissioner and Commander-In-Chief. Dated the 12th Day of April 1920*, 1 July 1920, F.O. 371/5121. The Palin Commission Report.

(ii) Palestine. *Disturbances in May, 1921. Report of the Commission of Inquiry with Correspondence relating thereto.* Cmd. 1540, 1921. The Haycraft Report.

(iii) *Correspondence with the Palestine Arab Delegation and the Zionist Organisation.* Cmd. 1700, 1922. The Churchill White Paper.

(iv) Mandate for Palestine. Letter from the Secretary of the Cabinet *to the Secretary-General of the League of Nations Regarding the Mandate of Palestine and the Holy Places commission.* Cmd. 1708, 1922.

(v) League of Nations. *Mandate for Palestine, Together with a Note by the Secretary-General Relating to Its Application to the Territories Known as Trans-Jordan.* Cmd. 1785, 1922.

(vi) *Report of the Commission on the Palestine Disturbances of August, 1929*, Cmd. 3530, 1930. The Shaw Commission Report.

(vii) *Palestine. Statement of Policy with Regard to British Policy.* Cmd. 3582, 1930. The White Paper on the Shaw Commission Report.

(viii) Palestine. *Report on Immigration, Land Settlement and Development, by Sir John Hope Simpson.* Cmd. 3686, 1930.

(ix) Palestine. *Statement of Policy by His Majesty's Government in the United Kingdom.* Cmd. 3692, 1930. The Passfield White Paper.

(x) *Palestine Royal Commission Report.* Cmd. 5479, 1937. The Peel Commission Report.

(xi) *Policy in Palestine. Despatch Dated 23rd December, 1937, from the Secretary of State for the Colonies to the High Commissioner for Palestine.* Cmd. 5634, 1938. The terms of reference of the Partition

Commission.

(xii) *Palestine Partition Commission Report.* Cmd. 5854, 1938. The Woodhead Report.

(xiii) *Correspondence between Sir Henry McMahon and the Sherif Hussein of Mecca, July 1915-March 1916.* Cmd. 5957, (Miscellaneous No.3), 1939.

(xiv) *Statements Made on Behalf of His Majesty's Government during the Year 1918 in Regard to the Future Status of Certain Parts of the Ottoman Empire.* Cmd. 5964, (Miscellaneous No.4), 1939.

(xv) *Report of a Committee Set Up to Consider Certain Correspondence between Sir Henry McMahon and the Sherif of Mecca in 1915 and 1916.* Cmd. 5974, 1939.

(xvi) *Palestine Statement of Policy.* Cmd. 6019, 1939. The White Paper of May, 1939.

C. Published Documents

(i) Arabic

Watha'iq al-Muqawam al-Falastiniyya ali'Arabiyya dida al-Ihtilal al-Baritani wa al-Sahyuniyya (Documents of the Palestinian Arab Resistance against British Occupation and Zionism). ed. Kayyali, Abdul-Wahhab. Beirut, 1968. Referred to as Documents.

(ii) Others

1. *Papers Relating to the Foreign Relations of the United States. The Paris Peace Conference 1919.* Department of State, Washington, US Government Printing Office, 1947.
2. *Documents on British Foreign Policy 1919-1939.* vol. iv. eds. Woodward, E.L. and Butler, R. First Series. London, HMSO.

D. Interviews

(i) Hajj Amin al-Husseini, Beirut, Summer, 1966
(ii) Emile Ghory, Beirut, August, 1967

E. Newspapers and Periodicals

(i) Arabic

Al-'Arab, Jerusalem
Al-Ahram, Cairo
Al-Ashma'i, Jerusalem

Al-Hilal, Cairo
Al-Iqdam, Cairo
Al-Jami'a al-'Arabiyya, Jerusalem
Al-Karmal, Haifa
Al-Kawkab, Cairo
Al-Manar, Cairo
Al-Mufid, Beirut
Al-Munadi, Jerusalem
Al-Muqtabas, Damascus
Al-Mustaqbal, Paris
Al-Rai'i al-'Am, Beirut
Al-Shura, Cairo
Al-Urdun, Damascus
Al-Yarmuk, Haifa
Falastin, Jaffa
Fata al-'Arab, Damascus
Mir'at al-Sharq, Jerusalem
Mulhaq al-Hayat, Beirut
Suriyya al-Janubiyya, Jerusalem
Suriyya al-Jadida, Damascus

(ii) Others

The Illustrated Sunday Herald, London
Le Jeune Turc, Constantinople
The Jewish Chronicle, London
The New Palestine, New York
The Palestine News, Cairo
The Times, London

F. Books and Articles

(i) Arabic

A'mal al-Wafd al-Suri al-Falastini (The Activities of the Syrian-Palestinian Delegation). Cairo, 1923

'Allush, Naji *Al-Muqawama al-'Arabiyya fi Falastin*, 1917-1948 (The Arab Resistance in Palestine) Beirut, 1967

—— *Al-Mu'tamar al-'Arabi al-Awwal* (The First Arab Congress). Published by the Supreme Committee of the Decentralization Party in Egypt. Cairo, 1913

Darwaza, 'Izaat *Al-Wadiyya al-Falastiniyya* (The Palestine Question), Saida, 1959

Sifir, 'Isa *Falastin al-'Arabiyya bayn al-Intidab wa al-Sahyuniyya* (Arab Palestine between the Mandate and Zionism), Jerusalem, 1937

Yasin, Subhi *Al-Thawra al-'Arabiyya al-Kubra fi Falastin 1936-1939* (The Great Arab Revolt in Palestine), Damascus, 1959

—— *Harb al-'Isabat fi Falastin* (Guerrilla Warfare in Palestine), Cairo 1967

(ii) Others

Antonius, George *The Arab Awakening:The Story of the Arab National Movement*, First published 1938. Beirut, n.d

Ashbee, C.R. A *Palestine Notebook, 1918-1923,* London, 1923.

Azoury, Najib *Le Reveil de la Arabe,* Paris, 1905

Barbour, Nevill *Nisi Dominus: A Survey of the Palestine Controversy,* London, 1946

Ben-Gurion, David *Israel: Years of Challenge,* London, 1964

—— *We and our Neighbours,* Tel Aviv, 1931

Bentwich, Norman and Helen *Mandate Memoirs, 1918-1948,* London, 1965

Boustany, W.F. *The Palestine Mandate: Invalid and Impracticable,* Beirut, 1936

Churchill, Winston 'Zionism versus Bolshevism', *The Illustrated Sunday Herald,* 8 February 1920

Cohen, Israel *The Zionist Movement,* London, 1945

Cuinet, Vital *Syrie Leban et Palestine, Géographie, Administrative, Statistique, Descriptive et Raisonée,* Paris, 1896

Erskine, Mrs Steuart *Palestine of the Arabs,* London, 1935

Esco Foundation for Palestine, Inc *Palestine: A Study of Jewish, Arab and British Policies,* 2 vols., New Haven, 1949

Harington, General Sir Charles *Plumer of Messines,* London, 1935

Hertzberg, Arthur (ed.) *The Zionist Idea; A Historical Analysis and Reader,* New York, 1959

Herzl, Theodor *The Complete Diaries of Theodor Herzl,* 5 vols. Edited by Raphael Patai. Translated by Harry Zohn. London, 1960

The Jewish State: An Attempt at a Modern Solution of the Jewish Question. Translated by Sylvia D'Avigdor. London, 1946

Hourani, Albert *Arabic Thought in the Liberal Age, 1798-1939,* London, 1962

—— 'Ottoman Reform and the Politics of Notables', in William R. Polk and Richard L. Chambers (eds.) *Beginnings of Modernization in the Middle East: The Nineteenth Century,* Chicago, 1969, pp.41-68

Howard, Harry *The King-Crane Commission,* Beirut, 1963

Hurewitz, J.C. *Diplomacy in the Near and Middle East,* Vol.II: *A Documentary Record, 1914-1956,* Princeton, 1958

Hyamson, Albert *The British Consulate in Jerusalem in Relation to the Jews of Palestine, 1838-1914,* 2 parts, London, 1939-1941

Jeffries, Joseph *Palestine: The Reality,* London, 1939

Kedourie, Elie 'Sir Herbert Samuel and the Government of Palestine', *Middle Eastern Studies,* vol. v, January, 1969

Khalidi, Walid (ed.) *From Haven to Conquest: Readings in Zionism and the Palestine Problem until 1948,* Beirut, 1971

Kisch, Lt.-Colonel F.H. *Palestine Diary,* London, 1938

Knightley, Phillip and Simpson, Colin *The Secret Lives of Lawrence of Arabia,* London, 1969

Kohn, Hans *History of Nationalism in the East,* London, 1929

Laqueur, Walter *Commission and Nationalism in the Middle East,* 3rd ed. London, 1961

Lawrence, T.E. *Revolt in the Desert,* London, 1927

Luke, Sir Harry and Keith-Roach, Edwards (eds.) *The Handbook of Palestine and Trans-Jordan* 3rd ed. rev. London, 1934

Mandel, Neville 'Attempts at an Arab-Zionist Entente, 1913-1914', *Middle Eastern Studies,* vol.i, April, 1965

—— 'Turks, Arabs and Jewish Immigration Into Palestine: 1882-1914', *St. Antony's Papers,* No.17, *Middle Eastern Affairs,* no.4, London 1965

Marlowe, John *Rebellion in Palestine,* London, 1946

—— *The Seat of Pilate: An Account of the Palestine Mandate,* London, 1959

Meinertzhagen, Colonel Richard *Middle East Diary: 1917-1956,* London, 1959

Mogannam, Mrs. Matiel E.T. *The Arab Woman and the Palestine Problem,* London, 1937

Monroe, Elizabeth *Britain's Moment in the Middle East, 1914-1956,* London, 1963

Mowat, Charles Loch *Britain Between the Wars 1918-1940,* rev. ed first published, 1955. London, 1968

Newton, Francis *Fifty Years in Palestine,* Wrotham, England, 1948

Pearlman, Moshe (ed.) *Ben Gurion Looks Back,* London, 1965

—— 'Chapters of Arab-Jewish Diplomacy 1918-22', *Jewish Social Studies,* April, 1944

Polk, William 'The Arabs and Palestine', in William R. Polk, David M. Stamler and Edmund Asfour (eds.) *Backdrop to Tragedy: The Struggle for Palestine,* Boston, 1957, pp.225-304.

Ra'Anan, Frishwasser *The Frontiers of a Nation*, London, 1955
Rabinowicz, Oscar K. *Fifty Years of Zionism: A Historical Analysis of Dr. Weizmann's 'Trial and Error'*, London, 1950
—— *Winston Churchill on Jewish Problems: A Half Century Survey*, London, 1956
Royal Institute of International Affairs *Great Britain and Palestine, 1915-1945*, London, 1946
—— *Political and Strategic Interests of the United Kingdom: An Outline*, London, 1940
—— Survey of International Affairs. Edited by Arnold Toynbee, 1925 (vol.i), 1930, 1934, 1936, 1937 and 1938 (vol.i)
Ruppin, Arthur, *The Jewish Fate and Future*, London, 1940
—— *Three Decades of Palestine; Speeches and Papers on the Upbuilding of the Jewish National Home*, Jerusalem, 1936
Samuel, Viscount Herbert *Memoirs*, London, 1945
Sereni, Enzo and Ashery, R.E. (eds.) *Jews and Arabs in Palestine: Studies in a National and colonial Problem*, New York, 1936
Sidebotham, Herbert *British Interests in Palestine*, London, 1934
—— *England and Palestine: Essays Towards the Restoration of the Jewish State*, London, 1918.
Simon, H.J. *British Rule and Rebellion*, Edinburgh, 1937
Sokolow, Nahum *History of Zionism: 1600-1918*, 2 vols. London, 1919
Stein, Leonard *The Balfour Declaration*, London, 1961
Storrs, Ronald *Orientations*, London, 1937
Sykes, Christopher *Crossroads to Israel*, Cleveland, 1965
—— *Two Studies in Virtue*, London, 1953
Wavell, Colonel A.P. *The Palestine Campaigns*, London, 1928
Weizmann, Chaim *Trial and Error: An Autobiography of Chaim Weizmann*, London, 1949
Yale, William *The Near East; A Modern History*, Ann Arbor, 1958
Young, Major Sir Hubert *The Independent Arab*, London, 1933
Zeine, Zeine N. *Arab-Turkish Relations and the Emergency of Arab Nationalism*, Beirut, 1958.

INDEX

'Abdullah, Prince 91, 198, 201, 202, 206, 207
'Abdul Latif Salah 178, 191
'Abdul Rahim 223
'Abdul-Qader Husseini 180, 211
Abu-al-Hol 17
Acre 11
Advisory Council 87, 88, 118
Agricultural Loans Scheme 73
al'Ahd 39, 166
Ahmad al-'Aref 38
al-Ahram 221
'Ajaj Nweihed 183
Akram Zu'ayter 182, 183
Allenby, General 45, 46, 67, 84
Alliance Israélite Universelle 14
American Jewish Committee 151
Amery, L.S. 56, 135
Amin al-Hussein 54, 79, 94-5, 110, 115, 130, 132, 136, 140, 141, 145, 165, 175-6
Anglo-Arab Treaty 119, 131
Anglo-Palestine Bank 38
Anglo-Palestine Company 25
Antebi, Albert 18, 25, 263 32
Anti-Zionist Society 32
Antonius, George 14
Aqsa Mosque University 166
Arab Bank 176
Arab Bureau 43, 45
Arab Congress (Paris) 30-3
Arab Decentralisation Party 31
Arab Economic Agricultural Conference 116, 119
Arab Executive Committees: of 3rd Congress 88, 89, 91, 93; of 4th Congress 111, 112; of 5th Congress 115-19 *passim*; of 6th Congress 130, 133, 135; of 7th Congress 137, 141, 149, 160, 162, 171; *see also* Palestinian Arab Congresses
Arab Higher Committee 191, 194, 196, 198, 201, 202, 203, 206, 207, 210, 218, 222
Arab Independence Party *see Istiqlal*ist Party

Arabic language 49
Arab National Bureau 212
Arab 'national charter' 166
Arab National Committees 189, 190, 192, 197, 208, 210
Arab National Conference 167
Arab National Fund 176
Arab Nationalism 30-41 *passim*, 155: and anti-British feeling 1930-5, 164-84 *passim*; and British Mandate 1920-3, 84-124 *passim*; and British policy in Palestine 1917-20, 43-79 *passim*
Arab National Movement 88, 116
Arabs in Palestine: agitation against the British 1930-5, 155-83 *passim*; and British Mandate 84-124 *passim*; and British policy, 1917-20 43-79 *passim*; early opposition to Zionism 16-41 *passim*, relations with British and Jews, 1923-9 130-51; revolt against British, 1936-9 187-223 *see also fellaheen*, notables
Arab Women's Congress 168
Arab Youth 145
Arab Youth Conference 177
'Aref al-'Aref 79
'Aref Nuralla 183
Aref Pasha Dahudi Dajani 61, 131
Al-Asma'T 22, 24
Attlee, Clement 200
'Awni 'Abdul Hadi 157, 168-9, 191, 194, 199, 200, 201
al-Azhar Society 34

Balfour, Lord 44, 47, 48, 134-5: *see also next entry*
Balfour Declaration 40, 45-6, 49, 51, 56-7, 78, 84: *et passim*
Basle Programme 19
Beersheba 11
Beirut 11, 15
Beisan 29, 30, 32, 91, 107, 133
Ben Gurion, David 19, 175, 199
Bentwich, Norman 146

239

For Product Safety Concerns and Information please contact our EU
representative GPSR@taylorandfrancis.com
Taylor & Francis Verlag GmbH, Kaufingerstraße 24, 80331 München, Germany

9 781032 904849